Particular and Universal

By the same author

Or (1999)

MM's Revolution (1998)

Happening (1997)

Realization (1996)

Poems for People of the Future (1992)

Engendering (1990)

SOLUNA: Collected Earlier Poems (1989)

Selected Poems (Indian Edition) (1989)

Realization, II (1988)

Realization, I (1986)

Selected Poems (Chinese/English) (1985)

Revolution (with Dan Boord) (1985)

Light (1983)

O (1982)

Sleep (1981)

Poems (1977)

Girls (1976)

MADISON MORRISON

Particular and Universal

Essays in Asian, European and American Literature

Crane

Contents

For Richard Beck

Particular and Universal

中文序

松柏

　　認識慕禮生教授在 1983 年，當時他應國科會之邀請擔任國立台灣大學外文系及外文研究所客座教授。本人有幸聆聽他所開當代英美詩課程，研讀自艾略特以來許多英美當代詩人的作品，獲益良多。慕教授也是位熱衷於寫作的詩人，年輕時即擬訂了一套完整的寫作計劃，洋洋灑灑共二十六本詩集。當時覺得真是不可思議，但是經過積年累月的辛勞，他目前已出版了十七本，另外有三本也在排版編印中。

　　慕教授自 1969 年取得美國哈佛大學英美文學博士學位以後即在美國奧克拉荷馬大學英文系及英文研究所任教。開設課程計有惠特曼研究、史蒂文斯研究、美國文學 (1865 年至現代)、美國現代史詩、現代美國詩、美國超現實主義作品、美國文學與電影欣賞等。也先後指導博士論文共七本。1991 年他應國立臺灣師範大學之聘，擔任英語系及英語研究所客座教授。1992 年起則改聘為專任教授。開設課程計有英國文學史 (涵蓋中古英文至二十世紀四個學期的課程)、英文文藝創作、西洋史詩傳統、文類研究、史賓塞研討、密爾頓研討、文藝復興時期文學及詹姆斯梅崁研究等。每學期也精心指導學生論文，歷年至今在臺灣師大指導的碩士論文共有十五本。

　　在這期間慕教授也曾應邀赴印度、泰國及義大利等國之大學擔任客座教授。慕教授喜歡旅遊，也藉此瞭解各國不同的文化。在其漫長而成功的學術生涯中曾多次應邀遠赴德國、義大利、印度、泰國、新加坡、南美等國家作巡迴演講，講題所涉領域甚廣，包括古典、中古、文藝復興、及現代歐洲文學；美國文化；古印度文化；中國文學與山水畫等。實際題目計有〈英國文學的世界觀〉、〈惠特曼民主思想中的印度傳承〉、〈中國山水畫的發展〉、〈西洋史詩中的寓言與諷喻〉、〈但丁神曲的魅力〉、〈古文明、文藝復興、與現代文化〉…等，不一一細述。

這些頻繁的學術活動、涉獵寬廣而精闢的演講、以及三十年致力於英美歐洲文學的教學經驗，也足以表現慕教授豐富的學識與閱歷以及對文學的執著與熱愛。除了以上所述二十六本的文藝創作計劃外，慕教授也經常撰寫文學評論。本書即收錄七篇他這幾年所寫的評論：前三篇討論英美現代詩人的東方思想，第四篇探討老子道德經，後三篇則著重於歐洲及英國文學。本書命名為《獨特性與普遍性》，也足以反應慕教授博大精深的治學功力。長年居住台灣及經常的旅遊，讓他思考東西文化彼此互動的關係。慕教授的文筆優雅洗鍊，加上豐實的文學素養以及深入的見解與哲理，使得本書讀來頗耐人尋味，足以媲美葉慈的散文評論，值得讀者仔細閱讀。以下簡述各篇主要內容，謹供讀者參考。

一‧古典印度文化和惠特曼的民主思想

惠特曼和其師承愛默生一樣，都代表著美國文壇第一波的東方思潮。(愛默生不但是梭羅和惠特曼的印度導師，亦是當時首屈一指的漢學家)，在所有美國詩人中，惠特曼在全球享譽最盛，這或許是因為他的作品提供了跨越東西文化的典範。他確認荷馬的《伊利亞得》和《奧德塞》乃「脫胎於亞洲」的作品。他在劄記中提到一個未完成的計劃，名為〈我，歐里希斯〉，這是一部企圖融合現代美國和埃及傳統的作品。他有名的詩篇《自我之歌》(比照印度史詩〈薄伽梵歌〉"Bhagavad Gita," 又名頌主之歌)可說是〈我，克里胥那〉。因為這裡所說的主，乃是印度教經典《奧義書》(Upanishad) 中所提到的巴瑪特曼 (Parmatman, 最高我或宇宙魂)，亦即〈薄伽梵歌〉中的神祇，都代表神聖的自我。本書首篇討論惠特曼在美國詩壇的地位，也正可引導緊接的第二、三章有關美國現代主義詩人及其所繼承惠特曼跨越東西文化的理念。

首篇的前半部評論惠特曼對十九世紀民主思想的新詮釋。後半部則解讀他四首最重要的長篇詩作，分別為〈自我之歌〉、〈橫越布魯克林渡口〉、〈熟睡的人〉及〈印度之旅〉。學者常評論這些作品所蘊含的古印度思想，慕教授的創見在於把印度的神學和惠特曼詩與散文中的民本思想聯結起來，尤其著重在〈民主遠景〉以及 1855年和 1872 年爲《草葉集》所作的序。

二・葉慈、艾略特和龐德詩中亞洲文化因素

葉慈深知惠特曼，梭羅及愛默生都吸取了印度思想。葉慈的第一位師承威廉・莫里斯 (William Morris)，兼容並蓄，在作品中集結了歐洲古典、中古和現代三個傳統。他的第二位師承海倫娜・布魯瓦斯基 (Helena Petrovna Blavatsky) 則融合了印度、埃及及歐洲的密教傳統。葉慈接納了這些悠久的傳統，最後終能在自己的作品內揉合了東方印度、日本和中國以及歐洲古典、基督教與現代六個不同傳統。在他加入通神社期間，他慢慢吸收了印度思想。在葉慈致力於愛爾蘭劇院 (Abbey Theater) 期間，他吸取了日本的歌舞劇及能劇傳統。旋後他在和龐德交往期間也再次激起他對日本文化的嚮往。龐德也引起葉慈對中國傳統文化的興趣。他們兩人也一起研讀古印度史詩《摩訶婆羅多》(Mahabharata)。

艾略特在哈佛研讀梵文的同時，也修習佛教和印度教經典。慕教授在本章主要探討艾略特兩篇作品中所呈現的佛教及印度教兩大亞洲文化精髓。在討論龐德的東方思想時，他則把重點放在龐德的史詩《詩篇》(Cantos) 中所蘊含的孔子思想。《詩篇》一書可說是西方第一部系統性地以中國哲學思想爲依據而寫成的史詩巨作。

三・史蒂文斯，威廉斯，及佛洛斯特的本土佛教意念

不像上章所談的三位賦居國外，閱讀原文經典的現代詩人，史蒂文斯 (Stevens)，威廉斯 (Williams)，及佛洛斯特 (Frost) 以間接的方式濡沐東方思想與文化。葉慈、艾略特和龐德的詩融合了許多東方思想，而本章所介紹這些留居故土的美國詩人作品卻也流露濃厚的佛教思想，而且更難能可貴地呈現了廣博的宇宙觀，雖然他們以塑造個人獨特的風格與想法爲途徑：佛洛斯特一生描述簡樸的鄉野生活；威廉斯篤守他自己的信念：「唯在物中方有觀念」；雖從某方面看來，史蒂文斯是較具世界性的，但在細節處理上卻是美國式的

專研獨特。何以這三位留居本土的美國詩人都在他們的作品中表達了帶有異國風味的佛教概念？慕教授在第三章將試著闡釋這點疑惑。

四‧老子道德經的詩與哲學

　　慕教授對道德經的解讀認為其上篇〈道經〉具有哲學的普遍性，而其下篇〈德經〉則注重詩的具體意象及細節。此章對道家重要經典的探討與第三章對儒家信念的概述相輝映。連同第一章對印度教義的詮釋，這幾篇探討主要亞洲哲學的章節，應當對西方以及亞洲研讀文學的學子有所助益，因為本書前四章以幾篇文學作品為例對東方哲學重新加以審視。

　　此章為本書中唯一探討東方文學的一篇，並間接為詩下定義，也討論詩與哲學的關係。慕教授將此章置於全書的中心，以連結本書前三篇關於東方價值觀的文章，以及後三篇關於西方哲學的重要議題：獨特性與普遍性，詮釋循環 (the hermeneutical circle)，主體與客體 (subject and object)。

五‧寓言與西洋史詩

　　本章研究十二位西洋名家作品中的寓言形式 (allegory)，包括前古典時期的希臘、亞歷山大、與羅馬；中古時期與文藝復興時代的義大利；英國的文藝復興；十七世紀的西班牙；以及浪漫時期的英國。慕教授將此章置於兩篇探討普遍性與獨特性的章節之間，因他認為寓言實際上乃銜接兩者間的橋樑。而且他強調西洋史詩自始至終都以寓言的形式表達。本章集合作者在印度、泰國、中國、及美國的教學經驗，提供亞洲，歐陸，與英語語系國家學子從事英美文學研究時的必要背景知識。

　　在回顧「寓言」一詞的不同意涵後，接著作者按作品年代為序，探討荷馬的《伊里亞得》(Iliad) 及《奧得賽》(Odyssey)，海希奧德 (Hesiod) 的《神譜》 (Theogony)，阿波羅尼 (Apollonius) 的《阿岡諾提卡》(Argonautica)，維吉爾 (Vergil) 的 《伊奈德》(Aeneid)，

奧維德 (Ovid) 的《變形記》，但丁的《神曲》 (Divine Comedy)，阿里奧斯多 (Ariosto) 的《奧蘭多歷險記》 (Orlando Furioso)。在此稍作停頓來思考塔索 (Tasso) 對於傳統史詩及寓言觀點的修正。慕教授指出，雖然《耶路撒冷的解放》 (Gerusalemme Liberata) 一書對史賓塞 (Spenser) 的《仙后》 (Faerie Queene) 情節發展中有關鍵性的影響，但事實上卻是塔索 (Tasso) 的理論決定了密爾頓 (Milton)《失樂園》(Paradise Lost) 的寫作大綱。接著作者簡要討論賽凡提 (Cervantes) 的《唐吉訶德》(Don Quixote) 及拜倫 (Byron) 的《唐璜》(Don Juan)。

本章先談論寓言 (allegory) 與寓言式的解讀/改寫 (allegoresis) 的主要區別；幾世紀以來對荷馬與維吉爾 (Vergil) 的解讀方式；文藝復興時期結合寓言的《伊奈德》與道德寓意的《變形記》；早期現代史詩與現代思想的關聯，如賽凡提對康德 (Kant) 的預示；以及拜倫對惠特曼與龐德所愛用的開放式結尾 (open-endedness) 所提供的先例。本章各重要史詩之英譯由慕教授執筆。

六‧英國文學的普遍性

從實用的觀點來看，英語已成為一種世界語言，因此英國文學也變成了普及全球的重要研究學科；但是從哲學的角度來看，起源於中世紀末的英國文學，本質上一直都具備著包容的世界觀。本書第五章探討英國文學之所以擁有普遍性的幾個重要因素：因為它結合了不同的外來文化 (希伯來、希臘、羅馬、歐陸，以及晚近的亞洲與非洲文學)、集結了全球信仰體系的基礎 (羅馬、羅馬天主教及更廣義的基督教，新古典主義和啓蒙運動，浪漫主義及理想主義等思潮)，以及晚近對於國際主義運動的支持。本章前半部探討歷史上有關「普遍性」及「獨特性」的辯論；後半部則縱覽自盎格魯撒克遜時期至二十世記的英國文學。作者將把重心放在英國文壇的幾員大將上：如喬塞 (Chaucer) 和馬羅萊 (Malory)；希德尼 (Sidney)、史賓塞 (Spenser) 和莎士比亞 (Shakespeare)；密爾頓 (Milton) 和德萊敦 (Dryden)；波普 (Pope)、斯威夫特 (Swift) 和約翰生 (Johnson)；

布雷克 (Blake)、渥茲華斯 (Wordsworth) 和拜倫 (Byron)；狄更斯 (Dickens)、但尼生 (Tennyson) 和重要的現代主義名家。本章末尾，作者也嘗試將傳統英國文學的主幹與現今興起之非母語作家之英文作品作一連結。

七・晚近現代英國文學中的經驗思想

本章研究上自荷馬、歷經但丁及早期文藝復興，而至西班牙黃金時代的體驗文學。在西班牙的黃金時代，「流浪漢」(picaró) 式的主角出現，也因而發展出新的人物描寫手法。慕教授認為此種新的描寫技巧對於經驗哲學的發展有著舉足輕重的關係，他強調經驗主義的概念並非由洛克 (Locke)、休姆 (Hume) 和康德 (Kant) 最早提出，而是起源於西班牙的拉撒里羅 (Lazarillo)，他以作者的身分以寫作來重新體驗 (rehearse) 親身的歷險經驗。緊接著慕教授思考從康德、黑格爾 (Hegel) 到裴特 (Pater) 有關「體驗」或「經歷」的定義，再研究第一、二代英國浪漫派作家的「體驗」文學。為了延伸這主要名辭的含義，以涵括歷史或人類的集體經驗，作者接著研究幾位維多利亞時期的理論家：卡萊爾 (Carlyle)、紐曼 (Newman) 和米爾 (Mill)；安諾德 (Arnold)、羅斯金 (Ruskin) 和裴特 (Pater)。緊接著是兩位維多利亞時期的代表詩人：但尼生 (Tennyson) 和布朗寧 (Browning)；及兩位維多利亞中期的主要小說家：狄更斯 (Dickens) 和艾略特 (George Eliot)。十九世紀末，經由裴特的重新定義，「體驗」或「經歷」的概念演變為當時花俏公子 (the Dandy) 的理論基礎。作者認為這樣一個特殊角色不僅表現於拜倫和王德爾 (Wilde)，而且也包括了惠特曼及許多現代主義大師。最後本章以討論康拉德 (Conrad) 和葉慈 (Yeats) 作為終結，留待後學者將此概念繼續延伸至詩人艾略特、龐德、史蒂文斯和其後大家。最末這篇文章首先簡要概述西方文學，並重申前述各章所思考的兩大主題：文化互動與詩與哲學的問題也都涵蓋於本書的標題《獨特性與普遍性》之中。

Preface

When he met Oscar Wilde for the first time the young William Butler Yeats was astonished. Never before, he reports, had he heard "a man talking with perfect sentences." Yeats had met not a book but a man posing as a book, one who claimed that he never traveled anywhere without Walter Pater's *Studies in the History of the Renaissance*. From Wilde, Yeats learned what it is to be singular, how a particular point of view is capable of grasping the universal. We may take from this two lessons: that we are capable of encompassing the universe; but also that the universe may be larger than we think, certainly larger than Oscar Wilde thought. Here we might recall Jean-Paul Sartre's humbling deflation of our ambitions. There is more, he remarks, in a grain of sand than in our conception of the universe. The western preoccupation with particular and universal, it might be noted, is by no means universal.

Both the poet and the philosopher attempt to make sense of experience, each following an appropriate strategy. As the philosopher renders experience through an analytic prism, so the poet creates a synthesizing opticon to project it. Some philosophers, some poets engage in both activities. Lao-zi is both philosophical and poetic, Dante both poetic and philosophical. Each writer diffracts his own experience and by reprojecting it enables others to view their own more clearly. The Italian poet-philosopher and the Chinese philosopher-poet differ in their rhetoric: one is systematic and expansive, the other, fortuitous and cryptic. Yet both regard experience in the same way: as intensely personal and as philosophically meaningful. The work of both, like that of Homer, Valmiki, Shakespeare and Whitman, has nearly universal appeal.

My first essay attempts to answer the question, What is it that lifts Whitman out of his role as American Poet and recasts him as Universal Sage? Surely not any philosophical system, for among western poets he is the first non-Aristotelian. He accomplished something that few other writers ever have. For out of his democratic experience Whitman created a universal language. His incorporation of an exotic system of thought links him with the expatriate Modernists, Yeats, T. S. Eliot and Ezra Pound, the subjects of my second essay. His intuitive method in this links him with the subjects of my third essay, Wallace Stevens, William Carlos Williams and Robert Frost. In their rhetoric of personal experience and intercultural exchange all follow Whitman.

Lao-zi's Dao De Jing has proven central to the western reception of Asian thought. My exposition of Daoist principles complements the earlier summary of Pound's Confucian principles, the study of Whitman's Vedantic element and the citation of Buddhist precepts relevant to Modernist poets. Next I turn to the panoply of western culture as represented by the progression of the long poem from Homer to Byron. Philosophy in the form of allegory seems to me essential to the epic. As in those cultures unified by the allegorization of Ramayana, so in ancient Greece and Rome, and the cultures that emerge from them, allegory may be the fundamental means whereby particular experience is rendered universal. Allegory, theology and philosophy are all of a piece. When integrated with profound experience they issue in the highest poetry.

Like the second and third, the final two essays form a pair. Together they bring to conclusion my meditation on particular and universal. The sixth examines the universal in a single national literature, the seventh, the particular, in one of its prominent phases. With Tennyson we return to the question with which we began: How is it that he, like Whitman, in the now universal medium of English, managed to create a universal grammar of particular experience?

My dedication indicates my principal indebtedness, to a former student latterly turned teacher. I should also like to thank Meghmala Tarafdar for help with Sanscrit terms, Fang Po for help with Chinese quotations, and Mowbray Allan for help with the concept of Experience and much else.

1

Classical Hindu Culture and Whitman's Democratic Thought

The democratic poet would begin to discover the ideal world not in external figures, but in himself—not as an individual, but as an embodiment of the evolving nation and race.
                                                                    —Tocqueville

I am not in them, they are in me.
                                                                    —Krishna

I have taught one doctrine, the infinitude of the private man.
                                                                    —Emerson

Whitman embraces, then shies from, Emerson, because his mentor has said it all. Western democratic theory and Hindu thought find their first synthesis in the apothegms of the Concord sage, their exposition in the poems and ancillary prose of Tocqueville's democratic poet. We apprehend both bodies of thought somewhat obscurely, the first perhaps because of our very nearness to it, the second no doubt because of our distance from it. Their resolution too remains something of a mystery, one which we intuit in the major canonical poems of *Leaves of Grass*, one which we puzzle over in the prose.

Much has been said of democracy, much remains to be understood. The wise are hesitant to pronounce. "Nothing," writes Henry Adams of Jefferson and Madison's administrations, "was more elusive than the spirit of American democracy." Not a set of laws, but a spirit. Not a set of philosophical formulations, but a movement: "Jefferson's writing may be searched from beginning to end without revealing the whole measure of the man, far less of the movement." Adams is perhaps soberly recapitulating what he has found more exuberantly phrased by Whitman. "We have frequently printed the word Democracy," says the poet. "Yet I cannot too often repeat that it is a word the real gist of which still sleeps. It is a great word, whose history, I suppose, remains unwritten, because that history has yet to be enacted."

When we put "Democratic Vistas" alongside *The Second Treatise on Civil Government* we sense a generic mismatch. Why? Both Locke and Whitman are speaking of democracy. Yet the thing itself has changed, from an Enlightened idea to a Romantic emotion, the distinction suggested by Adams: "No one questioned the force or the scope of an emotion which caused the poorest peasant in Europe to see what was invisible to poet and philosopher [if not invisible to Whitman], the dim outline of a mountain-summit across the ocean, rising high above the mist and mind of American democracy."

What is this thing, democracy, this estate "all men are naturally in" (Locke) but must unnaturally construct and then construe? "A state of perfect freedom to order their actions," "a state of equality wherein all the power and jurisdiction is reciprocated." Not the power of which Adams speaks—the force of an emotion—but the force of law. And not freedom *from* but freedom *within:* "freedom of men under government is to have a standing rule to live by, common to everyone in that society."

The last word is crucial and predictive. For what we are dealing with are three democratic revolutions, the first political, the second social, the third yet to be named but the subject of Emerson, Whitman, Thoreau's radically libertarian, egalitarian, fraternal thought. I shall limit myself to Whitman and to the narrower focus of the Hindu contribution to these new ideas.

The three revolutions trace a progression from the intellectual to the emotional to the religious, as Tocqueville predicted: "The people reign in the American political world as the Deity does in the universe. They are the cause and the aim of all things; everything comes from them, and everything is absorbed in them." Only the last clause escapes the Frenchman's Biblical frame, a clause better glossed by my epigraph from the Bhagavad Gita: "I am not in them, they are in me." But here we must ask, Who is this me, this divine Self, poetically rendered as Krishna? Only then may we understand how the people and the poet become one in Whitman.

The divine Self is of course the *Atman,* a term that may be translated as either Self or Soul, two aspects of an entity that stand in need of distinction. By Self we do not mean self, which would translate *svayam,* my ordinary personal identity. We mean instead that larger identity which compounds itself through the experience of the cosmos. But whereas the Self is limited by time and space, the Soul is not, and though in a sense, then, the Soul is transcendent, in a more important sense it cannot be, for the Soul depends upon the Self for its experience. It is this Self that Whitman has in mind when he titles his epyllion "Song of Myself." It is this Soul that he has in mind when, in that poem, he speaks of himself as "the poet of the Soul." It is the relationship of Self (body) and Soul that informs the first two of the following lines:

> I have said that the soul is not more than the body,
> And I have said that the body is not more than the soul,
> And nothing, not God, is greater to one than one's self is.

2

To understand the crucial term of the third line—a universalized "God" we need to bear in mind another Upanishadic concept, *Brahman,* the universal principle, which, in the monistic synthesis central to the doctrine, is identified with the *Atman.* Finally, this *Atman* writ large is the *Parmatman,* the God of the Gita, among whose attributes are love, perfection, eternity. Now we understand the closing lines of "Crossing Brooklyn Ferry" as representing *Atman* in its identity as *Parmatman,* both terms simultaneously translated "soul."

> We fathom you not—we love you—there is perfection in you also,
> You furnish your parts toward eternity,
> Great or small, you furnish your parts toward the soul.

All is not strictly Hindu—how *could* such poetic English words, used with such license, be identical with their theological Sanscrit counterparts? But the correspondences nonetheless should be clear.

As a young boy Krishna went out into the yard to play. Whereupon his mother observed him eating a handful of dirt. Opening his mouth to remove it, she was offered therein a vision of the heavens and the earth, sun and moon, the vastness of the universe. "I am not in them, they are in me." And yet the first clause, while denying it, speaks another truth: Krishna *is* the god incarnate. Whitman, late in life, conceived a poetic project, never executed, which he titled "I, Osiris." "Song of Myself" might well be thought of, by analogy, as "I, Krishna."

Perhaps we can now supply the middle term: the People = Whitman = the Deity. "I am persuaded that in the end democracy directs the imagination from all that is external to man and fixes it on man alone," says Tocqueville, thereby moving us from Wordsworth's natural to Whitman's human universe. "Democratic nations may amuse themselves for a while with considering the productions of nature, but they are excited in reality only by a survey of themselves," he continues, in a chapter of *Democracy in America* titled "Sources of Poetry Among Democracies." Might we retitle Whitman's poem "Song of Myselves" (the People)? And do the observations of Tocqueville, in conjunction with Hindu theology, help us better understand the sequence of the poem's actual titles: 1855: no title (the ineffable *Brahman*); 1856: "Poem of Walt Whitman, an American" (the representative democrat); 1860: "Walt Whitman" (the Self)? The poem's true title, the 1881 "Song of Myself" (cp. Bhagavad Gita, Song of the Lord) then makes explicit what had earlier been merely implicit. This is the song of the *Atman* through which we know all, the *Brahman,* a doctrine expressed in the Brihadaranayaka Upanishad (I, iv, 7) as follows: "Of all these, the Self alone is to be realized, for one knows all these through it." Likewise in the Tantras, where the Self, called "the witness of all," is seen as

3

pervading everything (II, 46-48): "All gods and goddesses—nay, the whole universe from Brahma to a blade of grass—are his forms." From the god to his creation, from Whitman to his *Leaves of Grass*.

Not only the terms themselves—*freedom, equality, brotherhood,* but their sequence, is instructive. The great revolutions—of 1776, of 1789, of 1905, of 1949—are principally *political*. They begin with the need for freedom from tyranny. The Declaration of Independence iterates the doctrine of equality, the basis of subsequent *social* revolutions, accomplished in the manumission of slaves, women's suffrage, the extension of civil rights into every aspect of life. The third revolution is the most radical yet. It may eventuate in the realization of universal brotherhood but is directed by a more profound egalitarianism, one neither political nor social but cosmic. All things are equal, it says. All people, it says, are of equal value. It finds noxious the very notion of hierarchy. It is this revolution that prompts the American student to say, to his teacher: "That is your opinion. My opinion is different" (meaning equally valid). Though Whitman celebrates the political revolution, and participates in the social, it is our third revolution that he passionately advocates ("He most honors my style who learns under it to destroy the teacher"). The principal prose text is "Democratic Vistas."

Asked what Aeneas believes in, the American student says "freedom." Asked "What is democracy?" "Equal opportunity," he replies. "We are the World," says the Chinese student of the popular song of brotherhood, "that is a Chinese idea" (四海一家 [four seas one family]). From the Vedic Seers on, Indian poetics stress *rasa*, emotion. The great Hindu poems are religious. We are dealing here, as Adams understood, in these popular conceptions of democracy, not with ideas but poetic emotions, not with emotions but religious beliefs. These beliefs inform "Democratic Vistas," their irrational content and illogical exposition rendering Whitman's text difficult of explanation. "I shall use the words America and democracy," he begins, "as convertible terms." Unlike Montesquieu and Locke, who address the problem of the body politic, unlike Jefferson and Madison, who create a national social polity, Whitman universalizes democracy and so transforms it into something else. "The problem of humanity all over the civilized world," he says, "is social and religious." The solution to the problem, he claims, is democracy. His view has become the American faith. But what does Whitman—and what do we—mean by democracy?

Whitman means many things. First, he means *individualism,* thereby grossly reducing democracy's complex ideologies and manifestations to Emerson's "infinitude of the private man." "The ripeness of Religion," says Whitman, "is doubtless to be looked for in this field of

4

individuality." By democracy he also means freedom, not the freedom from political tyranny spoken of in The Declaration but rather the modern doctrine of one's freedom to realize oneself, to realize, for that matter, anything desirable (cp., for example, the cant phrase "freedom from poverty"). "The doctrine," says Whitman, "that man, properly train'd in sanest, highest freedom, may and must become a law . . . unto himself . . . *this* . . . is the only scheme worth working from."

Turning then from individualist to collective democracy, Whitman recommends as the greatest "lesson" Lincoln's "The government of the people, by the people, for the people." Here by democracy he means not the carefully balanced representative mechanism designed by those conservative founding fathers but a liberal mid-nineteenth-century *populism.* Yet, he adds, "Democracy too is law," referring again not to the body of adjudicated precedent, nor to the Constitution with its political and social rights, but rather to "the unshakable order of the universe," the "superior law," "not alone that of physical force," but "that of the spirit." "Would you have in yourself the divine, vast, general law?" he asks. "Then merge yourself in it." Again, not a political, not a social, but a religious doctrine, heavily indebted, as elsewhere, to Hindu theology.

Addressing the "purpose" of democracy—an interesting topic, implying as it does democracy's *dynamism,* Whitman is also of several minds: "The purpose is not altogether direct; perhaps it is more indirect," he says. We should not, that is, limit the formulations of democratic purpose to the straightforward language of political and social thinkers. "For it is not that democracy is of exhaustive account, in itself," he continues. "Perhaps, indeed, it is (like nature,) of no account in itself," that is, indefinable. To which he appends an even more fanciful figure: its "end," he says, "may be the forming of a full-grown man or woman." Democracy is to rival the God of Genesis. Or, in another Miltonic trope: "to justify God, his divine aggregate, the People" (not, we might note, the American people, but the people of the world). For democracy's "most alluring record"—its highest justification, says Whitman, is that it "alone can bind . . . all nations, all men, of however various and distant lands, into a brotherhood, a family," though again into a mystical, not literal, brotherhood. "At the core of democracy," Whitman himself concludes, "is the religious element."

Democracy for the poet, then, is religion. But what does Whitman understand by religion? Certainly not the Christian faith, though one whose individualism and sense of mission Christianity feeds. "Religion, although casually arrested, and after a fashion, preserv'd in the churches and creeds, does not depend at all upon them." This universal religion of the spirit is instead "a part of the identified soul," which is to say, the

5

Parmatman as we find it embodied in the world. "Bibles may convey and priests expound," Whitman continues, "but it is exclusively for the noiseless operation of one's isolated Self"—the *Atman*—"to enter the pure ether of veneration, reach the divine levels, and commune with the unutterable," that is, with *Brahman*. How, though, are we to identify this Self, this Soul, its activity leaving no trace? By attending, says Whitman, to the divine literatus. For, says the poet, concluding his account of democracy, "This SOUL—its other name, in these Vistas, is LITERATURE." For Whitman democracy is religion, religion, literature. Democracy, then, must be literature.

Which all brings us to the second major topic of the prose, the democratic poet. He, Whitman argues, is not only the exponent of the new democratic religion but its creator too, for "a great original literature is surely to become the justification and reliance, (in some respects the sole reliance,) of American democracy." Without its poet, democracy fails, as without democracy so does the American poet. I shall here conflate what Whitman says in the Vistas with what he has already said in the 1855 Preface.

There, we recall, despite protest to the contrary, Whitman had devoted much of his energy to dismissing the past. "The poems distilled from other poems will probably pass away," he had somewhat rashly predicted in his final paragraph. So much for Vergil, Dante, Milton; so much too for Homer and Vyasa. The expression of the American poet was to be "transcendent and new," "not direct or descriptive or epic." In "Democratic Vistas" (1871) Whitman concludes that "There can be no complete or epical presentation of democracy in the aggregate, or anything like it, at this day." Thus he dismisses not only the past but the present. Then, in the 1872 Preface, he speaks of "an impetus" that has urged him "to an utterance, or attempt at utterance, of . . . an epic of Democracy." The ambiguity of the latter phrase, a reprise of his 1855 statement, "The United States themselves are essentially the greatest poem" (itself an echo of Emerson's "America is a poem in our eyes"), is deliberate. In a world where democracy is literature, history supplants poetry, a dangerous trend for the democratic epic poet. Falling into line, Whitman in the Vistas takes the further step of reducing the canon of democratic literature to "the Declaration of Independence and . . . The Federal Constitution." If in the process, however, he seems to withdraw authority from his own project, not so. By moving forward into an indefinite future the realization of democracy (its "history," we remember him saying, "yet to be enacted"), he has likewise pushed the realization of his own project forward and therefore out of reach of the critic. He has, in other words, become authority itself. "How long it takes," he says slyly, "to make this American World see that it is, in itself, the final authority and reliance!" Yet, by making of himself the authority on democracy, has Whitman not contradicted democratic principles? So it would seem. "How much," exclaims the poet of democracy, entangled in his own contradictions, "is still to be disentangled, freed!"

At the heart of Whitman lies another paradox. This poet of the democratic future has chosen as his spiritual authority the traditions of the most ancient past. What, we must ask, is the relationship between those Hindu beliefs and democratic ideals that Whitman both expounds in his prose and embodies in his verse? Before we turn to examine the poetry, let us consider some general parallels.

Above all, both doctrines are idealistic. Freedom, equality and brotherhood, as newly construed by the mid-nineteenth century, all represent, practically speaking, unattainable goals. Likewise, the spiritual perfection recommended by Upanishadic, Sankhya, and Buddhist doctrines, remains for most an ideal, not a reality. All three principal democratic ideals, moreover, have their equivalents in Indian thought and practice. *Moksha*, the principle of release from *samsara*, the round of worldly suffering, corresponds to the ideal of *freedom*, the appetite for both perpetually renewed by the world's constraints. *Nirvana*, which portends a world of dissolved distinctions—between self and other, right and wrong, this and that—corresponds to the ideal of *equality*. As Krishna tells us (Bhagavad Gita V, xviii), the aspirant must "see with an equal eye the learned and the modest Brahmin, the cow, the elephant, the dog, the outcast." At its furthest reaches the Sankhya doctrine asserts the equality of man and God (of *Atman* and *Parmatman*). "Nothing," as Whitman had said, "not even God, is greater than one's self is." *Bhakti yoga*, which represents God as father, brother and friend—the last term suggesting Whitman's "friendliness," one of the democratic virtues listed at the close of the 1855 Preface, is parallel with *brotherhood*. *Bhakti*'s doctrine of love, furthermore, adumbrates the spiritual dimension of Whitman's own "amativeness."

In terms of the mid-nineteenth-century's expanded conception of democracy, observable in Emerson, Whitman and Thoreau (as well as more generally), Hindu thought might be said to promote *individualism*, i.e., the celebration, even deification of the self. The terms of the Sankhya philosophy, as embodied in the Gita, are highly moral: by achieving self-knowledge one may realize tremendous powers for good within oneself. Whitman reflects this doctrine too, as when he says, elliptically, "The supernatural of no account, myself waiting my time to be one of the supremes, / The day getting ready for me when I shall do as much good as the best, and be as prodigious." The principle of self-reliance, again shared with Emerson and Thoreau, has both Hindu roots (*svayam nirbhar*) and democratic manifestations. In philosophical terms,

Sankhya doctrine maintains that truth is self-proven (*svasidh*) and to the Soul self-evident. In Whitman's language, "Wisdom is of the soul, is not susceptible of proof, is its own proof." Finally, the *dynamism* that we have identified as characterizing latter-day notions of democracy has its counterpart too in the Gita's theory of transmigratory existence. "Myself moving forward then and now and forever," in Whitman's rendering. Only his *populism* is missing from Hindu doctrine.

To explore further these parallels and, where possible, locate their nexus, we turn now to four poems: "Song of Myself," "Crossing Brooklyn Ferry," "The Sleepers" and "Passage to India."

"Night Poem," the 1855 title of the third of these, retitled in 1870 "The Sleepers," suggests that Whitman was pairing this work with his untitled poem of "the rich running day," later titled "Song of Myself." "I celebrate myself," reads the latter's first line in 1855, "I stop some where waiting for you," its last. The relation not only of first and last lines but of first and last words within those lines is intentional ("myself" closely translates *atman*, the Sanscrit reflexive). Study of the opening and closing lines of the other poems of 1855 confirms our sense of artful design. "The Sleepers," for example, begins, "I wander all night in my vision," referring us to the poet's Vision of Democracy that had preceded his decision to create a Poetry of Democracy ("Speech," Whitman had said in his first poem, "is the twin of my vision").

Between day and night is dusk, the time at which "Crossing Brooklyn Ferry" has its natural setting (commuters returning home from Manhattan). Between the publication of the 1855 edition, which fully embodies the Hindu thought that Whitman had sedulously studied, and the 1856 edition, in which "Crossing Brooklyn Ferry" first appeared, the poet's father died. Accordingly, this poem of passage across water (it begins with "Flood-tide" and ends with "soul") represents other rites of passage, perhaps recapitulating as well the historical passage from Hindu to Buddhist thought. Taken together, the poems of day, dusk and night, "Song of Myself," "Crossing Brooklyn Ferry," and "The Sleepers," to arrange them in the order of the deathbed edition (1891-1892), whose text I shall use, form a trilogy, whose first and last parts begin with "I" and end with "you," and whose last line reads, "I will duly pass the day O my mother, and duly return to you." The "mother" is the mother of all things.

The motif of outward voyage and return, which plays upon larger patterns of natural recurrence, constitutes of course a fundamental epic structure not limited to the western tradition but a notable component thereof, whereby circular voyages vie with open-ended ones as though in a contest to determine which is the more appropriate figure for life itself.

(Odysseus returns home but Aeneas voyages outward to found a new home; Don Quixote comically tropes the Homeric pattern, as Ahab, tragically, the Vergilian.) Both directions of heroic movement owe something no doubt to the sun's course, which in one sense begins in the East and ends in the West, in another sense voyages outward and returns.

Whitman's work partakes of both traditions, as his title "Passage to India" suggests, but in the four canonical poems that we are looking at the pattern of outward voyage and return predominates. Thus the "Song of Myself" persona returns to the earth that has borne him; the Brooklyn commuter, to Brooklyn; "The Sleepers"'s European immigrant, in his dream, to his native land. Only "Passage to India" exhorts us to sail farther, though that course of action, as Magellan's servant Henriquez first demonstrated, eventually leads us homeward.

Whitman's poems, however, are not epics and are not entirely western. "Song of Myself," though I have called it an epyllion, may owe more structurally to those episodic anthologies, the Ramayana and Mahabharata, that Emerson, Thoreau and Whitman had, along with other religious, poetic and philosophical texts from the Orient, so enthusiastically assimilated. The fundamental motif in "Crossing Brooklyn Ferry" owes more to a central Buddhist metaphor—the passage from this shore to that (from *samsara* to *nirvana*)—than to any western figure. Likewise, "The Sleepers," in its reversals of westward progress, its double motifs ("The homeward bound and the outward bound"), its continental linkages ("The Asiatic and African are hand in hand, the European and American are hand in hand") is not traditionally western. That his general penchant was for Asia, not for Europe, is made clear by Whitman's acknowledgement of the Occidental's general debt to the Orient, in religion (to "those autochthonic bequests of Asia," "The Hebrew Bible, the mighty Hindu epics"), in poetry (to "the Iliad . . . certainly of Asiatic genesis"), in thought ("Probably both the Druids and Pythagoras drew their philosophy from the same source . . . the Indus or the Nile?"). "An oriental origin to all," he says in summary, his examples helping us to see what he means by "oriental."

That Whitman is working in the form of a trilogy may have to do with his trinitarian penchant. It is not the Christian configuration so much as the Romantic— Man, Nature and God—that attracts him, as he himself suggests in "Carlyle from the American Point of View." "The most profound theme," he says, that can occupy the mind of man . . . is doubtless involved in the query: What is the fusing explanation and tie— what the relation between the (radical democratic) Me, the human identity of understanding, emotions, spirit &. on the one side, of and with the (conservative) Not Me, the whole of the material objective universe and laws, with what is behind them in space and time, on the other side?"

9

"Song of Myself" takes up the radical democratic Me, "Crossing Brooklyn Ferry," the conservative Not Me, "The Sleepers" exploring "the other side," not just the nighttime realm of sleep but that which lies behind human identity and nature. But the trilogy may also owe something to the triadic structure of Hindu doctrine, divinity and cosmology. For example, *sukarma*, the action of good deeds, describes "Song of Myself"; *vikarma*, the action of ill deeds, a central concern of "Crossing Brooklyn Ferry"; *akarma*, the neutral bodily functions (among which, sleep), the world of "The Sleepers." Likewise Brahma, Vishnu and Shiva, or the cosmic cord of the Upanishads, with its strands of white, red and black, suggest themselves as parallel.

Others have dealt with the element of Hindu doctrine in "Song of Myself." Rather than rehearse these points, let us instead return to our principal theme, the democratic element. The central text is section 17:

> These are really the thoughts (1) of all men (2) in all ages and lands, (3) they are not original with me,
> (4) If they are not yours as much as mine they are nothing, or next to nothing,
> (5) If they are not the riddle and the untying of the riddle they are nothing,
> (6) If they are not just as close as they are distant they are nothing.
> This is (7) the grass that grows wherever the land is and the water is,
> This is (8) the common air that bathes the globe.

In summary, then, democracy according to Whitman is (1) universal, (2) eternal, (3) dependent upon no authority, (4) consensual, (5) both mysterious and explanatory, (6) immediate, (7) natural, and (8) essential. By "The thoughts of all men" he of course is also referring to his own poetry, but then democracy, as we have understood, is literature. If we do not normally think of literature as universal, dependent upon no authority, consensual, or natural, this, we recall, is democratic literature. Moreover, "Song of Myself" embodies the universal, natural religious doctrine of consensual democracy. But what of more specific ideals—freedom, equality, brotherhood—as they manifest themselves in the poem?

The greatest *freedom*, for Whitman, is the freedom to be oneself (the last word a literal translation of *atman*). Here the poet frees us from any and all other obligations, religious, cultural and philosophical. "Song of Myself" celebrates the freedom achieved in the political revolution, and it promotes the liberation implicit in the ongoing social revolution, but at its core is the celebration of personal experience. "Not I, not any one else can travel the road for you, / You must travel it for yourself." How we feel about these lines may determine how we feel about Whitman's work, about democratic literature, even about democracy itself.

Generally speaking, Whitman's democratic bias leads him away from Wordsworth's egotistical mode and toward a more compassionate humanism. Common sense, along with common experience, give to his

10

work what is all too frequently lacking in Blake or Milton. But is experience, we must ask, the only basis for literature? "You must travel the road for yourself," says Whitman, but who built the road? Nor does experience begin and end with the individual. The traveler who precedes us on the road, like the one who follows, can tell us of his travels, which then become a part of our experience. "Not any one else can travel that road for you." Which road? There are many roads to travel. How choose among them? Whitman has chosen, has constructed, his road, and tells us that we must take it. But are we not also free to choose, or build, another? A wiser than Whitman once asked if the road itself existed.

Freedom in "Song of Myself," however, is not nearly so central a theme as *equality*, whose political aspect in turn is less central than its social and religious aspects. In this, Christian compassion and Hindu cosmology prove more important to Whitman's doctrine than democratic theory. The view of "the wicked" as "just the same as the righteous" has its parallel in much religious thought, but Whitman's equalizing principle of sympathy seems Christian in origin, rather than Hindu. His "Congressman, Cuff, I give them the same, I receive them the same" promotes social equality, though Whitman's meaning verges toward the religious (we are all equal in the eyes of God). "Out of the dimness opposite equals advance," he says, sounding political or social to the modern ear, in fact echoing the religious Dao (道). "Always," he continues, substance and increase, always sex," the line now introducing a Hindu element. "Always a knit of identity, always distinction, always a breed of life."

The so-called "catalogues," principally the longer sections 15, 16 and 33, but including as well other passages of one-line montage, illustrate *equality;* yet they also express *brotherhood* ("all the men ever born are also my brothers," says the poet, temporally enlarging the doctrine). These sections, as their misnomer suggests, have been little understood, principally because their social has been allowed to obscure their religious dimension. True, Whitman treats social occupations as equal (15); but he also treats geographical places as equal (16); the animals, the vegetables, all details of creation, as equal (33). We have to do here less with the European sense of equality, political or even Christian, than with the Hindu sense of self-realization in the cosmos. That Whitman's rubric for these sections is birth, procreation and death is suggested by the opening of section 8, one of the briefer instances of the mode, where three couplets introduce us to a baby asleep in its cradle, "the youngster and the red-faced girl," and the suicide sprawled "on the bloody floor of the bedroom." The remainder of the section, followed by those mentioned, then releases upon us the perpetual cornucopia of reality, interweaving among egalitarian juxtapositions images of natural

11

difference (the sequence of the seasons, in 15), of natural *inequality* (the patriarchs, again in 15, who sit "at supper with sons and grandsons and great-grandsons"), of racial, social and political *distinction* (the "hue," "caste," and "rank" of 16). All these inequalities, however, in some sense resolve into equality, as the democratic poet incorporates them into his consciousness. In section 33 Whitman intersperses his so-called "catalogue" with narrative, dramatic incident, thematic rubric, and philosophical generalization so as to represent the equality of all situations. Defining his enterprise in heroic and Christian terms, he allows all history and time to march through him. The last of these sections, 41, universalizes Hesiod, in a Theogony of ancient gods, divine men and animals, in another Works and Days, where the natural world is internalized by the poet, who ends by designating himself "a creator," his "ambushed womb" suggesting rather the *hiranyagarbha*, the generative golden egg of Hindu tradition, than the Biblical Logos.

Some of Whitman's democratizations in "Song of Myself," on the other hand, are neither so ambitious nor so admirable. His patriotism, for example, leads him to a narrow view of history, as reflected in the choice of incidents for his two narrative sections. Likewise his mode of narration there, limited as it is to fictionalized autobiography: "Now I tell what I knew in Texas in my early youth," he opens section 34, which goes on to recount an episode from the history of Manifest Destiny. "Would you hear of an old-time sea-fight?" he begins 35, introducing another nationalistic tale. "List to the yarn, as my grandmother's father the sailor told it to me." Both Whitman's ethno- and egocentric treatment—tendencies that Pound and Eliot will overcorrect for—make of an otherwise cosmopolitan work something more provincial. His democratic reductions of past literature impress us as skillful but also faintly ridiculous, as when Barnardo's thrilling "Who's there?" and Hamlet's plangent "What a piece of work is a man?" conflate to become "Who goes there? . . . What is a man anyhow?"; as when Whitman reduces the elegant pathos of Homer's Odyssean invocation to the *Schwärmerei* of "Shoulder your duds dear son, and I will mine . . . Wonderful cities and free nations we shall fetch as we go." When he says of his reader (and poem), "It is you talking just as much as myself," Whitman anticipates much nonsense of the sort answered by Berrigan's riposte in "People of the Future": "while you are reading these poems, remember / you didn't write them, / I did." Whitman's democratic theory of truth, "Only what proves itself to every man and woman is so," has more serious weaknesses. "What is known I strip away," a provocation to ignorance, rather than promoting, threatens the enlightened world that Whitman elsewhere proposes. If "Song of Myself" expresses the limited attachment (*moha*) advocated by the Gita (which tells us that, even though we should not be attached to the world, we should not hate it; otherwise we could not play our proper role in it), then "Crossing Brooklyn Ferry" advocates the detachment (*nirmoha*) of the Buddhist tradition ("Give up attachment and desire," says the Dhammapada). Whereas the doctrine of "Song of Myself" can be largely understood by reference to a theory in which the accidents of the self, becoming *Atman*, merge with *Brahman*, the principle which unifies the phenomenal world, the later poem intermingles a variety of notions from the various Hindu traditions and may finally be read as Whitman's most Buddhistic work. How these elements combine in a democratic text will be our subject here.

The movement of the poem traces the larger pattern, typical of Buddhist thought, from differentiation to non-differentiation back to a higher sense of differentiation. Here "non-differentiation" combines an element of Buddhist selflessness (*anatman*), "myself disintegrated" in Whitman's phrase, with the broader Upanishadic doctrine of one and all (*sarvatmaya*). The latter, elaborated in temporal terms, expresses the corollary that all souls are the same age; in moral terms, that young and old should be equally respected. This accords with Whitman's democratic views. In short, says the doctrine, there is no difference between past, present and future. Hence Whitman's "similitudes of the past and those of the future." Those other souls of the Buddhist cosmos who "enter the gates of the ferry and cross from shore to shore," once reborn in the future, will again undertake the passage from *samsara* to *nirvana*. The doctrine resolves differences of place as well as time: "It avails not, time nor place—distance avails not." Whitman's brilliance here lies in turning the scene of his poem into the future, where he personally addresses us, each and all, as "you":

Just as you feel when you look on the river and sky, so I felt,
Just as any of you is one of a living crowd, so I was one of a crowd,
Just as you are refresh'd by the gladness of the river and the bright flow, I was
refreshed,
Just as you stand and lean on the rail, yet hurry with the swift current, I stood yet
was hurried . . .

The river gains from its metaphorical Hindu associations with experience. But the sense of far and near, of past, present and future, are all merged in the consciousness of the eternal moment, a psychological feature, the westerner might say, of the *nirvana* toward which Whitman is moving. As in the formal aspects of his work, so in its imagery Whitman absorbs the Hindu esthetic (the flames of the foundry "casting their flicker of black contrasted with wild red and yellow light," an Indian triad of colors). In Hindu deathbed practice, a flame is lit, whose extinction signifies the death of the individual. But the flame is also a characteristic

13

Buddhist metaphor for the self.

In section 5 "curious abrupt questionings stir within" the poet, suggesting the Buddhist theory of knowledge through questioning. (The poem placed after "Crossing Brooklyn Ferry" in the deathbed edition is "Song of the Answerer.") Also Buddhist are the lines at the close of the section, with their emphasis not upon soul but body: "I too had receiv'd identity by my body, / That I was I knew was of my body." Such reasoned self-knowledge stands in contradistinction to the intuitive Hindu process of self-realization.

In section 6 Whitman combines a Buddhist figure—the rebirth of the Buddha in the enlightened reader—with a series of Hindu metaphors in illustration of "what it was to be evil." "I too knitted the old knot of contrariety," he says, averting to the Gita's distinction between *jatil*, knotted, and *saral*, straight, the latter used of a person who thinks and acts in unison, unlike the poet, whose wishes, he says, he "dared not speak." "Nor," he introduces the passage, "is it you alone who know what it is to be evil," echoing in his complicity with the reader the Hindu view that when there is an evil everyone participates in it. The list of vices that Whitman confesses to incorporates the five emphasized in the Gita: *kama* (lust), *krodha* (anger), *lobh* (greed), *moha* (attachment) and *hath* (pride, vanity or stubbornness, as reflected in the word "lied"). The animals that allegorize the lower vices, "The wolf, the snake, the hog," might all have been drawn from the animal fables of good advice collected in the Hitopadesha. The final lines of the section, with their mention of the role, great or small, "that is what we make it," also incorporate doctrine from the Gita, which tells us that we all have roles to play; no matter that your role is inferior, you must play it well.

Section 7 brings to climax the Buddhist movement in the poem. "Who was to know what should come home to me?" asks Whitman, alluding to two Buddhist doctrines, those of the Return and of No-knowledge. Thereafter the poem itself returns from non-differentiation to its opposite, perhaps, as suggested earlier, recapitulating the broad historical trend of Indian thought whereby Hinduism returns to supplant Buddhism. At any rate, the doctrinal distinction of section 8 between "my highest name" and "my face" is interpretable in the Gita's terms, *nama* (name) and *rupa* (appearance), used to express the doctrine of soul consciousness: we communicate soul to soul not body to body (though it is through the body that we reach the soul).

The final section 9 (the number itself suggests the avatars of Vishnu, among which the Buddha is sometimes counted as the ninth) reintroduces terms compatible with Buddhist emphases. "Objects than which none else is more lasting" suggests the doctrine of No-permanence, in which transience is paradoxically regarded as the only permanence. At

14

the same time—and in keeping with this syncretistic tradition—the argument includes an urging of the "necessary film," appearance, "to envelop the soul," thereby reverting to Hindu doctrine, which, as shown earlier, informs the poem's closing lines.

To deal properly with these exotic elements involves a certain antisepsis. The poem's speaker is, after, all, a resident of Brooklyn and lover of Manhattan, passing among the objects of his affection. The measure of his greatness is the measure of his human sympathy ("crowds of men and women attired in the usual costumes, how curious you are to me!"), the tone of this meditation determined by the prediction of his death, an event never literally referred to. The cast of the poem's imagery is *chiaroscuro*, as in the image of seagulls: "how the glistening yellow lit up parts of their bodies and left the rest in strong shadow," its visual effects reminiscent of the work of Winslow Homer, Whitman's contemporary, but not at all of oriental painting. The poet's projection of nostalgia into the future ("you . . . are more in my meditations than you might suppose"), and then back into the present ("I loved well those cities . . .") may be a tour de force, but we must bear in mind that all is not rhetoric. When Whitman speaks of "others who look back on me because I look'd forward to them," his words pull the reader up short. And not simply with the truth that we register as Tu Fu 杜甫 and Li Po 李白 congratulate themselves in the knowledge that we shall be reading them a thousand years thence. "Crossing Brooklyn Ferry," though Romantic, is also romantic in the larger sense—of expressing nostalgia for life in the midst of its being led. It is this, rather than its doctrinal features, that places it among the world's great lyric poems.

Let us turn now to our third major poem. I have suggested analogies between Whitman's trilogy and various trinities of Hindu myth and western thought. If we take Man as the subject of "Song of Myself" and Nature as the object of meditation in "Crossing Brooklyn Ferry," then "The Sleepers" is preeminently the poem of God. If we do not immediately recognize the divinity, it may be that we are thinking in western rather than Hindu terms. For just as "Song of Myself" has at its heart the creative Brahma, and "Crossing Brooklyn Ferry," the solicitous Vishnu, so "The Sleepers" embodies Shiva. Having dealt successively with democratic theory and philosophical doctrines in the first two poems, I should like now to take up the question of Whitman's use of myth.

Among the earliest deities of the Vedic period, preceding by eons the synthetic Hindu divinities just mentioned, are Indra and Varuna, a solar and lunar dyad, maintainers of the universal order (*rita*). Indra, an identity that Whitman assumes in "Song of Myself," like the sun, shines during the day. Like the democratic poet, he presides over friendship and ratifies contracts (democracy's ultimate basis is in law). Varuna, by contrast, presides over the night, nothing, it is said, escaping him. He judges all equally by peering into the natures of men as they sleep. He is omnipresent, knows the past and the future, is unequalled in authority. Varuna, in short, describes the persona of "The Sleepers," from whom, says Whitman of himself, they can hide nothing, "and would not if they could." Stepping, like Vishnu (another early deity), "With light feet, swiftly and noiselessly," the poet bends "with open eyes" over their "shut eyes," "pausing, gazing, bending, and stopping."

Myth, in the poem as in mythology itself, is multi-layered. The later Shiva, anticipated in the Vedas but only elaborated in the Mahabharata, figures too in "The Sleepers"'s subliminal mythology ("I am a dance," says Whitman). Though also a god of fecundity and creation, he is principally the god of destruction (the two, however, interlinked in the Hindu vision). An episode of the great epic recounts his destruction of the triple city of the universe—heaven, sky and earth, the latter two having been propped apart in the earlier Indian creation myths.

Similarly Whitman collapses what had earlier been distinguished. Shiva, in the myth, then causes those pairs, differentiated and named at the time of creation, to unite, thereby dissolving their separate identities. And so Whitman reproduces Chaos, the original state that in many cosmologies precedes creation; having joined his opposites, the poet moves behind them to their origins:

> Now I pierce the darkness, new beings appear,
> The earth recedes from me into the night,
> I saw that it was beautiful, and I see that what is not the earth is beautiful.

As Whitman himself had said of Emerson, "He pierces the crust that envelops the secrets of life." But in piercing the darkness he arrives at night, which "pervades" and "infolds" both "the new-born emerging from the gates, and the dying emerging from the gates." What is this night? The text that stands in need of explication is the cosmic love sonnet that concludes section 1:

> I am she who adorn'd herself and folded her hair expectantly,
> My truant lover has come, and it is dark.
>
> Double yourself and receive me darkness,
> Receive me and my lover too, he will not let me go without him.
>
> I roll myself upon you as upon a bed, I resign myself to the dusk.
>
> He whom I call answers me and takes the place of my lover,
> He rises with me silently from the bed.

Darkness, you are gentler than my lover, his flesh was sweaty and panting,
I feel the hot moisture yet that he left me.

My hands are spread forth, I pass them in all directions,
I would sound up the shadowy shore to which you are journeying.

Be careful darkness! Already what was it touch'd me?
I thought my lover had gone, else darkness and he are one,
I hear the heart-beat, I follow, I fade away.

Whitman's principal source here is not the Vedic but the early Greek creation myth. Hesiod, we recall, derives Erebos, the dark, from Chaos, in the first differentiation. Night, the second born, then couples with Erebos to produce Ether and Day. As in the early Vedic myths, however, the actors in Whitman's primordial scene remain nameless, the One creating a Second. The "she" of Whitman's text is undoubtedly Hesiod's Night, product of Chaos's second parthenogenic act. "She" now awaits her lover, "Erebos, the dark," as Hesiod calls him. "My truant lover has come, and it is dark," says Whitman's figure, who proceeds to transform Erebos into "darkness," thereby preserving the Vedic tradition of obscure original principles. This doubling of Erebos, then, explains the double figures of darkness and lover who dominate the sonnet's octave. The gesture, in the tenth line, of spreading the hands forth and passing them in all directions suggests that Whitman is conflating with the feminine Hesiodic principle the masculine Egyptian principle Ra, god of the sun, whose rays are often represented as hands spread forth. In the final lines the speaker acknowledges the unity of darkness and the lover ("darkness and he are one"), the final fade presumably presaging the dawn of creation.

This fundamentally Greek structure is complemented elsewhere in the poem by motifs that parallel Vedic mythology. Thus the four linked continents—Asia, Africa, Europe and America—mentioned earlier, might be identified with the four parts of the world bodied forth as the limbs of Purusha, an Indian Adam Kadmon who also figures in the creation myths. More generally, the underworld aspect of Whitman's scene corresponds to Indian conceptions: in the Vedic Hell, the kingdom of Yama had represented a paradise for the good; in the Hell of the Puranas, a purgatory for the wicked. Whitman—in his characteristically democratic gesture—includes the not-so-virtuous side by side with the virtuous ("I swear they are averaged now," he says). Even more generally Hindu, however, is the sense we have in Whitman of a world which the gods maintain without having instituted. As he says in "Song of Myself," "I do not talk of the beginning or the end, / There was never any more inception than there is now." By thus balancing his allusions to the Greek and Vedic creation myths with this steady-state perspective the poet reinforces the non-sequential, non-hierarchical, non-ethnocentric tendencies that we have identified as so important to his democratic stance.

As in "Song of Myself" and "Crossing Brooklyn Ferry," so in "The Sleepers" the democratic and the Hindu elements blend into one another. Whitman's "journeymen divine," though American craftsmen, suggest the Vedic half-gods (what later generations viewed as divine beings were, in their time, says the Hindu, merely men). Due to the mythic ambiance here, American history is more successfully universalized than it had been in "Song of Myself." In section 4 the ship heading helplessly on, though it may suggest a premonition in 1855 of an impending national tragedy, The Civil War, remains generalized. In section 5 Whitman successfully democratizes Homeric motifs by transuming the figure of Priam in Washington. In the mythic scene of section 6, the red squaw— of Asiatic origins—visits Whitman's mother, thus paired with the *pater patriae* of the preceding section, in a scene which successfully renders the Edenic America. Elsewhere, Hesiod himself is democratized in Whitman's transmogrifications of Hypnos and Thanatos into sleep and peace, the latter universal modern desideratum replacing the classical equalizer, death. Under the protection of sleep's mythic spell Whitman restores a dreamlike hierarchy, one in which the scholar kisses the teacher and the master salutes the slave, only to balance it out with reciprocal, egalitarian gestures.

In "Poetry To-day in America—Shakspere—the Future" (1881) Whitman quotes approvingly Sainte-Beuve's distinction of 1866 between the poet of "perfect"—we might translate *accomplished*—work, and the poet "who leaves you much to desire, to explain, to study, much to complete in your own turn." This early characterization of modern poetry by itself proves the critic's stature. In one sense its latter terms define the whole Whitman project, in another more specific sense the enveloping moves that Whitman makes in the major poem of 1871. And yet, ironically, it is the former term, *accomplished*, that best characterizes "Passage to India." This summative poem, like works of the later Stevens, may seem abstractly orotund, until its poetic is understood.

"Singing my days," reads the first, apparently naked, line. "Singing the great achievements of the present," the poet continues, as though directly affronting the reader's sense of epic propriety. Upon reflection, however, we realize that "my days" are our days, the singing a continuing activity, the invocation both "feudal," as Whitman might say, and democratic. Just as we have heard him out on the splendors of technology, suddenly, at the stanza's end, the poet turns, in his hopelessly flat apostrophe, to "The Past! The Past! The Past!" Is this but more democratic reduction, such as we have seen in Whitman's travesties of lines from Homer and Shakespeare? In one sense the poem merely reworks familiar arguments; and yet its central subject, "the Past," is surely new. This *is* the juncture of past and future, like it or not, that the theory has predicted. "O you temples fairer than lilies pour'd over by the rising sun," the Bard bathetically emotes, as he embraces precisely those high cultural and religious traditions hitherto so much maligned. Whitman, in short, has made of the arch-enemy of democracy—tradition—the subliminal hero of his Ode to the Past. Having done with day, dusk and night, he turns to the fourth body of Brahma, the dawn, including in its hopeful light what he had earlier omitted.

Like his incorporation of Victorian diction, Whitman's marriage of Capitalism and Christianity ("not for trade or transportation only, / But in God's name") strikes the modern liberal reader as extinguishing, not kindling, that light. But for Whitman these features merely indicate a desirable popularization of his work. At fifty-two he is not, at any rate, in conservative dotage but rather profound consolidation, having mastered a skillful duplicity whereby, for example, in the poem that precedes this one ("Proud Music of the Storm") he can rehearse the repertoire of grand opera only to dismiss it. In "Prayer of Columbus," the poem that follows ours, he lets Tennyson loose on a figure who to the popular ear may have seemed memorialized but who to the more attentive reader appears limned as a kind of degenerate Ulysses. Such practice may not be to everyone's taste, but a deliberate ambiguity is clearly what Whitman is up to.

The question that he is raising might be put more sympathetically: how within democracy can the older traditions be maintained? The answer: by an Odyssean cunning. By speaking openly but disguising one's intentions. By denying the older traditions but embodying them. These procedures may grow out of Whitman's modulation from the early canonical mode, in which democracy is promoted over culture, to the middle, essayistic mode of the "Songs," which reflect the popular values of oratory, hymnody and opera, on to the new mixed genre of the work before us, where cultural motifs from the history of civilization shape the exposition of ideas. It is this new genre itself—Whitman's unacknowledged legacy to Pound—that makes the reader uncomfortable. More uncomfortable, though, than the mere reader of poetry, is the democratic apostle who, in place of Whitman's early native and naïve vision finds the project of democratic idealism encumbered with Professor Longfellow's conservative European reading lists. "Lands found and nations born," says Whitman, the former signifying his rediscovery of the past, the latter, further extensions of the new ideology.

Our specific subject here is Whitman's handling of the epic tradition.

We could without difficulty trace its presence through the poem's tropes on Homer ("Struggles of many a captain, tales of many a sailor dead"), Dante ("Reckoning ahead O soul, when thou . . . frontest God"), and later figures. More to the point is to seek Whitman's true model, one which Sainte-Beuve happens to have mentioned in the passage quoted by Whitman: the Aeneid. For indeed, Whitman is not so much America's Homer as her Vergil. Like the Roman poet, he assimilates past to present and projects Empire into the future, offering it a social, political and cultural model. If Vergil's deliberate effort focuses upon Book VI of the Aeneid, Whitman constructs "Passage to India" with similar intent.

"Down from the gardens of Asia descending radiating," he writes, translating a Biblical subject into modern dactylic hexameter; thus he alludes metrically to Vergil, rhetorically, to Milton. "Finally shall come the poet worthy that name," he continues, "The true son of God shall come singing his songs," a figure that collapses Christ with Vergil's *"Augustus Caesar, divi genus,"* the offspring of a god. And so Whitman renders unto Democracy what Vergil had rendered unto Caesar Augustus. Moreover the passage of prophecy that follows takes as its model Vergil's prophecy, one spoken, we recall, by Aeneas' father. Whitman, then, as both father and son—he himself the hero as well as author of his poems—speaks prophetically to his collective progeny, Democratic Man.

It is of course Columbus—to whom Whitman next turns—not Caesar, who issues in for America its golden age, the "golden world," as Whitman has it. Like Vergil, who had done so in his Fourth Eclogue, Whitman employs motifs compatible with Christianity, as he searches out the "Comrade perfect." The Dantesque passage already quoted from concludes with the achievement of "love complete": "the Elder Brother found, / The Younger melts in fondness in his arms," an echo not only of the reunion of Prodigal Son with older brother but of the underworld reunions described by Homer, Vergil and Dante. At the close of the poem, having traced out this European epic tradition, Whitman, in a generous but prudential gesture, draws in, by allusion, figures from his own contemporary world: Melville ("Away O soul! Hoist instantly the anchor!"), Thoreau ("Have we not stood here like trees in the ground long enough?"), and Poe ("Reckless O soul, exploring, I with thee, and thou with me, / For we are bound where mariner has not yet dared to go"). Finally, however, affirming his own exclusive divinity, he exhorts himself and us ("O my brave soul!")—America and the brave new world generally—to "farther farther sail," on into that democratic vision of the poet's own making. This voyage across "the seas of God," though it may require daring, is ultimately safe, conducted as it is under Whitman's benevolent supervision.

Like Vergil, then, the American Poet has humanized the gods and immortalized men. Like Aeneas, who had voyaged from Asia to Africa to Europe—leaving women behind to do so, Whitman, himself companionless, marries the continents (*his* higher goal). Like Vergil he celebrates the past, present and future of Empire. Each poet effectively dispenses with a burdensome heritage by transforming it for his successors into a difficult but accessible vision, in the process creating a myth that no one can fully believe in, but no one dare gainsay.

2

More Asian Importations in Yeats, Eliot and Pound

For nearly two millennia European culture was governed by two traditions, the Biblical and the classical, always, if grudgingly, allowing a third to flourish, openly or secretly, at its margins. Sometimes the third tradition was exotic, as in the case of the Egyptian (Isis was worshipped as far north as Trier, as late as 800 A.D. at Marseilles). Sometimes it merely amalgamated the dominant traditions, as in the case of the neoplatonic. Sometimes it combined one of them with an occult element, as in the case of the Rosicrucian. Latterly the third tradition has aspired to originality and comprehensiveness, in the seemingly endless series of movements that we denominate Romanticism, Realism, Naturalism, Symbolism, and so forth.

These movements, though often discussed as though they were secular, are in fact religious. The desuetude of Christianity in the eighteenth century and the decay of classical learning in the nineteenth bring about the disappearance, first of the Judeo-Christian, then of the Greek and Roman pantheons. Since no substantial divinities have yet arrived to replace them, the modern movements have found it impossible to institutionalize themselves for more than a few generations. Explorations in search of a new god, however, continue, and expeditions into oriental culture have for the past two centuries proven the most long-lived of such ventures. If the eighteenth century represents the germinating, and the nineteenth, the sprouting, then the twentieth represents the flourishing of this new third tradition.

Much attention has been given to these three phases in England and America: to the seminal work of early orientalists like Sir William Jones; to the cultivation of the Orient in the work of Emerson, Thoreau and Whitman; to its subsequent exfoliation. Studies of twentieth-century poetry have dealt in some detail with its continuing influence, beginning about mid-century with the successive waves of Buddhist transplantation, for example. What has not been so carefully considered is the Asiatic element in Anglo-American poetry of the first half of the century. The case of Ezra Pound has received considerable attention, but he has been regarded for the most part as an anomaly rather than as part of a general trend.

In this essay I shall take up the cosmopolitan Yeats, Eliot and Pound, in whom a conscious and deliberate process of orientalization is at work;

22

in the essay that follows, I shall take up the more provincial Stevens, Williams and Frost, in whom the process by comparison is intuitive and random. As well as limiting the number of figures under study, I have chosen to consider altogether only four Asiatic elements: the Vedantic, the Buddhist, the Confucian and the Daoist.

In one sense Yeats, Pound and Eliot, so closely associated, all but by arrangement divide among themselves the three traditions, Eliot taking the Biblical (Christian); Pound, the classical; and Yeats, by virtue both of his vacillation between those two and of his early embrace of the occult, the third. In another sense, however, all three poets vie with one another in synthesizing the three traditions. We might in fact say that this process of judging the cultural traditions constitutes the unifying theme of their work in verse and prose. It may be the probity of their judgments, rather than any overwhelming poetic excellence, that for later generations has proven such an obstacle in succeeding them.

In 1895 William Butler Yeats, at the age of thirty, published his *Collected Poems*, divided its slim but carefully considered contents into two sections, "Crossways" and "The Rose," and thereby suggested the superimposition of rose on cross found in Rosicrucian imagery. In so doing he established a model both for the syncretism of the Modernists and for his own characteristic vacillation. The rose of his second title stands, among other things, for primitive Ireland (dark Rosaleen), the cross in his first title, for the modern Catholic dispensation. His difficulty in choosing between traditions came to fullest expression in the late poem "Vacillation," where the rhetorical question "What theme had Homer but original sin?" reflects not only Yeats's powers of synthesis but also his indecisiveness in the face of a choice between two major traditions. Made discontent by his own vacillation he sought, from beginning to end, a third tradition, first in the mystical and the primitive, later in the exotic. Never coming to rest in any single tradition, he succumbed, so to speak, by providing an heroic epitaph for the Christian grave that he finally occupied in Drumcliff Churchyard.

Nor was it only in conservative old age that this latter-day Milton summarized the values of the two major traditions. The heroic theme permeates Yeats's work from the earliest "Wanderings of Oisin" (1889), whose structure is modeled on the Odyssey's; to the emerging interest in that Irish Achilles, Cuchulain; through the poems of explicitly Homeric content; and on to the stoic spirit off his last years. In speaking of his earliest intentions he writes, "I wanted, if my ignorance permitted, to get back to Homer, to those that fed at his table," the last words imitating those of a classical Athenian dramatist. The Christian element in his work is most characteristically merged with a second tradition, as in its

23

late marriage, in *Purgatory*, with the classical Oedipal theme, but it also receives remarkably pure expression in the life and work, perhaps nowhere more clearly than in the naming of his daughter for the mother of the Virgin and his son for the patron saint of the Church Militant. Both births, moreover, received commemoration in the form of poetic prayers.

I have mentioned Milton, but it was to Shakespeare, whom the Irish poet praised for his variety and multiplicity, and more especially to one of his creatures, Hamlet, that Yeats in his indecisiveness was indebted. Curiously Hamlet occurs twice in juxtaposition with the Buddha. In a section of the *Autobiography* first published in 1914 Yeats describes a reproduction of a portrait over his mantle piece depicting his most influential poetic mentor, William Morris:

> It is 'the fool of fairy . . . wide and wild as a hill,' the resolute European image that yet half remembers Buddha's motionless meditation, and has no trait in common with the wavering, lean image of hungry speculation, that cannot but because of certain famous Hamlets of our stage fill the mind's eye.

Hamlet, who later recurs as an unsatisfactory alternative to the Buddha in "The Statues," we might regard as an image of the heroic weakened by Christianity. (In *The Trembling of the Veil*, Part IV, "The Tragic Scene" Yeats had asked, in relation to certain Christian poets he had known, "Why are these strange souls born everywhere today? With hearts that Christianity, as shaped by history, cannot satisfy.") The Buddha, then, for Yeats represented an alternative to Christ, one strengthened by his association with the primitive figure of fairy, seen as persisting through reincarnation, recalled for the moment as a ghost hovering in the meditative visage of Morris.

Having identified the oriental alternative to a tortured Christian humanism, Yeats still cannot choose it. After he has loaned to a friend his copies of *Esoteric Buddhism* and Renan's *Life of Christ*, the friend, the poet tells us (again in his *Autobiography*), proceeded to offer himself to the Theosophical Society as a *chela*, "vexed now," says Yeats, "by my lack of zeal, for I had stayed somewhere between the books, held there perhaps by my father's skepticism." On still another occasion, and as it often does in *A Vision*, Yeats's indecisiveness took the form of an inclusive range of reference. In a passage from *Estrangement*, "Extracts from a Diary Kept in 1909," the poet discusses his newly instituted mode of self-documentation:

> To keep these notes natural and useful to me I must keep one note from leading on to another, that I may not surrender myself to literature. Every note must come as a casual thought, then it will be my life. Neither Christ nor Buddha nor Socrates wrote a book, for to do that is to exchange life for a logical process.

The Buddha, placed out of chronological order between the Greek and Christian martyrs, is in fact the only one of the three for whose words we have no certain quotation. By comparison with the father of western logic and the god whose word defines the Way, he might further be said to represent the only valid example of what Yeats wished to illustrate.

Sometimes a Buddhistic feeling made its presence felt, as in Yeats's desire, expressed in "Byzantium," to escape from "all complexities of mire or blood," a parallel for the release (*moksha*) from the world of suffering (*samsara*) that we find in Buddhist doctrine; typically, though, and again in accord with another Buddhist tradition, one that equates the ultimate peace (*nirvana*) with that very world of suffering, Yeats could represent his final wisdom, in "The Circus Animals' Desertion," for example, as an acceptance of the "foul rag-and-bone shop of the heart." A more explicit example, however, of the Buddha's importance in the poet's work is to be found in "The Statues." Though he principally treats the relationship of modern Ireland to ancient Greece, Yeats, in a not altogether necessary third stanza, here goes out of his way to acknowledge the Buddhist vision, giving it preference over his version of medieval Christianity. In the second stanza, speaking in a quasi-historical way, he has the Greece of Phidias reject "all Asiatic vague immensities," a gesture that we might read as Yeats's own rejection of his earlier infatuation with Hindu doctrine, were it not for our knowledge that in old age he returned to the sources of Indian philosophy, helping to translate a selection of the Upanishads. How, we might wonder, did the Irish poet come to this interest in Vedantic thought, which preceded his recorded interest in the Buddha?

"Was the *Bhagavad Gita* the 'scenario' from which the gospels were made?" he muses in the 1909 diary. Although Hindu thought predated Christian, Yeats insisted that his own "vague speculations" had preceded those of the Hindu thought that he encountered at the age of twenty, when Mohini Chatterjee visited Dublin. Yeats himself, as a member of the newly-organized Blavatsky Lodge, was instrumental in making the arrangements: "We persuaded a Brahmin philosopher to come from London," he writes in the *Autobiography*. "It was my first meeting with a philosophy that confirmed my vague speculations and seemed at once logical and boundless." Again a synthetic spirit is at work, as Yeats seeks to resolve the philosophical character of Greek thought with the infinitude of the Biblical divinity but finds that resolution only within the terms of in an exotic tradition.

Although it has never been clear who it was that first stimulated the Irish poet's interest in Hindu thought, an important influence must have been his philosophical mentor, Madame Blavatsky, whose encyclopedic works are rife with Vedantic reference. The *Autobiography*, if only indirectly, intimates several other such stimuli. "I sometimes wonder what he would have been," says Yeats of his friend, the poet A. E. Russell,

> had he not met in early life the poetry of Emerson and Walt Whitman . . . and those translations of the Upanishads, which it is so much harder to study by the sinking flame of Indian tradition than by the servicable lamp of Emerson and Whitman.

Earlier Yeats had spoken of an "ambition, formed in Sligo in my teens, of living in imitation of Thoreau on Innisfree." The American naturalist had himself been inspired by Hindu asceticism. The emphasis on the names of two other American predecessors suggests Yeats's debt to them as well for the transmission of the Indian tradition. Finally, the very opening pages of the *Autobiography*, which record his earliest recollections, include a description of the dining room in the house of his maternal grandfather, William Pollexfen, an influential figure in the poet's early development. The passage concludes by enumerating "a jar of water from the Jordan for the baptizing of his children and Chinese pictures from rice-paper and an ivory walking-stick from India that came to me after his death." In the midst of this survey of three generations and three traditions we are given a vicarious glimpse of what may have been Yeats's first impression of China.

Unlike three early poems on Indian subjects that are more atmospheric than philosophical (even the subsequent "Mohini Chatterjee," like "A Dialogue of Self and Soul," does not treat very seriously the idea of reincarnation, so central to Yeats's mature thought), the late oriental poems, especially those with Chinese subjects, are among his most thoughtful meditations. Unlike Auden, however, who gathered impressions of China first hand, Yeats traveled in imagination only. And unlike the evidence that we have of the poet's contact with Hindu philosophy, a rather uncharacteristic Confucian epigraph, inspired perhaps by the sustained contact that he had recently had with Ezra Pound, graces the 1914 collection *Responsibilities*. Otherwise Yeats's China is predominantly Daoist, or more generalized. By the latter I mean that China represents for him a philosophical view and a civilization seen broadly as alternatives to those of the West.

For the demise of western civilization is a major theme of the late poems, which intermittently suggest its reconstruction in the Orient. "Lapis Lazuli" is here the principal text. As has often been noted, the crucial terms on which Yeats's argument turns are "tragedy" and "gaiety." What has not been so clearly seen is the way in which the ensemble of poems that opens this last volume orchestrates that opposition. In the famous work based upon a carving in lapis lazuli

26

presented to him by Harry Clifton, Yeats meditates upon the decline of the West on the eve of the second World War, predicting not only its ruin but its reconstruction: "All things fall and are built again." The questions that we naturally ask are when, where, and by whom? To which the next line gives the clue: "And those that build them again are gay." Those who are "gay," for Yeats, are not those who turn away from tragedy, but those of philosophical temper whose vision incorporates and transcends it. Such are the "Chinamen" who, at the end of the poem, having climbed the hill, stare back on "the tragic scene," and whose eyes, in the last word of the poem, are described as "gay." At which point, by a backward motion, those figures of philosophical fortitude, Lear and Hamlet, who had also been described in unlikely terms as "gay," are now drawn into the compass. Readers of the poem have sometimes been led, perhaps by Yeats's description of their eyes as "ancient," to regard the Chinese figures (who at any rate are graven in an old piece of stone) as belonging to the past. But the figures for Yeats are very much alive in the present. At this point we should have the whole text of the closing lines before us:

> Two Chinamen, behind them a third,
> Are carved in lapis lazuli,
> Over them flies a long-legged bird,
> A symbol of longevity;
> The third, doubtless a serving-man,
> Carries a musical instrument.
>
> Every discoloration of the stone,
> Every accidental crack or dent,
> Seems a water-course or an avalanche
> Or lofty slope where it still snows
> Though doubtless plum or cherry-branch
> Sweetens the little half-way house
> Those Chinamen climb towards, and I
> Delight to imagine them seated there;
> There, on all the tragic scene they stare.
> One asks for mournful melodies;
> Accomplished fingers begin to play.
> Their eyes mid many wrinkles, their eyes,
> Their ancient, glittering eyes, are gay.

The crucial turn in the passage occurs seven lines from the end, as the poet shifts his attention from the scene represented before them to his own extension of it. For it is Yeats who enables the Chinamen to complete their journey, to arrive at the half-way house, and to gaze upon "the tragic scene" that he himself had earlier conjured up. Music is called for, and, in a significant phrase, "Fingers *begin* to play." The scene occurs in the future, the accomplishment of an ancient civilization hopefully transposed by Yeats's synchronic, syncretistic imagination.

Nor does Yeats's orientalism here conform to the western stereotype of hermetism. By contrast with the solitary Hamlet and Lear the Daoist scholars with their serving-man are engaged in a sociable party, not a solitary retreat. By contrast with the destruction of civilization represented throughout the first half of the poem, their activity represents its perpetuation. The sense of historical progression in "Lapis Lazuli" finds its counterpart too in "Nineteen Hundred and Nineteen," interestingly enough in Yeats's other most important "Chinese" passage:

> When Loie Fuller's Chinese dancers enwound
> A shining web, a floating ribbon of cloth,
> It seemed that a dragon of air
> Had fallen among dancers, had whirled them round
> Or hurried them off on its own furious path;
> So the Platonic Year
> Whirls out the new right and wrong,
> Whirls in the old instead . . .

Yeats's figure of the dragon combines its destructive western with its restorative Chinese powers. There is, moreover, a double movement in the last three lines, for the new right and the new wrong are both replaced by their older counterparts.

I have suggested that our reading of "Lapis Lazuli" will gain by considering its immediate context in *Last Poems*, where it follows "The Gyres," with which Yeats opens the volume, and precedes a poem titled "Imitated from the Japanese," done from a prose translation of a hokku. The opening stanza of "The Gyres," Yeats's last treatment of the figure that schematizes the double movement of his cycles, further identifies the poet's point of view with that of the Chinamen in "Lapis Lazuli":

> The gyres! The gyres! Old Rocky Face, look forth;
> Things thought too long can be no longer thought,
> For beauty dies of beauty, worth of worth,
> And ancient lineaments are blotted out.
> Irrational streams of blood are staining earth;
> Empedocles has thrown all things about;
> Hector is dead and there's a light in Troy;
> We that look on but laugh in tragic joy.

The joy of the Chinamen, reflected in their "glittering eyes," "gay" in the face of the "tragic," is like the mood of those who laugh in "tragic joy." That "joy" is not to be understood in its customary sense Yeats makes clear by contrasting its use here with its use in the poem that follows "Lapis Lazuli" ("Seventy years have I lived," says its speaker, "and never have I danced for joy"). The gaiety, then, of the ancient Chinese view, with which Yeats has identified his own (for he himself now joins the company of those "poets who are always gay"), is neither comic nor joyful but rather profoundly resigned.

28

Yeats's on-going argument, however, does not end here, and we would misrepresent his final view if we characterized it as oriental. In a poem titled "Sweet Dancer," which immediately follows "Imitated from the Japanese," a solitary girl gone mad in her own dance suggests, if indirectly, that the gaiety of the Chinamen is not, for the Westerner, a plausible solution within his cultural context. The lines from "The Gyres" quoted above, where new replaces old, also contradict the motion of history reported in "Nineteen Hundred and Nineteen," where the old had replaced the new. Yeats's fully cyclical view implies a continual reversal of all things. Nonetheless, two final examples should be noted in support of his sympathy for the Orient and his sense of the new course that civilization is taking.

In the twelfth of the "Supernatural Songs" he had represented civilization as "brought under a rule . . . by manifold illusion"; "man's life," the poet says, "is thought"; he "cannot cease ravening" through history "that he may come into the desolation of reality." After which the following lines occur:

> Egypt and Greece, good-bye, and good-by Rome!
> Hermits upon Mt. Meru or Everest
> Caverned in night under the drifted snow . . .
> . . . . know
> That day brings round the night, that before dawn
> His glory and his monuments are gone.

A more balanced and complete version of the cycles, this fanciful vision nonetheless clearly dismisses the West, explicitly in terms of the three traditions that we have spoken of. Once again the poet represents in sympathetic terms the vantage point of the Oriental who views from a mountainside the tragedy of history.

By 1939, the year following the composition of "Lapis Lazuli," and the last of his life, Yeats's thoughts had apparently turned away from the Orient. He continues, however, to worry the theme of western civilization's decline ("Gyres run on," he says in "Upon Ben Bulben," his last poem; "When the greater dream had gone . . . confusion fell upon our thought." "Long-Legged Fly," also dating from that year, represents a ray of hope "That civilization may not sink, / Its great battle lost." To that end the poet recommends shutting the door to the chapel housing Michelangelo's fresco of Adam and Eve and suggests that the auditor "move gently" if he wishes to recall the glory of Helen of Troy, now greatly fallen in stature. The refrain, repeated with variations for Helen and Michelangelo, is in the first stanza given to "our master Caesar," who is seen

> in the tent
> Where the maps are spread,

> His eyes fixed upon nothing,
> A hand under his head.
> *Like a long-legged fly upon the stream*
> *His mind moves upon silence.*

Like the rest of the poem, the stanza may be read in purely western terms, but, as we shall see in dealing with other Modernist poets, the use of the term "nothing" in their work often represents a poetic shorthand for those philosophies of No-knowledge (*wu zhi* 無知) and Actionless Action (*wu wei* 無爲) which many Westerners regard as characteristic of eastern thought. Here the mind moving upon silence suggests as well the quietude (*ji jing* 寂靜) of Buddhist doctrine. Though the oriental alternative is not so explicitly established as in other examples that I have discussed, nevertheless Yeats clearly indicates that our Caesar, like Helen of Troy and Michelangelo, must reform his practice. Or, to generalize further, the poet once more proscribes the central classical and Biblical myths and substitutes for them an orientalized posture in the interests of the continuation of civilization.

If we turn next to T. S. Eliot, it is not to give him precedence over his senior, Ezra Pound, but to treat in order three poets progressively devoted to an orientalization of their work. So different from that father's studio in which Yeats received his early education, and where oriental things must have had no great importance, the Harvard of the first decades of this century, where Eliot went as an undergraduate and to which he returned to study Sanscrit and Pali along with western idealist philosophy, was a hotbed of comparatist thought and oriental studies. Perhaps for this very reason the young poet is at pains to exclude from his early poetry any oriental reference. But the impact of his education makes itself strikingly felt in the major poems of his middle and late periods.

Unlike Yeats, who always absorbs his sources then to project and criticize them in his own voice, Eliot in *The Waste Land* prefers the method that Pound had already adopted of naked quotation, though he seasons it by translating most of his oriental materials into English, paraphrasing them and, through a process of juxtaposition and allusion, assimilating them to his western materials, some of which he offers in the original, some again in translation. This at least is how he treats Augustine's Confessions and the Buddha's Fire Sermon at the close of Section III, which takes as its title the one ascribed to the Buddha's original address. This last point is worth reflecting on, since the first three section titles all represent quotations, the first from the Anglican service, "The Burial of the Dead," the second, "The Game of Chess," from a work of secular literature. The fourth and fifth titles, "Death by Water" and "What the Thunder Said" do not quote other titles but make

30

reference, as Eliot's notes inform us, to the occult Tarot deck and the Brihadaranyaka Upanishad. Since the note to line 218 states that the "substance of the poem" is "what Tiresias sees," Eliot's intention would seem to be an embrace of Biblical, classical, occult, Buddhist and Hindu traditions. It is interesting to note, in the light of Yeats's and Pound's contemporary work, that there is no Chinese element in the poem.

By contrast with Yeats's full, modulated, philosophical discourse, the spare lines in which Eliot offers what he calls his "collocation" of "eastern and western asceticism" may strike us as rather brittle and inconclusive:

> To Carthage then I came
>
> Burning burning burning burning
> O Lord Thou pluckest me out
> O Lord Thou pluckest
>
> burning

The "poetry" of Eliot's work, however, consists not only of the source materials and their juxtaposition but of their mediation by the presiding critical voice of the notes. Eliot's lines themselves also mediate our contact with their sources in Augustine and the Buddhist tradition, for though the first and third lines quote (and the fourth in part repeats) Augustine, they do so only in translation and in a most fragmentary way. The remaining two lines, with their single repeated word, merely allude to the Fire Sermon. A passage from that text, in the translation of Henry Clarke Warren, to which Eliot makes reference, indicates another aspect of the poet's artistry:

> Perceiving this, O priests, the learned and noted disciple conceives an aversion for the eye, conceives an aversion for forms, conceives an aversion for eye-consciousness, conceives an aversion for the impressions received by the eye. . . . And in conceiving this aversion, he becomes divested of passion, and by the absence of passion he becomes free, and when he is free he becomes aware that he is free; and he knows that rebirth is exhausted, that he has lived the holy life, that he has done what it behooved him to do, and that he is no more for this world.

It is a passage to which Eliot, both in his reference to its provenance (complete with mention of the "Harvard Oriental Series") and in his encomium, both of Mr. Warren and the Buddha, earnestly directs our attention. Without much exaggeration, then, we might call it a part of the poem, especially since we have nothing else in the text, aside from the section title and the note itself, that refers to the Buddha.

How, then, does the passage function in relation to the lines that we have quoted? Though it is relevant to the whole third section, it relates

31

more particularly to the lines immediately preceding those that we have quoted, ones which describe the modern Thames, which introduce Elizabeth and Leicester (only to superimpose images of a modern sexual encounter), and which end with another voice. Because it mentions Margate, where Eliot wrote part of the poem, this voice merges with the poet's own. We have, then, a progression in the poem parallel with that in the passage from the Sermon whereby "the disciple conceives an aversion for the impressions received by the eye" and whereby "he becomes divested of passion": ("after the event" the poem's seducer weeps, promising "'a new start'"). Following two transitional lines Eliot, in the evocation of Augustine, represents another figure who has "lived the holy life," "who has done what it behooved him to do," who is "no more for this world." Not only is Augustine thereby merged with the Buddha (the poet has placed the Augustine lines between lines that allude to the Fire sermon, and *vice versa*), but both are merged with an Eliot-like voice. Might we not now read Eliot's note as meaning that in Augustine he has found a western equivalent of the Buddha, and *vice versa*? The Eliot-like voice at Margate, several lines before, had said, "I can connect nothing with nothing," words which may refer both to Eliot's state of nervous exhaustion at the time of composition and to the connection that, as poet, he is about to draw between Augustine's and the Buddha's acts of renunciation.

The third section ends with the single word "burning," whose image is gathered up at the end of the poem into the line that Eliot quotes from Dante: *"Poi s'ascose nel foco che gli affina"* (then he hid himself in the fire which refines them). In the *Purgatorio* these words had described the conclusion of a scene in which the soul of Arnaut Daniel pleads with Dante, asking his friend to bear witness to his suffering. It is, incidentally, this same sufferer whom Dante had characterized as *"il miglior fabbro,"* a phrase that Eliot uses in dedicating the poem to Pound.

So much, at any rate, for the poem's Buddhist element. Two notes to its fifth section refer the reader to Eliot's Hindu sources. The first, to line 402, reads in part: "'Datta, dayadhvam, damyata' (Give, sympathize, control)" and refers us to the Upanishad already mentioned. The second note, to the poem's last line, reads: "Shantih. Repeated as here, a formal ending to an Upanishad. 'The Peace which passeth understanding' is our equivalent to this word." As in the passage at the end of the third section, the poet again is interested in collocating eastern and western religious traditions. The first example is the less obvious of the two.

Eliot accurately summarizes for us the themes of the first part of the fifth section as "the journey to Emmaus, the approach to the Chapel Perilous . . . and the present decay of eastern Europe." The first two of these are Biblical: in line 375, "Jerusalem Athens Alexandria," Eliot

32

expands his subject by reference to classical and perhaps to Egyptian tradition as well. At line 396, with the mention of Ganga—the modern Ganges River—he turns to India. The three Sanscrit words, quoted in the note as though they formed a single phrase, are in fact culled from his source and even in the poem are first parceled out in the text as introductory to three verse paragraphs. Only in the next-to-last line of the poem are they gathered together. The important point is that Eliot has reversed the order in which the words occur in the Upanishad, whereby (in translation) they would read: control, sympathize, give. Why has he done so? Though no conclusive answer can be offered, there are two possible explanations, both of which may be valid: (1) the reversal creates a more Christian order of values and thereby Christianizes Hindu doctrine, and (2) it suggests a return to origins, a movement in keeping with the general endeavor of the poem.

Whatever Eliot's intentions may have been, the repetition of those three words in the penultimate line, along with the closing ("Shantih shantih shantih") incontestably gives the poem a Sanscrit conclusion. Since he himself has drawn our attention to the customary function of those last three words in Hindu tradition, we may well interpret him as suggesting that *The Waste Land* itself be read as an Upanishad, a word which in Sanscrit means holy text. As Eliot in 1927 coyly remarked, "The poem turns out more positive than we used to think."

I do not propose to discuss in any detail the whole of *Four Quartets*, their blend of the oriental and occidental traditions having been frequently remarked upon. Many of the techniques that we have observed in *The Waste Land* have been extended and refined in the later poem. The universalization sought by the poet in the earlier work is in one sense more fully achieved here. At the same time, Eliot's conversion to Christianity, a process completed in 1927, colors the poem and shifts its predisposition from one of neutrality to one of *parti pris*. A quotation contemporary with its composition (1937) expresses the new spirit: "The division between those who accept and those who deny Christian revelation, I take to be the most profound difference between human beings." What is sometimes perceived, then, as the ecumenical tendency of *Four Quartets* should not be overemphasized.

This, however, is not to deny the technical skill with which Eliot now absorbs into his own ruminations those elements of Hindu tradition that he had earlier presented among his "fragments." Section III of "The Dry Salvages," beginning "I sometimes wonder if that is what Krishna meant," is perhaps his best effort at such absorption. At any rate it constitutes his most concerted exposition of Vedantic doctrine. Careful examination of the whole passage reveals the extent to which, despite his use of "quotation" (again the source has been translated, then paraphrased), Eliot has dissolved Vedantic thought in his own and *vice versa*. Even Heraclitus, quoted in the original at the outset of "Burnt Norton," is now made to undergo the same process of modification and absorption. As in *The Waste Land*, scenes of contemporary reality interrupt a meditation woven of generalization, image and paraphrase, only to be reinterrupted in turn by the latter.

> And on the deck of the drumming liner
> Watching the furrow that widens behind you,
> You shall not think "the past is finished"
> Or "the future is before us."
> At nightfall, in the rigging and the aerial,
> Is a voice descanting (though not to the ear,
> The murmuring shell of time, and not in any language) . . .

Whereupon follows an evocation of Krishna, into which Eliot weaves, as well as Vedantic ideas, the imagery of Buddhist tradition ("Here between the hither and the farther shore . . ."). Finally, after such elaborate preparation, the text of the Bhagavad Gita is finally quoted (albeit still in translation)—

> "on whatever sphere of being
> The mind of a man may be intent
> At the time of death"

—only to be quickly reabsorbed into the envelope of Eliot's imaginative evocation. As a recreation, or "imitation" of the great Hindu text, the passage ranks with the translation by Eliot's master, Sir Edwin Arnold, whose *Light of Asia*, a versified history of the Buddha, Eliot had also absorbed. That the modern poet does not, however, accept with any equanimity the Hindu or Buddhist dispensation is suggested by Eliot's parting allusion to the tradition later in "The Dry Salvages," where he mentions "distress of nations and perplexity . . . on the shores of Asia" as well as "in the Edgware Road." For Eliot Krishna has had his day; the return to the Anglican fold is imminent.

> 道不行乘桴浮於海
> (If my teaching's not accepted, I'll take a raft and float off on the sea.)
>
> —Confucius

Ezra Pound's relationship to the Orient is a much larger subject. As with Eliot and the Hindu tradition, much will be foreshortened and simplified here. As with Yeats and Japan, much will be omitted. The central point, however, can be made without exaggeration: that Pound conceived of the *Cantos* as Confucian. Moreover, quibble as we may, his

34

conception is essentially correct. Chinese ideas, however misunderstood, traduced or unchinese in their application—or, contrariwise, however clearly grasped, trenchantly modernized and brilliantly applied—constitute an essential matrix of his thought and esthetic practice. As with much in Pound's life and work, there may be no general agreement, but let us consider the evidence.

The Chinese element enters Pound's oeuvre by three principal modes of appropriation. The first involves direct sources, which he variously quotes, translates, paraphrases, or otherwise subsumes. The second involves models—such as the ideogram, or the analect—more generalized than the sources, products partly of those sources, partly of his own imagination. The third involves those attitudes which epitomize the cultural values, either as expressed in Pound's sources and the traditions of commentary or as abstracted from them by the poet and his western compeers. It is often the practical use of these materials, rather than a misunderstanding of them, that irritates the curatorial scholar.

For Pound was a programmatic evangelist, devoted to technical innovation, moral reform, and the radical criticism of western civilization. In all three areas Chinese sources and models were instrumental. "To break the pentameter," he says, "that was the first heave." To this end various sources contributed, including the nineteenth-century French *vers libre* and the Anglo-Saxon alliterative half-line, but also the *model*, as we have defined it, of Chinese poetry (one that ignores the rigors of character count, pitch and stress patterns, regular caesura and end rhyme in favor of its so-called "ideogrammic" qualities—grammatical sparseness, an "imagistic" tendency, the actual use of ideograms, whose visual component Pound was misled into overestimating). The second "heave," we might say, was to break up the well-developed paragraph, that building-block of discursive western prose. Unlike the first heave, which Pound frequently discussed, the second he merely exemplified in his letters and critical prose, which progressively introduce conversational diction, fragmentary syntax and a journalistic paragraph of one or two sentences. This whole development might be seen as culminating in the essay on Aristotle's Nichomachean Ethics, where colloquial annotation substituted for excursus as critical procedure. That essay also illustrates a third object of attack, western philosophical abstraction. Here the Confucian analect—or more broadly, the Chinese tradition of gnomic wisdom — contributed a model of brevity and concreteness whose function for Pound's prose may have been analogous to the model of the ideogram for his poetry. The ideogram—the model extended into the ideogrammic *method*—then served as model for a fourth attack, whose object is the continuous, coherent structure of the long poem in western

35

tradition. The *theory* of the ideogram—as enunciated by Fenellosa and elaborated by Pound—served in turn as model for a new theory of poetry ("For Ars Poetica," says Pound in a letter of 1935, "get my last edtn of Fenellosa's 'Chinese Written Character,' vide my introduction"). Finally, and perhaps most importantly, the responsibility of Confucianism served for Pound as corrective to what he regarded as the irresponsibility of Greek and Christian thought, a natural consequence of their tendency toward transcendence. The embrace of Confucianism enabled him to cross the line between moral philosophy and religion—as vague for Pound as it is for most Chinese—so that as early as 1922 "the writings of Confucius," along with Ovid's Metamorphoses, became for the poet "the only safe guides in religion."

The central figure in all this was the Sage himself, and here it might be well to summarize Pound's views, as expressed in prose, of the man and his philosophy. Pound first mentioned Confucius in a letter of 1917, proposing to Margaret Anderson that he write an essay on the subject for *The Little Review*. The first text of the Confucian classics that he translated was the Da Xue 大學, which he calls *The Great Digest* (1928); next he translated the Zhong Yong 中庸, which he calls *The Unwobbling Pivot* (1947); finally, in 1950, he translated The Analects (論語). This last work he then epitomized in a seven-page "Digest," with which he introduced the *Guide to Kulchur*. Confucius, at first seen as an alternative to western, especially Greek, thought, gradually evolved to become the center of Pound's own classical Chinese world view until he finally metamorphosed, as in the following, quasi-mystical metaphor, into a universal original: "From Kung to Mencius a century, and to St. Ambrose another six or so hundred years, and a thousand years to St. Antonio, and they are as parts of one pattern, as wood of a single tree." Confucius, as in Chinese tradition, had been sanctified.

Pound's penchant for pitting Chinese thought against its Greek counterpart, however, had been facilitated precisely by his early relinquishment of Christianity. Though Dante's humanist, catholic vision remained a powerful influence to the end, Pound unequivocally denounced Old Testament culture: "Nothing cd. be less civil, or more hostile to any degree of polite civilization than the tribal records of the Hebrews." In so doing he rejected Protestant Christianity: "The revival of these barbarous texts in the time of Luther and Calvin has been an almost unmitigated curse to the occident." Unlike Yeats and Eliot, then, who sublimated their Christianity later to express it sympathetically, Pound freed himself early on to address the classical by itself, which he embraced in the form of Homer and rejected in the form of Greek philosophy, as embodied in Aristotle and Plato.

In this he preferred the practicality of Confucius to their idealism: "not even a half-masted tyrant wd. give Plato a ten acre lot whereon to try out his republic." He preferred the method of the Analects for its direct address of problems, regarding Greek philosophy as "befuddling itself with the false dilemma: Aristotle OR Plato, as if there were no other roads to serenity." He preferred the concrete ethical basis of Chinese thought to the abstract theoretical nature of western thought. Aristotle, he says, "was interested in mind not in morals" and as a consequence promulgated "an amoral tradition." In the whole of western philosophy, Pound found "an unconscious" agreement to avoid moral discussion, one, he says, "which wd. be inconceivable in the Ta Hio [大學], in the steadfast Mean [中庸], or in the Analects." "Kung (Confucius)," he pronounces, "we receive as wisdom. The greek philosophers have been served up as highbrows." Even the injunction "Know thyself" he regards as "glib," the Great Learning representing by contrast "an examination with a clear purpose."

Thinking of ancient Greece as the object of Renaissance emulation, Pound predicted that "this century may find a new Greece in China." Gradually ancient China came to replace ancient Greece as Pound's *paideia*. A late revision of his many reading lists mentions "the FOUR BOOKS" (四書) first, "HOMER: Odyssey" second, "The Greek TRAGEDIANS" third and "DIVINA COMMEDIA" fourth, in a list of seven titles. Thus what began as the new third tradition finally becomes for Pound his first, the Homeric-Attic and Christian-Humanist filling out the triad. The Confucian classics, Pound explains, "contain answers to all problems of conduct that can arise. A man who really understands them," he adds, "may regard the other six components of this list as amenities rather than necessities."

Another, more general justification, clarifies his stand: "Rightly or wrongly we feel that Confucius offers a way of life, an Anschauung or disposition toward nature and man and a system for dealing with both." Though his unspoken theme is still the superiority of Chinese to Greek thought—expressed, ironically, in terms drawn mostly from the latter tradition—he is edging toward a Sinocentric view. With the composition of the Chinese history cantos the balance shifted toward China. Confucius had become not so much an alternative to Aristotle as a source for the definition of culture, which for Pound has become Chinese. In one of the radio broadcasts that he made during World War II his language and thought would take their most Chinese coloration: "Kung," he says, "is to China as water to fishes [cp. 如魚得水]. Meaning Confucius, the Confucian doctrine is the true habitat of the son of Heaven [天子] , and from the Emperor down to the common people, the

duty or *root* is ONE [cp. 自天子以至於庶人，壹是皆已修身爲本].
Chinese thought had been reduced to Confucian thought (Pound had
always rejected the Taoist and Buddhist elements), which was now seen
as the source of political stability and positive change. "Whenever and
wherever order has been set up in China," says the poet in a kind of gloss
to the Chinese history cantos, "whenever there has been a notable reform
or constructive national action, you find a group of Confucians 'behind
it,' or 'at the center.'"

In *Guide to Kulchur*, at the end of the chapter titled "Kung," Pound
says of Confucius' thought, "it is root volition branching out." An earlier
chapter begins, "Ideas are true as they go into action." In "Canti," he says,
"There is no mystery about the Cantos, they are the tale of the tribe."
Pound's poem, in other words, applies Confucian thought to the history
of mankind. To say, however, there is "no mystery" in this is not to say
that all is immediately apparent. In a passage from Canto CXVI, one that
James Laughlin appended to Pound's original version of *Selected Cantos*,
the poet says notoriously, "I cannot make it cohere." Make what cohere?
we must ask. Later, on the same page, Pound draws a useful distinction:

> i.e. it coheres all right
> even if my notes do not cohere

The cosmos coheres even if the *Cantos* do not. They refer, that is to say,
to another world, one in which "it" all "coheres." Therefore the poem,
though it seems to be epic—and Pound so conceived it at first—is in fact
visionary. Like Eliot, Joyce and others in his tradition, Pound never
escaped Dante, remaining — despite his apparent apostasy — deeply
Christian, in his zeal and martyrdom, but also in his vision. That he
recognized the vestiges of this belief is suggested in a letter to W. H. D.
Rouse of 1935 on the subject of the latter's translation of the Odyssey:
"Possibly you are Greek enough to take complete cynicism as part of my
divine equipment and that I am so Xtian that a lying god tickles my
funny bone." The final movement of the *Cantos* is, after all, a *paradiso*,
as Pound had planned it from the start. But a *paradiso* with a difference,
one in which the godhead is played, if not by Confucius, at least by the
Confucian *logos*, its theme, as the ninety-ninth canto has it,

> Our SAGE FOREBEAR examined to
> stimulate anagogico

An exegesis of the *Cantos* is not possible here, nor even a complete
discussion of their Confucian element. I propose instead: first, to
consider those cantos most devoted to Confucius in relation to Pound's
prose accounts of Confucian principles; second, to weigh this oriental
element against the classical and the Christian. As text I shall take the

Selected Cantos, drawn up by Pound in 1966, by which time the poet had completed most of the writing and, more significantly, had identified himself with the Confucian point of view.

The final selection of twenty-four cantos (and parts thereof) draws attention to the Homeric analogy. "And then went down to the ship" begins the poem, the abridged version of which ends, "You in the dinghy (piccioletta) astern there!" In between, images of water, as we shall see, serve to unify its themes. Thus the Odyssean sea of Canto I gives way in Canto IV to a variety of watery forms, as the European narrative mode is replaced by "a thin film of images" connecting Greek and oriental (mostly Japanese) materials. Canto IX introduces the Christian ("JHesus," an emblem of the Church's power and magnificence) in the form of the Odyssean Sigismundo Malatesta, as Homeric, oriental and modern are united in the parenthetical line "and we sent men to the Silk War."

The canto that follows, XIII, along with two later selections devoted to expounding Confucian ideas, might best be introduced by returning momentarily to Pound's "Digest of the Analects," the most compact but complete prose summary of Confucius that he offers. I have reduced the poet's digest in turn to twelve principles, retaining the order in which Pound presents them. The first is to admit ignorance (the ground of the scholar-poet's quest). The second, to use correct terminology (Pound once thought of placing the ideograms *zheng ming* 正名 on the cover of the collected Cantos). The third is *zhi* 止, moderation. The fourth and fifth are *ren* 仁 and *zhi ren* 知人, in Pound's version, *"Humanity? Is to love men"* (仁者人也知者知人也). The sixth is timeliness ("the lord of a feudal kingdom shd not demand work of his people save at convenient and/or suitable time" 使民以時), a principle broadly applied in the *Cantos.*

The seventh, eighth and ninth are included in the following quotation: *"Duty in the home, deference among all men. Affection among all men and attachment in particular to persons of virtu (or virtue)."* "Duty" here translates and combines *xiao* 孝 and *qi jia* 齊家, the Confucian principles of filiality and order in the home (from which order elsewhere proceeds). "Deference" translate *ti* 悌, brotherly deference, but applies it outside the home as well. "Affection" repeats *ren* 仁, benevolence, the central Confucian principle, and "attachment . . . to persons of . . . virtue" translates 見賢思齊 (when you see someone virtuous emulate him). *"Seek friends among equals"* translates the principle 無友不如己者. The eleventh, *"I am pro-Tcheou (in politics) . . . . They examined their predecessors"* refers us to another passage in Confucius (周監於二代，

郁郁呼文哉！吾從周), which Pound then generalizes, "(The full text being: they examined the civilization and history of the Dynasties which preceded them)," thereby expounding his own method as well as that of Confucius and the Zhou dynasty before him. The twelfth principle consists of "*The six words, and the six becloudings* (六言六蔽)," those things that suffer "without the love of learning," or, in the anonymous translation that Pound uses, the love "of being benevolent" (仁), "of learning" (知), "of being sincere" (信), "of straightforwardness" (直), "of boldness" (勇), and "of firmness"(剛).

The "Digest," as a summary of Confucian principles, is, like the Analects themselves, vivaciously unsystematic. Moreover, Pound is deliberately tendentious, drawing attention to his own aims and even seeking Confucius' support for his current economic views. Principles absent or underemphasized include *zhong* 忠, loyalty, *shu* 恕, compassion, *li* 禮, the rites, *chun zi* 君子, the conduct of the gentleman, and the *wang dao* 王道, or governance of kings.

Confucian principles omitted at one point in Pound's work, however, are often introduced at another, a practice that should warn the student against attributing to the poet an incomplete knowledge of his subject. Thus in Canto XIII, published much earlier than the "Digest," we already have passages bearing on the governance of kings (the prince represented as patron of learning and the arts), on the conduct of the gentleman, on the principle of loyalty (in examples drawn from the Master's own life). Having earlier introduced Italian Renaissance materials, Pound is in this canto at pains to distinguish the Confucian from the Christian view (Kung "said nothing of 'life after death'"); in the canto that follows, XIV, he has Calvin in hell and Augustine "gazing toward the invisible." The idyllic quality of the first Confucian canto may be classical; at any rate this "moral backbone" of the poem, as Pound termed it, deemphasizes the austerity of the Master's ethical vision in order to emphasize its felicity. Though Pound's exposition is remarkably complete, we might note the omission of such central concepts as *ren* 仁 and *shu* 恕.

The first page of the canto translates a passage from the Analects in which several disciples propose exemplary activities. When asked who is right, Confucius replies, "They have all answered correctly / That is to say, each in his nature." The last phrase paraphrases Pound's source (亦各言其志也已矣!), in which Confucius says, more literally, that each speaks according to his goal or interest. Pound's deliberate choice of "nature" here is significant, for in so translating he not only draws into his compass another Confucian principle (*xing* 性) but establishes one term of a polarity important in the poem. For Canto XLV, that chant in exorcism of *usura*, concludes with the emphatic statement of its evil principle: "CONTRA NATURAM." By a process of conflation, then, the civilized oriental celebration of the natural is contrasted with the occidental perpetuation of the unnatural, a perversion which in Pound's view extends from the misuse of money to all manner of "sin against nature."

One of the intervening cantos, from a group indexed as "Jefferson—Nuevo Mundo," offers the first example of the western Confucian ruler. Canto XXXI opens with Jefferson writing to Washington on the subject of "water communication," specifically the need for a canal to connect the eastern and western United States. Pound probably has in mind the analogous activity of Yu 禹, the Xia dynasty emperor whose policy of flood control is legendary. He next quotes Jefferson in correspondence with Thomas Paine, instigator of the American Revolution. Jefferson speaks of the pamphleteer's "wish to get a passage to this country / in a public vessel," and assures him that arrangements have been made that will also "accommodate you / with passage back." Again we have a modern reprise of a legend, Paine's outward voyage in the service of principle, and his return, echoing those of Odysseus. In such a way the canto establishes two parallels with American experience, one Chinese, one Greek — all within the rubric of the governance of kings (or presidents).

Cantos LII and LIII form a pair, the first devoted to the mythic world of ancient China as reflected principally in Lu Shi's Spring and Autumn Annals (呂氏春秋), the second to the historical world of China from earliest times to the death of Confucius. In his arrangement Pound places Canto XLV, "With *Usura*," twelfth, thereby closing out the first half of *Selected Cantos;* the thirteenth, Canto LII, is the first in which Pound himself assumes the voice of Chinese wisdom ("Know then:" it opens). Canto LIII is, like most of the Chinese history cantos, a long-winded *mélange* of Confucian principles, mythic fragments and historical anecdotes. The early emperors are introduced in ideogram, as is the principle "MAKE IT NEW," quoted from the inscription that appeared on the bathtub of the emperor Tang 湯. Pound's source, from which he takes the last four characters, reads 苟日新，又日新，日日新 (if you make something new today, make it new tomorrow, make it new every day).

Canto LIII and the passage that follows it, from Canto LXII, also form a pair, as Pound suggests in his index: "Chinese Cantos—John Adams." Both concern the principle of *wang dao* 王道, LIIII choosing its examples from early Chinese history, LXII, from the early history of the American Republic; both likewise concern the lives of active men of

41

wisdom, LIII taking Confucius, LXII, John Adams as exemplary. In the Chinese canto Pound punctuates his historical sketch and thumbnail biography with the ideograms *Zhou* 周 (the name of the dynasty), *Zhong Ni* 仲尼 (another name for Confucius) and *Zhou* 周 again. In this he may be reflecting a pattern in one of the Analects quoted above in the summary of the "Digest," where Confucius' words begin and end with the character *Zhou* (周). Against these origins the poet, in *Selected Cantos*, directly juxtaposes "Mr. A," our first "Confucian" president. Though Pound's attitude is hardly reverential ("we may take it . . . he was the Prime snot in ALL American history"), he nonetheless dubs him "pater patriae," an appellation usually reserved for George Washington. In praising his "fairness" (cp. *zheng* 正), "honesty" (cp. *cheng* 誠), and "straight moving" (cp. *zhi* 直), he refers to qualities all discussed in the Analects.

The two examples that Pound selected from the Pisan Cantos (Laughlin adds another passage) show the poet first recombining elements from his three principal traditions, then assimilating elements previously excluded. Canto LXXXI opens, "Zeus lies in Ceres' bosom / Taishan is attended of loves / under Cythera," an image that searches Chinese tradition for a myth comparable in antiquity and religious power to those of archaic Greece, one it then enfolds within a Greek matrix. In direct juxtaposition to his images of ancient religions the poet then quotes a modern Spaniard to the effect that Catholicism has lost its religious power. And yet a change in Pound's exclusive mentality is imminent. With a reference to Kuan Yin 觀音, an early Chinese divinity who absorbed the *boddhisattva avalokiteshvara* ("Light as the branch of Kuanon"), he admits the Buddhist tradition. The canto concludes, in one of his few sympathetic references to the Old Testament, with a passage whose refrain, "Pull down vanity," is now famous. Another Hebraic reference appears in the following polyglot passage from Canto LXXXIV:

> quand vos venetz al som de l'escalina
> $\eta\theta o\zeta$ gradations
> These are distinctions in clarity
> ming[2] 明 these are distinctions
> John Adams, the Brothers Adam
>   There is our norm of spirit
> our   chung[1] 中

The first four lines combine Christian, classical and oriental sources in images of mystical attainment, ethical hierarchy and philosophical clarity (the ming[2] 明" derived from the Great Learning's doctrine of clarity, "大

學之道在明明德," where the last four characters may be translated, "in understanding of the clear virtue/nature," the latter endowed from heaven). The next three lines bring American, Hebrew (and by implication, Christian) materials into relation with Chinese doctrine, so that by a kind of modernized typology John Adams becomes the antitype of Confucius as well as the second Adam (Pound's earlier encomium had said, he "saved us"). Whereas earlier in the canto Pound had used three languages (Renaissance Latin, English and Chinese) in the phrase "humanitas (manhood) / or jên²" to indicate the interchangeability of principles, in this quotation he intends an intercultural ideogram whose "radicals" are drawn from all his major traditions.

"Our general notion of Confucius," he says in the *Guide to Kulchur*, "has perhaps failed to include a great sensibility." The passage excerpted from Canto LXXXV begins "LING² 零," sensibility. "Our dynasty," Pound adds in the voice of Yi Yin 伊尹, the Shang statesman, "came in because of a great sensibility." Two western counterparts to this Confucian ruler, Elizabeth I of England and Cleopatra, make their appearances, the former translating Ovid (that guide to religion), the latter writing of currency (Pound's gauge of civilization). The passage selected from Canto CVIII introduces "ELIZABETH," transformed by Pound, after Renaissance precedent, into a principle of love, "Angliae amor." The name of the Elizabethan jurist Coke is juxtaposed in a later line with the "Iong Ching" 庸經, thereby connecting English law with the Confucian classics. The passage flickers to a close with another allusion to the Emperor Yu. In Canto XCV Pound then frames the words of Confucius with two lines in his late mystical mode:

That the crystal wave mount to flood surge
近   chin⁴
乎   hu¹
仁   jên²
The light there almost solid.

The theme of flux, frequently expressed through water imagery, gives way at the moment of luminous stability to the theme of permanence, expressed as light passing water-like beyond the bounds of its nature. The Chinese reproduces the words with which Confucius closes his prescriptions: if you follow such-and-such a principle, you will be "quite close to benevolence." By situating the words in the context of religious vision Pound characterizes Confucian wisdom as a state of beatitude. "LOVE," the first word of the Canto, we might then reread as Pound's translation of *ren* 仁, which, along with *amor* forms another triad.

His quotation from the *Zhong Yong* 中庸 here, unlike the earlier citation of single characters, represents a kind of ventriloquism in which

Pound assumes Confucius' voice. In lines that follow upon the passage quoted he then himself begins to write Chinese:

$$\begin{array}{ll} 一 & \text{i}^{1.5} \\ 人 & \text{jên}^2 \end{array}$$

Using the simplest characters in the language, those for the cardinal "one" and for "man," he composes a phrase that initiates a new theme, picked up in Canto XCIX, "The whole tribe is from one man's body," though also contradicted in the statement, "This is not a work of fiction / nor yet of one man" (which incidentally clarifies the difficulty of placing *Cantos* in the tradition of single-author, fictive poems). Having assumed many *personae* in the course of his work, the last mask that Pound adopts is that of Confucius, whose philosophy he now compounds in a final moral essay on the subject. His treatment here is both more primitive and more practical, more encyclopedic and more conversational than his earlier efforts in prose and verse. Two ideograms, *zhao* 兆, omen, and *en* 恩 grace or gratitude, disembodied from their contexts, reflect Pound's concern with the religious backgrounds of Confucian thought (omens precede political disaster, gratitude underlies the principle of filiality). The poet lists many principles, including "the 9 arts" 九經, "the six kinds of action"六藝, and the four *duan* 端: *ren, yi, li,* and *zhi* 仁義禮智. Many other principles are reiterated; some are mentioned for the first time. Among the latter perhaps the most important is *shu* 恕, compassion, which Pound now calls "tree's root and water-spring." Having thoroughly assimilated Confucius, the voice of the canto combines the oriental and the occidental. "The basis is man / . . . but the four TUAN / are from nature," it says, thereby conveying both the assurance of Confucian doctrine and the uncertainty of Greek dualism. Pound speaks for the Master but also improvises his own Confucian dicta. The canto ends with the poet's organic metaphor, one that has its origin in the language of tradition: "The fu jen [富人, the man rich in wisdom] receives heaven, earth, middle / and grows."

Having completed his final statement of Confucian principles, Pound dropped the subject to pursue different interests, turning to the European Dark Ages, the development of English law, and other matters. In so doing he reasserted his identity as Odyssean intelligence, though gathering perhaps within that persona, especially in the long silence of his last years, the figure of the Sage whose teaching has not been accepted.

3

A Native Buddhist Strain in Stevens, Williams and Frost

My previous essay dealt with the Asian element in the poetry of Yeats, Eliot and Pound, three cosmopolitans who, despite origins in places as far-flung as Sligo, St. Louis and Hayley, Idaho converged upon London in the early years of the century to live the rest of their lives either there or in other centers of civilization. Their contact with Asia, though indirect by comparison with that of some later-day western poets, nonetheless involved scrutiny of the original traditions. This scholarship eventuated in prose commentary and verse that weighed in the balance Asian and western values and contributed to their stature as three of the most important cultural critics of the age.

Wallace Stevens, William Carlos Williams and Robert Frost, by comparison, were provincial and unlettered. All three deliberately chose not only to remain in America but to live at a distance from its literary centers. Stevens, having begun his career as a lawyer in New York, accepted the quiet life of Hartford, Connecticut, scarcely leaving that small city once he had established himself in a large insurance firm. Williams, though at the periphery of certain artistic circles in New York, chose the life of a small town doctor in Rutherford, New Jersey. Frost, after an early episode in England, returned to cultivate the scene north of Boston, one of America's notably provincial regions. Though the literary essays of Williams come to several hundred pages, they are entirely without oriental reference. The critical writings of Stevens and Frost amount to little more than occasional prose, in the case of Stevens, late essays on a philosophical theme, in the case of Frost, prefaces to his own work and general essays. Unlike the cosmopolitans, none wrote seriously in prose about the Orient.

And yet, by a curious paradox of the imagination, the thought of Stevens and Williams, and on one or two occasions that of Frost as well, is in a sense as orientalized as that of their learned contemporaries. As we might expect, this "oriental" element is more diffuse, more difficult to specify, more subject to debate. None of the three set before himself, like Yeats, a Chinese jade, like Eliot, the text of the Bhagavad Gita, like Pound, the Confucian corpus, to compose a major poem. Furthermore, by contrast with the Confucian, Vedantic and Daoist strains in Pound, Eliot and Yeats, the oriental element in Stevens, Williams and Frost is markedly Buddhistic. Since Buddhism is by far the least textual of all four traditions, we must seek other methods than those used earlier to document its presence in their work. Accordingly, I must ask the reader's indulgence now to consider parallels, analogies and similarities rather than sources.

Moreover, as what I have said would imply, the oriental element in the provincial poets is largely an unconscious one. Subject, as agnostics raised in Christian families, to the same problems of faith encountered by the cosmopolitans, Stevens, Williams and Frost relinquished Christianity early on, but unlike Yeats, Eliot and Pound (with the one exception of Frost, who returned to school briefly to study the Latin classics), they did not cultivate the classical. Instead, they developed a native independence from European culture, which took in Williams the most aggressive form of Americanism, though it also found fierce expression in Stevens (mingled there with a modern Francophilia) and implicit embodiment in Frost's preoccupation with rural New England. It was perhaps this very sense of originality that at first obscured from all three the ways in which they had adopted traditional alternatives to western civilization. For though each was aware of his Emersonian, Thoreauvian and Whitmanesque past, none was conscious of the degree to which those figures represented precedents for his own embodiment of oriental thought.

Of the three provincial poets Stevens expressed the greatest interest in exotic things. Having learned that Harriet Monroe, the editor who had published him in *Poetry* magazine, had a sister in Peking, he importuned Miss Monroe to make arrangements whereby her sister would send him some things of her own choosing from China. "For a poet," as he says in a letter of September 23, 1922, "to have even a second-hand contact with China is a great matter." After a box of jasmine tea had arrived, an event that he characterized as a reversion to innocence, another box appeared containing *objets d'art*. In a letter of the next month, October 28, Stevens speaks at length of "the five, really delightful things" that it contained:

> One of these, the chief one, is a carved wooden figure of the most benevolent old god you ever saw. He has a staff in one hand and in the other carries a lotus bud. On the back of his head he has a decoration of some sort with *ribbons* running down into his gown. The wood is of the color of dark cedar but it is neither hard nor oily. And there you are. But the old man, Hson-hsing, has the most amused, the nicest and kindliest expression: quite a pope after one's own heart or at least an invulnerable bishop telling one how fortunate one is, after all, and not to mind one's bad poems. He is on a little teak stand as is, also, each of the other things. The other things are a small jade screen, two black crystal lions and a small jade figure. The jade pieces are white. We have placed the screen behind the prophet,   so that if he desires to retire into

its cloudy color he can do so conveniently and we have set the lions in his path, one on each side. The heads of these noisy beasts are turned back on their shoulders, quite evidently unable to withstand the mildness of the venerable luminary.

He concludes his description by saying, "The old man is so humane that the study of him is as good as a jovial psalm."

I have quoted the passage at length, because it gives us a rare glimpse of the western poet's imagination as it plays over the surface of oriental things. Having only the day before received it, Stevens had had no opportunity to determine the principal figure's identity, though presumably by copying his name from the box (which he or the editor of the *Letters* has mistranscribed—it should read "Hsou-hsing"), he enables us to identify Fu Shou Xing Gong 福壽星公, the god of longevity. How keen, then, Stevens' intuition, for he first refers to the figure as "the most benevolent old god," and then imagines him to be "telling one how fortunate one is." The god, in charge of human longevity, often bestows that good fortune as an act of benevolence. That he is also called Lao Ren Xing 老人星, literally, old man star, accords well with Stevens' description of him twice as "the old man," but more pointedly as "the venerable luminary" (Fu Shou Xing was originally a star in the constellation of Canopus, whose annual appearance in February signaled good fortune). That the figure is "humane" and possessed of "mildness" might have been observed from his expression. Of greater interest is the series of human identities that the poet metaphorically bestows upon him: "quite a pope," he calls him, "or at least an invulnerable bishop," and, finally, "the prophet." These epithets, along with the comment that "the study of him is as good as a jovial psalm," tell us several things: first, of Stevens' desire to please his correspondent, both for her role in securing the present and for her favors as editor. He may have been doing this by Christianizing the scene that he had arranged, for Harriet Monroe was known for doing the same in her editorship of *Poetry* ("Is literature limited to Christianity?" Pound at one point asks her in exasperation). But Stevens' own background and predilections (including a deathbed conversion to Roman Catholicism) must also figure in this extraordinary series of Catholic, Old Testament, and Protestant metaphors. Perhaps most interesting of all is that Stevens retained his humanized and western conception of the figure, writing to Harriet Monroe thirteen years later (April 5, 1935) as follows: "A little carved wooden figure of what I suppose to be a religious pilgrim, which [Miss Monroe's sister] sent me years ago, is one of the most delightful things that I have."

Stevens' comments illustrate the distinction that I have drawn between the conscious and unconscious reception of oriental materials. There are two complementary motions here. For just as the poet can consciously solicit oriental influence but, by transforming it into western terms, unconsciously deny it, so he can unconsciously receive it but elaborate its doctrines so as to give them a conscious coherence. Like any cultivated person of his time Stevens was inundated with images of the Orient; we know that he bought translations of Chinese poetry, to mention only one such source. Much of this oriental influence must have been absorbed unconsciously (in fact that is how, Stevens insisted, he was generally influenced). These unconsciously received sources often emerge later as part of a structure of thought. This does not mean that Stevens necessarily recognized the presence, say, of Buddhist doctrine in his poetry, but at the same time it does not mean that he was unaware of what he was doing.

The themes of absence, nothingness and impersonality have often been noted in his work, remarked upon because in general they contradict western expectations of presence, substance and personality. Attempts to explain them have focused on Stevens' indebtedness to French symbolist poets, to contemporary philosophy, even to the poet's aloof temperament. I do not wish here to substitute one set of influences for another but rather to suggest that comparative study may shed more light on Stevens' practice than influence study.

Edward J. Thomas, in his *History of Buddhist Thought*, summarizes the eight (or nine) stages of release, the *vimokkha*, at the sixth of which the adept, he says, "perceives that 'there is nothing' and attains and abides in the stage of nothingness." This nothingness, or negation, figures in several classic Buddhist doctrines, as for example, to use their Chinese formulations, *zhu fa wu wo* 諸法無我, the doctrine of No-self, *zhu xing wu chang* 諸行無常, the doctrine of No-permanence, the first two of the so-called three criteria, *san fa yin* 三法印, the third of which, consequence of the first two, is the peace of *nirvana, nie pan ji jing* 涅槃寂靜. Ceng Zhao 僧肇, a member of the Three Shastra Sect 三論宗, writes an essay called the Bo Ruo Wu Zhi Lun 般若無知論, which formulates another negative principle, that of No-knowledge. Let us, then, look at an early poem of Stevens', "The Snow Man," in the light of these doctrines:

> One must have a mind of winter
> To regard the frost and the boughs
> Of the pine-trees crusted with snow;
>
> And have been cold a long time
> To behold the junipers shagged with ice,
> The spruces rough in the distant glitter

Of the January sun; and not to think
Of any misery in the sound of the wind,
In the sound of a few leaves,

Which is the sound of the land
Full of the same wind
That is blowing in the same bare place

For the listener, who listens in the snow
And, nothing himself, beholds
Nothing that is not there and the nothing that is.

In *Early Buddhism* Rhys Davids lists among traditional metaphors for *nirvana* "the cool cave." Stevens' snowy landscape may represent its North American equivalent, just as his attention to misery and its elimination may represent a naïve concern with a Buddhist problem. At any rate, the poem's doctrine, that the listener be "nothing himself," which is reinforced by its impersonality—"One must have a mind of winter / to regard . . ."—is remarkably Buddhistic, the latter quotation recalling the words of the Buddha, who in the Surangama Sutra says, "this wonderful perception of sight is the true nature of our minds."

If we attend carefully, however, to early Buddhist doctrine, we shall notice that in Stevens, as in Williams, there is an important departure from its tenets. "The Tathagata's Nirvana," the passage quoted continues, "is where it is recognized that there is nothing but what is seen of the mind itself." This, we might say, accounts for Stevens' listener beholding the "nothing that is" there, but not for him beholding "nothing that is not there," a phrase which reflects the characteristic belief of Stevens and Williams in the existence of a concrete reality. Nirvana, the Buddha continues, "is where, recognizing the nature of the self-mind, one no longer cherishes the dualisms of discrimination." Here the poem's monistic tendency is true to Buddhist doctrine, but elsewhere Stevens' dualistic fluctuation between reality and imagination is not. "Nirvana," the Buddha concludes, "is where the thinking mind with all its discriminations, attachments, aversions and egoism is forever put away," a goal toward which Stevens sometimes aspires, but one which he more commonly rejects. Elsewhere, Buddhist doctrine, as in the Vajracchedika, says that the senses give only the experience of transient phenomena; no particular thing is real; at every moment it is passing into something else. At points in Stevens and Williams, as we shall see, a similar view is expressed, but not consistently. Thus, when the Vajracchedika says "all things are to be known and looked upon by one who does not rest upon the perception of things but on the perception of non-things," it expresses a view more extreme than any that Stevens or Williams would consent to.

It must also be said that "The Snow Man" is not typical of Stevens' early poetry, which by and large is devoted to the physicality of the real world and to the self. Both are robustly manifest in his "Comedian as the Letter C," a poem that he had been composing the summer before he wrote that first letter to Harriet Monroe. Earlier Stevens had represented China in terms of the Chinoiserie typical of his time (if the first of "Six Significant Landscapes" represents a considerable refinement thereof). In the later, longer poem he now speaks of "the Arctic moonlight," a false light, as "illusive, faint, more mist than moon, perverse, / Wrong as a divagation to Peking," suggesting thereby that his romance with Chinoiserie was over. At the same time, there are early flashes that suggest Stevens' awareness of the power of the Orient. "The Cuban Doctor" for example says, "I went to Egypt to escape / The Indian, but the Indian struck / Out of his cloud and from his sky." A collection of epigrams from *Ideas of Order* (1935) watches as "The sun of Asia creeps above the horizon." It is only, however, with *Parts of a World* (1941) that a considered oriental element makes its presence felt, as the beginnings of a negative Daoistic poetics, for example in the title "Poetry Is a Destructive Force." The most intriguing oriental essence, however, occurs in an earlier work, "Thirteen Ways of Looking at a Blackbird."

In Chapter I of the Dao De Jing 道德經 Lao-zi 老子 defines the two fundamental principles of the universe as *you* 有 and *wu* 無, something and nothing, and asserts their identity 此兩者同出而異名, in D. C. Lau's translation, "These two are the same / But diverge in name as they issue forth." What they proceed from is the "mystery." "Mystery upon mystery," Lau continues, "The gateway of the manifold secrets" 玄之又玄, 眾妙之門. The two operative terms here are *xuan* 玄 and *miao* 妙. Both have been much discussed. Both in a general sense mean "mystery." *Xuan* 玄, however, seems originally to have meant black, or dark, and refers accordingly to the unfathomable nature of the mystery. In philosophical terms *xuan* 玄 may be translated "abstruse"; when personified, it becomes "the Mother" and is correlative with another term in Lao-zi, *tian xia mu* 天下母, literally, the mother of everything under the heavens; the universe, or existence itself. *Xuan tong* 玄同 represents, in Suzuki's phrase, "the mystic experience of Identity," the lack of distinction between *chang wu* 常無 and *chang you* 常有, somethingness and nothingness, terms elsewhere associated with the female (*yin* 陰) and male (*yang* 陽) principles. *Xuan* 玄, then, in Lao-zi's words, is the gateway to *miao* 妙, the ultimate mystery, the intersection of time and the timeless. Stevens' blackbird, in keeping with Lao-zi's philosophy of constant mutability, is a changing entity, sometimes suggesting the self, sometimes death, sometimes commonplace reality. In the poem, however, all are represented as mysterious, and at several points the meaning of *xuan* 玄 seems apposite. Nowhere, however, does Stevens seem closer to Lao-zi than in section IV, where the philosophy of Yin and Yang 陰陽家 combines with the mystery of *xuan* 玄:

> A man and a woman
> Are one.
> A man and a woman and a blackbird
> Are one.

That we have no knowledge of Stevens having studied Lao-zi makes the passage all the more striking, for the language of the third line here, though easily reconciled with Daoist terms, is highly unorthodox in western thought.

Beginning with *Transport to Summer* (1947) a new wave of orientalism appears. "Chocorua to Its Neighbor," in which one New Hampshire mountain addresses another in monologue, represents a mythic sense unfamiliar in the West yet integrally Hindu. With this volume Stevens also begins to express a general Daoistic sense of the world's impermanence, one that culminates in the final lines of "An Ordinary Evening in New Haven," the central philosophical meditation of the late period:

> It is not in the premise that reality
> Is a solid. It may be a shade that traverses
> A dust, a force that traverses a shade.

Moreover, in this period a Buddhistic element enters again, nowhere more perfectly embodied than in "The House Was Quite and the World Was Calm." The house, in Stevens' symbology, represents the mind; the reader, its contemplative activity; the book, the book of nature. The "summer" of the poem's second line, as in the title of the volume, is reality; night is the self. The first and fourth lines create a progressively causal connection between the two terms of the poem's title by treating its words:

> The house was quiet and the world was calm.
> The reader became the book; and the summer night
>
> Was like the conscious being of the book.
> The house was quiet and the world was calm.

Here we feel a strong pulse of Vedantic thought, as summer, *Brahman*, is identified with night, the *Atman*. But the meditative mood of the poem is rather one of Buddhistic quietude. "The house," says Stevens, "was quiet because it had to be." As the Mahayana Shraddhotpada Shastra says, we should "quietly meditate upon the world," or, as a Neo-Confucian source

51

says, "penetratingly observe it," *qi guan wan wu* 寂觀萬物. In so doing we identify ourselves with it, as Stevens' reader becomes the book. "The quiet," the poem continues, "was part of the meaning, part of the mind: / The access of perfection to the page." The world, to cite again the Neo-Confucian source, itself achieves perfection in the process of meditation, 萬物靜觀皆自得. "And the world," says Stevens, "was calm":

> The truth in a calm world,
> In which there is no other meaning itself
>
> Is calm, itself is summer and night, itself
> Is the reader leaning late and reading there.

As Hua Yan 華嚴 Buddhism has it, principle and reality harmonize, *li shi yuan rong* 理事圓融 (*li* 理, originally the veins in a piece of jade: one cannot know the veins apart from the jade; the truth and the world are indivisible). When *nirvana* is achieved, the distinction between subject and object disappears (在涅槃的世界，沒有物我之分) and the truth is made manifest.

Stevens on occasion, then, could approximate the unified vision of certain oriental modes of thought. More characteristically, however, he struck an uneasy balance between Daoist, Buddhist or Vedantic monism and a thoroughgoing dualism. "Credences of Summer," one of several mid-length philosophical meditations, though it uses some Buddhistic language ("Exile desire / For what is not"), does so to celebrate "the rock of summer," that essential independent reality which, the poet says, "cannot be broken," because "it is the truth," a very unbuddhistic attitude. That truth, moreover, "is not a hermit's truth," Stevens adds.

Notes toward a Supreme Fiction reflects within itself this uneasy balance of eastern and western thought. Its invocation, addressed to the "supreme fiction" that for Stevens has replaced God, is quite Buddhistic, referring us to the "light of single, certain truth" in which the poet and the fiction "sit at rest, / For a moment in the central of our being" to experience a "vivid transparence" and a "peace." "It Must Change," the first of three prescriptive section titles, enunciates a principle in accord with the doctrine of No-permanence, and as a consequence the whole section takes on a Buddhistic coloration. In the same section the principles of Yin and Yang reappear: "Two things of opposite natures seem to depend / On one another, as a man depends / On a woman, day on night, the imagined / On the real." Though the poem contains an occasional oriental element, for the most part it is occidental, especially in its higher moments of religious vision. Certain passages, however, represent a marriage of the two spirits, as in the following lines, which move from a Buddhistic freedom from desire, through an evocation of the Vedantic Self, to a resolution in a pastiche of Hebraic monotheism (the latter echoing Jehovah's "I am that I am"): "There is an hour," Stevens begins, "in which I have

> No need, am happy, forget need's golden hand,
> Am satisfied without solacing majesty,
> And if there is an hour there is a day,
>
> There is a month, a year, there is a time
> In which majesty is a mirror of the self:
> I have not but I am and as I am, I am.

In some ways more poetically "advanced" than the volume that precedes it, *The Auroras of Autumn* (1950) reverts at crucial points to classical and Biblical imagery (it shows signs that Stevens was rereading the Bible, especially the Book of Revelation). The owl (Ascalaphus) in the title "The Owl in the Sarcophagus," along with the allegorical figures of sleep and peace, though transformed into what the poet calls a "mythology of modern death," are nonetheless classical in their origins, like the form of the elegy itself. "The Auroras of Autumn," the volume's opening sequence, like "Page from a Tale" and "Puella Parvulla," are markedly apocalyptic. In the midst of this fluctuation between classical and millenarian imagery, the third tradition enters in Buddhistic guise. In "A Primitive Like an Orb" "the giant of nothingness" makes an appearance alongside "the giant ever changing." Another poem, however, one with so Buddhistic a title as "What We See Is What We Think," ends with the line, "Since what we think is never what we see," thereby expressing Stevens' ambivalence toward, or rejection of, oriental doctrine.

What I have represented as an uneasy balance, or fluctuation, between East and West may of course be regarded as a measured eclecticism. "The Man with the Blue Guitar," Stevens' first mature speculative poem, adapts an Asiatic term to enlarge or reinforce a western philosophical vocabulary: "That I may reduce the monster to / Myself, and then may be myself / In the face of the monster." Here "myself" incorporates the Vedantic Self, a borrowing whose purpose is made explicit in the poet's restatement of an early theme: "A substitute for all the gods: / This self." Section XXII speaks of "an absence in reality" (roughly equivalent to the Buddhist *kong* (空), a generative force from which the poem, Stevens says, "acquires its true appearances," from which "it takes," to which "it gives," "in the universal intercourse," the last phrase suggesting as well the doctrine of Ceng Zhao 僧肇, *tian di jao he* 天地交合, the intercourse of heaven and earth. Similarly, in the later philosophical works Stevens combines eastern and western figures. "The Auroras of Autumn," whose first poem begins with a suggestion of the Greek Ophion ("This is where the serpent lives . . . Or is this another wriggling

out of the egg, / Another image at the end of the cave . . . ?") ends with a
reference that transforms the serpent into something Hindu:

> We saw his head
> Black beaded on the rock, the flecked animal
> The moving grass, the Indian in his glade.

A strongly Daoistic element is also present in this later sequence, not
only in the universal "mother," a principle like Lao-zi's *tian xia mu* 天下
母, but also in a virtual paraphrase of a line from the Dao De Jing's 道德
經 opening chapter (名可名非常名, "The name that can be named / Is
not the constant name" [Lau]). Having described reality as "a theater
floating through the clouds," Stevens says, of this thing that he has
named, it "is nothing," "Nothing until this named thing nameless is / And
is destroyed." In the section that follows we then encounter another
native version of Lao-zi in Stevens's inverted image of "the white creator
of black."

I have mentioned the Daoistic conclusion of "An Ordinary Evening in
New Haven," a poem everywhere permeated with that spirit, but the first
three words of its title suggest Buddhist "everyday-mindedness" (*ping
chang xin* 平常心 in its Chan 禪 formulation)." The Christian "New
Haven" has its analogue in a metaphor for *nirvana*, "the harbor of
refuge," cited by Rhys Davids. In section X of the poem Stevens says
that our spirit "resides / In a permanence composed of impermanence,"
an idea which approximates the *zhu xing wu chang* 諸行無常 or
doctrine of No-permanence. The extremity of the doctrine of Emptiness
(*kong* 空), however, is here resisted, both by innocence ("Alpha") and
experience ("Omega"), who respond to "the scene," or reality, as follows:
"For one it is enough; for one it is not; / For neither is it profound
absentia . . . ." The poem's closing sections reinforce its Daoistic burden,
as in XXVIII, where Stevens speaks of life as "things seen and unseen,
created from nothingness."

It was only with *The Rock*, the final section of *The Collected Poems*,
that Stevens produced a whole volume Buddhistic in its cast. Here, as
earlier, his emphasis is philosophical rather than moral, so that in
speaking of his parallels with Buddhism we most frequently have
recourse to the latter's metaphysics rather than its ethics. So too it must
be said that Stevens' concern with his own approaching death, a
naturalistic elegiac theme, is of more importance in this volume than any
religious vision. Nonetheless, the title "A Quiet Normal Life," though
primarily autobiographical, also embodies two Buddhist ideas that we
have mentioned, quietude and everyday-mindedness. Whereas its last
stanza expresses a Buddhistic spirit in its denial of "transcendent forms,"

its first stanza rejects an important doctrine, *jing you xin zao* 境由心造, the act of meditation creates the environment or world, one which "The World as Meditation," however, explicitly endorses. Generally, though, in the late meditations Stevens is less concerned with transformation than—as another title expresses it—with "The Plain Sense of Things." Nonetheless, the poems of *The Rock*, especially in their metaphors, continue to name Buddhist concerns. Thus "Vacancy in the Park," whose title again flirts with the notion of *kong* 空, incorporates in its second couplet another traditional metaphor:

> March . . . Someone has walked across the snow,
> Someone looking for he knows not what.
>
> It is like a boat that has pulled away
> From a shore at night and disappeared.

The Hinayana School initiated the figure of two shores, the near shore standing for *samsara*, the further shore, for *nirvana*. The Mahayana tradition then reconciled the opposites, either by declaring there to be no shores, or by identifying *nirvana* with *samsara* (as in Tian Tai 天台 doctrine, 生死即涅槃；煩惱即菩提). Stevens, in an otherwise Christian context ("To an Old Philosopher in Rome"), reaches a similar conclusion: "Impatient for the grandeur that you need / In so much misery; and yet finding it / Only in misery . . ."

In the Majjhima the first of the ten powers of the Buddha is listed as follows: "He knows what is possible as possible, and what is impossible as impossible." Though the title of the most ambitious poem in *The Rock*, "Prologues to What is Possible," may owe more to Kant than to Gautama, its doctrine, figuration and mood are strikingly like those of Buddhism, which Suzuki calls "the philosophy of infinite possibilities." "There was an ease of mind," the poem begins, "that was like being alone in a boat at sea." *Zi li* 自力, or self-reliance, as Emerson knew, is one of the features that most clearly distinguishes Buddhism from other religions (see 只有透過自身的努力，才能到達涅盤, only through one's own efforts can one reach *nirvana*). The waves on which Stevens' persona travels are compared in a bold metaphor to oarsmen, thereby identifying the natural and human phenomena "in the one-ness of their motion" (cp. the Hua Yan 華嚴 doctrine, 一即一切，一切即一, one is everything, everything is one). The vessel's "far-foreign departure" suggests not only a venture forth from *samsara* in quest of the other shore but, in its strangeness (the boat is "of unaccustomed origin"), an exotic belief as well. The traveler is likened to "a man lured on by a syllable without any meaning," which in the West would be a meaningless syllable but in the East might well be a mantra, "A syllable of which he felt, with an appointed sureness,"

55

That it contained the meaning into which he wanted to enter,
A meaning which, as he entered it, would shatter the boat and leave the
　　oarsmen quiet

As at a point of central arrival, an instant moment, much or little,
Removed from any shore, from any man or woman, and needing none.

The persona, quite simply, has achieved *nirvana*.

Lest, however, his reader anticipate Stevens' immediate conversion to Buddhism, a second stanza follows to examine, question and qualify the experience of the first stanza, which, the poet tells us, has "stirred his fear." After discussing the experience as "metaphor" and "hypothesis," Stevens concludes in a rather defiantly unbuddhistic way. "What self did he contain that had not been loosed?" he asks, flatly rejecting the doctrine of *wu wo* 無我, No-self. The poet instead returns "to what was real and its vocabulary," granting to the self the power to create "a fresh universe out of nothingness." On the very final page of *The Collected Poems*, in "Not Ideas About the Thing but the Thing Itself," the poet again turns away from these ventures into Buddhistic thought, settling instead for those sensations—a bird's first appearance in spring or his "scrawny cry" at dawn—which validate the existence of "reality," as Stevens had always fundamentally conceived of it.

諸佛世尊皆出人間終不在天上成佛也。
All the buddhas that the world knows are from the human world; after
all, they do not become buddhas in heaven.
　　　　　　　　　　　　　　　　—Ceng Zhao 僧肇

William Carlos Williams has often been regarded as something of an anomaly, for he appears to have had no religion, no theory of civilization, and no philosophy. These very features, along with his celebration of America, at the same time made him attractive to certain rebellious, rebarbative followers who, along with other, more moderate celebrants of the New World, found in him the most congenial alternative to the other figures so far discussed in this and the preceding essay. In the emphasis upon his native strain what have been ignored are William's religious conviction, cultural synthesis and philosophical insight. In a late poem he remarks, of "Deep Religious Faith," "it is / All that which makes the pear ripen / or the poet's line / come true! Throughout his career Williams meditated deeply on the relationship of American to more traditional cultures. Though his elder he served a kind of life-long apprenticeship to Ezra Pound, with whom he remained a friend to the end, despite the seeming incompatibility of their views. He struggled with Joyce and Eliot, making of the latter his *bête noir*, and through generous effort—

unreciprocated—accommodating the former, even writing on behalf of *Finnegans Wake*. His philosophy is accurately capsulized in the phrase, "no ideas but in things," one which, though anti-intellectual from a western point of view, is deeply in accord with oriental philosophy. Another gulf between Williams and his fellow Modernists lay in his life-style, for he alone inhabited a common human world. His career as a physician among the indigent and the lower middle class was as different from Stevens' career in surety claims, or Frost's rural isolation, as it was from the literary careers of Yeats, Eliot and Pound.

Williams' religious belief, never fully articulated but nonetheless apparent on every page of his work, was the immanentalism of the oriental view, expressed in Mahayana Buddhism as 是心則攝一切世間法出世間法, the (buddha) mind includes everything (or, literally, absorbs both secular and non-secular things). Unlike that of Stevens, though, Williams' native Buddhism was also ethical, his faith and metaphysics colored by his human sympathy. It is precisely the element of compassion (*zi bei* 慈悲), lacking in Pound, that was typical of Williams. "Complaint" might be taken as exemplary. The poet imagines himself, true to form, as having delivered "a great woman," "sick / perhaps vomiting," of her tenth child, whereupon, in the voice of Whitman, he says, "I pick the hair from her eyes / and watch her misery / with compassion." The poet delivered over three thousand babies in his lifetime, a fact that may have a good deal to do not only with his knowledge of people but also with his view of the world as emergent, of things as in a perpetual state of realization.

Although capable of modernizing the major myths of the Biblical and classical traditions, in such important poems as "Adam" and "Eve" and his lesser study, "The Birth of Venus," Williams more characteristically came at these subjects obliquely, casting off his judgments as though they were incidental to the matter at hand. His portrait of "The Bull," for example, depicts that creature as "godlike," resting for a moment "with half-closed eyes, / Olympian commentary on / the bright passage of days." The Christian often appears in its true paradoxical guise, as in "Pastoral," where Williams glimpses an old man "gathering dog lime," whose tread he describes as "more majestic than / that of the Episcopal minister / approaching the pulpit / of a Sunday."

Such pure moments of either Biblical or classical sentiment are few and far between. More frequently one tradition ironically inspects the other, as in "Venus over the Desert"; or the two are combined, as in "To Mark Anthony in Heaven." Adopting a rare historical view, the opening lines of "Choral: the Pink Church" represent the demise of the classical at the hands of the Christian: "Pink as a dawn in Galilee / whose stabbing

57

fingers routed / Aeschylus and murder blinked." The passage of greatest interest to us, however, comes at the end of "Burning the Christmas Greens," a ritual described in pagan terms but not without its Christian overtones ("Green is a solace / a promise of peace"). Williams celebrates the violent destruction of the flames; afterwards, when they have died down, he pauses to study the grate, in which, he says, "appeared a world! Black / mountains, black and red—as / yet uncolored—and ash white." "An infant landscape," he calls the scene, "as if we stood / ourselves refreshed among / the shining fauna of that fire." The black, red and white of this regenerative landscape repeat the colors of the three strands which, the Upanishad tells us, make up the cosmic cord. Moreover, the interpenetration of life and death, expressed in terms of paradox and cycle, is also distinctly Hindu.

Likewise the snake that appears in the first line of "A Sort of a Song," the poem that introduces Williams' most important philosophical idea:

> Let the snake wait under
> his weed
> and the writing
> be of words, slow and quick, sharp
> to strike, quiet to wait
> sleepless.
>
> —through metaphor to reconcile
> the people and the stone.
> Compose. (no ideas
> but in things) Invent!
> Saxifrage is my flower that splits
> the rocks.

Unlike Stevens' rock, which in "Credences of Summer" was "unbroken," or which later, in "The Rock," "the green leaves came and covered," Williams' rocks are split by the tough flowers of his poetry (we may choose among the poem's metaphors of striking, penetration and reconciliation). "Compose" suggests both verbal composition and meditative composure, though "Invent!" returns us to a western notion of poetry. It is notable that Williams' snake here has neither Biblical nor classical overtones. The central parenthetical phrase, repeated elsewhere in his work, may be regarded in two ways. The first would emphasize ideas but insist that they be found, or expressed in terms of, reality (cp. the Buddhist notion 佛法在世間，不離世間覺, the doctrine when applied in this world should express itself in the consciousness of this world). The second would emphasize reality and posit a kind of immanentalism. Again Williams is related to the thought of Ceng Zhao: 般若可虛而照，真諦可亡而知, truth is known by being made vacant (by getting rid of it); we can forget it but still know it.

In accordance with Buddhist doctrine much of his work also insists upon the suchness (*ru* 如) of things, perhaps nowhere more explicitly than in the title and opening line of "The Trees"; "the trees—being trees." A stanza later Williams interjects: "Christ, the bastards / haven't even sense enough / to stay out of the rain—." After the trees have spoken in their own voices ("Clacka tacka tacka," etc.), Williams commands them, "Loose desire!"; but they cannot: "desire / dead in the heart," he explains, "and memory broken." The elimination of desire (*ching jing wu yu* 清靜無欲) is a classic Buddhist goal, as is detachment from the past (see 念念之中，不思前境). Williams' insistence here upon the thing itself, it might be noted, is distinct from Christian essentialism—from the *haecceitas*, say, of Duns Scotus, which makes the evocation of Christ in the poet's blasphemous interjection relevant philosophically. The poem concludes with a classical trope in which the trees are regarded mythically ("These were men / from whose hands sprung / love"), but for the most part the poem denies them any human identity, thereby insisting upon their suchness.

That the trees themselves have no thought we expect. More original, and more Buddhistic, is Williams' extension of this principle into the human realm, as in "Spring and All," XXVI, where, at a ballgame, the poet says "The crowd is laughing / in detail, / permanently, seriously / without thought." Ceng Zhao's *wu zhi er zi zhi* 無知而自知, not to know and yet (spontaneously) to know, suggests a similarly serious thought in the absence of thought. A phrase from a later poem indicates that Williams was by no means innocent of Buddhist terminology. It occurs in "The Clouds," upon whose backs, the poet says, speaking of great geniuses of the past, "the dead ride, high! / undirtied by the putridity we fasten upon them— / . . . into the no-knowledge of their nameless destiny." The last phrase has no equivalent in classical or Biblical tradition but might be glossed in terms of a concept central to Lao-zi, *pu* 璞, "the uncarved block," meaning, among other things, an as yet undetermined fate. Namelessness, of course, is one of the attributes of the Dao (see 道常無名, the Dao is constantly without name). In a concluding figure that retreats from his earlier Buddhistic severity but is nonetheless oriental Williams describes the clouds as "a calligraphy of scaly dragons."

Partly because of its occasional nature, but more importantly because of his beliefs, Williams' work most often grows out of direct observation. The first poem of "Spring and All" includes the line, "One by one objects are defined—," whose double reference—to nature and to the writer's observant activity—stresses the naturalness of Williams' method and philosophy. Analogous to the Buddhist concept of suchness (*ru* 如) is the Daoist *zi ran* 自然, literally, self-so, or natural. In keeping with the Dao De Jing's philosophy of change it might be rendered as "the natural process." Thus the Dao emulates the natural process (*dao fa zi ran* 道法自然), the celebration of which is everywhere in Williams. An equally characteristic motif, in illustration of which the poet draws upon the metaphors of contemporary physics, is the simultaneity of all things. I quote from an early poem, "Spring Strains":

> creeping energy, concentrated
> counterforce—welds sky, buds, trees
> rivets them in one puckering hold!

"The myriad things grow in unison," says Lao-zi (萬物並作). "At the same time," he adds elsewhere, "one and many are born and grow" (萬物得一以生). Williams' phrase, "one puckering hold," may owe something to Einstein's model of the universe, to whose theory of relativity the "variable foot" is indebted, and whose natural religion he celebrates in "St. Francis Einstein of the Daffodils." Unlike the concept of simultaneity current among the cosmopolitan Modernists, where past, present and future are united in a philosophical or cultural focus, Williams' moment occurs in what D. H. Lawrence calls "the instant present," or immediate experience.

Chapter XL of the Dao De Ching says, 反者道之動, return is the movement of the Dao. This ontological concept, central to Lao-zi, suggests that energy is constantly emerging from the Dao and constantly returning to it. In a related statement Lao-zi says that the myriad things of the world are engendered of being, itself engendered of nothingness (天下萬物生於有，有生於無). We might consider several of Williams' images in this light. The first, a complete poem, titled "January Morning," VI,

> —and a semicircle of dirt-colored men
> about a fire bursting from an old
> ash can,

is one of a half dozen consecutive sections in that sequence, all beginning, "—and"; together they constitute a Whitmanesque series of vignettes in celebration of the fecundity of the world, of what Williams, in section VII, calls "the ever new river." The images in the poem quoted above may have had their genesis in a fleeting glimpse from a train as it crossed the Jersey plains, but they thoughtfully combine the earth and man in a circle half completed by the men, half by the poet or reader, all whom are warmed, if not engendered, by the primordial energy issuing from this receptacle for the remnants of earlier fire. Such an image, standing as here alone, would not have been considered poetic before the orientalization of the western imagination. A complementary passage, from "Spring and All, II," makes explicit the double, Daoistic movement of the Return:

> Pink confused with white
> flowers and flowers reversed
> take and spill the shaded flame
> darting it back
> into the lamp's horn

Again Williams expresses concepts—the reversibility of time and the issue of energy from a universal cornucopia—which, though conceptualized in modern western science, are more common to ancient eastern religion and philosophy.

Exactly how Williams came upon these ideas we may never know. Unlike his fellow Modernists, who assimilated the Orient in their youth, only to give it mature expression later, he was deeply oriental from the start (most of the passages that I have quoted are early ones). "It is impossible to recall," he says in the *Autobiography*, "whether it was in late childhood or early adolescence that I determined to be perfect." Later defining his subject matter, the ordinary people he encountered on his rounds, he speaks of his success in portraying "that secret world of perfection." "My 'medicine,'" he continues, "was the thing which gained me entrance to these secret gardens of the self. It lay there, another world, in the self." In Hindu terms Williams is speaking of the *Atman;* in connecting perfection with "the stinking ischiorectal abscesses of our coming and goings" he is identifying the Buddhist *samsara* with *nirvana.* "It is an identifiable thing," he says, "and its characteristic, its chief characteristic is that it is sure, all of a piece and, as I have said, instant and perfect." (For Williams' insistence upon instantaneity cp. the Buddhist 當下惜福, be grateful for the present moment; see also 當下涅盤, the present moment is *nirvana*.)

In Williams, however, there was no display of oriental learning, no reference or allusion, simply an intuition, one that leads the poet instinctively from early on to eschew western modes of logic, sequence and transcendence in favor of the concrete, instantaneous embodiment of perfection in the world of imperfection. It is not, therefore, surprising that his art, though verbal, should be so highly visual, musical and kinetic, as in the early "Overture to a Dance of Locomotives," whose single roman numeral, "I," suggests the poem's continuation in reality and whose last line, "The dance is sure" is elaborated in another later poem called "The Dance" ("But only the dance is sure!").

"Overture" includes many of the motifs that we have discussed. Time moves forward ("two-twofour — two-eight!") and backward ("Not twoeight. Not twofour. Two!"). All reality is seen as compacted into the present, which embodies the mystery; thus, though the hands of the clock "go round and round," "were they to / move quickly and at once the whole secret would be out." Lights hanging from the ceiling of the terminal are "packed with a warm glow," emitting energy but also attracting it ("inviting entry"). They "pull against the hour," says Williams, thereby again connecting time with energy. The motion of the train releases us from stasis into time, but as its wheels repeat the same gesture they remain, in an accurate observation, "relatively / stationary." Meanwhile, the rails, in a figure drawn from perspective, but also catching into itself the backward and forward motion of time and reality, "return on themselves infinitely." In a possible allusion to Heisenberg's Uncertainty Principle the poem ends with the line "The dance is sure."

Only late in life did Williams speak explicitly, or at any length, about the Orient. A reading trip to the West Coast in 1950 brought to conscious expression judgments that before had been implicit. In Seattle he discovered "the finest examples of Chinese carving" that he had ever beheld. "The Greeks," he said, "seem frozen beside them." A particular painting, "of a hundred crows in flight, nothing more," might, he said, "open our minds, were we before it, to many worlds." Characteristically, he applies his observation to a human one: "I think of Shapley of the Harvard Observatory and his active wish for many crossing cultures in a truly enlightened world to ease our plight."

His oriental enlightenment had been anticipated in "Choral: the Pink Church," whose lines on Galilee and Aeschylus, already quoted, give way to reminiscence:

> —and tho' I remember little
>   as names go,
> the thrust of that first light
>   was to me
>   as through a heart
>   of jade—
> as chinese as you please
> but not by that—remote

The Westerner is notorious for his inability to remember Chinese names (even a highly educated person cannot recall the name of a single Chinese painter, for example). The source of the "first light" to which Williams refers is not clear, for he is using the language of religious illumination, but the stanza that follows associates it with the light of dawn. When Williams speaks of his heart as jade,

```
transparent to the light
    through which the light
shines, through the stone,
    until
the stone-light glows,
    pink jade
—that is the light and is
    a stone
and is a church—if the image
    hold . . .
```

it is doubtful that he is thinking of a specific text, but the words of Lao-zi come to mind, "是以聖人被褐懷玉" (thus the sage harbors a piece of jade in his breast). At any rate, Williams represents himself as "chinese," by which he does not mean "remote," either in space, time, or, presumably, in degree of difficulty. Curiously, the line quoted from Lao-zi is preceded in the Dao De Jing by the assertion that his words are easy to understand and easy to act upon (吾言甚易知甚易行). The poem—as we have often observed to be the case among the Modernists—returns to Christian and classical terms ("Be ye therefore perfect even as your / Father in Heaven is perfect"; "Joy! Joy! / —out of Elysium!) to complete its thought.

The development of the poem's argument, however, is contradicted by the train of Williams' thought in the *Autobiography*, as he continues to contemplate the Orient. After leaving Seattle he proceeds on to Eugene, where again he is impressed by oriental collections: "On the first floor," he reports, "they have tapestries a lifetime might be spent in studying, such brilliance of color and skill have been lavished upon them." Like other orientalizing western artists Williams may be seeing his own work reflected in oriental art. His eye at last comes to rest on "a massive marble," "some personage or ruler (though no name is given), more than full scale, a draped figure in repose. The eyes," he continues, "are bemused, the face tranquil. The man is standing, as I remember it, a leather belt about his belly, the folds of his gown slightly caught at one point." Full of wonder in the presence of another world, he exclaims: "They have at least given the figure the whole platform!" He reports that he and his wife "sat on the bench opposite and were lost in admiration. The stained marble," he concludes, "seemed to make the whole campus outside us an absurdity."

Earlier in the passage, after having reached California, he offers a general cultural analysis: "The outstanding thing that I was aware of among all the West Coast cities was that they faced the Orient; that Europe had no more than a legendary hold on them; that airplanes or no airplanes they were remote from ancient, occidental cultures . . . ." "The young in the colleges," where he had been reading, "yearn for France, for New York, Boston, for that 'culture'"; "they cling to worn-out Europe as though the feudal were their king"; "while Japan, China and Korea lie across the water to their ruin." The apprenticeship to Ezra Pound had borne fruit.

I have placed Robert Frost last in our discussion of orientalism, partly because in him we find the exception that proves the rule, partly because, even in this eldest and most provincial of the American Modernists there are one or two strikingly oriental elements. His resistance to exotica, along with his expression of an attitude toward Asia prevalent at the time, may be found in the satirical lines of "An Importer":

> Mrs. Someone's been to Asia.
> What she brought back would amaze ye.
> Bamboos, ivories, jades, and lacquers,
> Devil-scaring firecrackers,
> Recipes for tea with butter,
> Sacred rigamaroles to mutter . . .

Though the poem ends with an ironic twist, turning a prejudiced conception of the East back on the general public that held it, the lines nonetheless also reflect Frost's own low regard for Asia, expressed as late as July 24, 1962 in a letter to John F. Kennedy, on the eve of the poet's good-will mission to the Soviet Union. Having mentioned the English- and the Russian-speaking worlds, Frost offers the young President some free geo-political advice. "The rest of the world would be Asia and Africa, more or less negligible for the time being though it needn't be too openly declared."

Again, however, the poet's conscious (and here political) sentiments need to be distinguished from his unconscious (religious and philosophical) affinities, for the work of this unofficial laureate of backwoods America, like that of his more worldly compatriots, on occasion bears a relationship to oriental thought. References to Asia in his work, however, are usually negative, if not derogatory; at any rate, few and far between. From London in 1913 he reports having passed up an opportunity to hear Tagore read. In 1918 he mentions a Buddhist friend in Franconia who "derives the present more from the future than from the past." Earlier, in 1906, he mentions a flap at the Pinkerton Academy, "where my poem about the heretofore turned up in the school library. "The Trial By Existence" represents "the gathering of the souls for birth," a theme hardly more radically expressed than in Wordsworth's Immortality Ode. After analyzing his fellow-teachers' reactions, wondering if the poem "had led them to question my orthodoxy," Frost adds that he has reconsidered, realizing "that a flock of teachers would be more apt to loathe me for misspelling Derry than for grafting Schopenhauer upon Christianity." Though the quotation does not speak openly of Asia, it implies Frost's awareness of the connection between Buddhist thought and advanced nineteenth-century western philosophy.

The poet's summary of the history of his own religious belief, provided for Amy Lowell at the latter's request on December 2, 1917, gives us as well a terse summary of western theological drift: "Presbyterian, Unitarian, Swedenborgian, Nothing." A letter to his intimate Sidney Cox of January 1, 1926 mentions Frost's dissatisfaction with the contentiousness of Christian theology. "Clash," he says,

> is all very well for coming lawyers, politicians and theologians. But I should think there must be a whole realm or plane above that—all sight and insight, perception, intuition, rapture . . . I have wanted to find ways to transcend the strife-method. I have found some. Mind you I'd fight a healthy amount. This is no pacifism. It is not so much anti-conflict as it is something beyond conflict—such as poetry and religion that is not just theological dialectic. I'll bet I could tell of spiritual realizations that at least for the moment would overawe the contentious. That's the sort of thing I mean. Every poem is one. I know I have to guard against insisting on this too much . . . .

Though the phrase "spiritual realizations" may suggest an oriental alternative, the terms of Frost's discussion are thoroughly Christian. He seeks to "transcend the strife-method," desires a realm "above" clash. Moreover, when his work, on rare occasions, expresses the sort of "intuition" that he speaks of here, it is likely, as in "All Revelation," to do so in terms of Christian vision. One would be hard pressed to find an example of "rapture" in Robert Frost. The last sentence quoted gives the game away, for being himself a contentious person, classical by temperament and dialectical by talent, Frost is not equipped to carry through on his yearning. Insofar as oriental thought is non-contentious, one might nonetheless expect to find such an element in Frost's work. In fact, aside from the one that incited controversy, there are only two other poems in which oriental thought plays a serious role. Both, however, are important works, and their oriental elements occur at crucial points in their arguments. The poems that I have in mind are "Birches," the best of the volume *Mountain Interval*, and "West-Running Brook," Frost's most sustained philosophical meditation.

The oriental element in the first of these is confined to a few lines near the end of the poem. Having lamented the pain of experience, which he assuages by reminiscing about the childhood joy of climbing birch trees and riding their branches back to the ground, Frost says wistfully, "I'd like to get away from earth awhile / And then come back to it and begin over." Having thereby expressed the wish for reincarnation, he is quick to distinguish it from its western alternative: "May no fate willfully misunderstand me / And half grant what I wish and snatch me away / Not to return." He then reverts to the theme of tree-climbing, now extending it metaphorically:

> I'd like to go by climbing a birch tree,
> And climb black branches up a snow-white trunk
> *Toward* heaven, till the tree could bear no more,
> But dipped its top and set me down again.
> That would be good both going and coming back.

Though the last line quoted again entertains the idea of reincarnation, it does so in the context of Frost's playful skepticism, one which effectively dismisses the belief in a Christian heaven along with the idea of transmigration, which it finally entertains here only as poetic property.

"West-Running Brook," on the other hand, represents a much more serious expression of oriental ideas. Like several other mid-length studies of marriages, "Home Burial" and "A Servant to Servants" among them, this dramatic poem concerns the relationship of man and wife; unlike those earlier works, however, Frost's mature treatment of the theme represents man and woman in harmony with one another. To the masculine and feminine principles he adds a third, symbolized in the brook: "As you and I are married to each other," says the wife, "We'll be married to the brook," Frost's parenthetical description of which discovers in it two elements, one black, one white, one a forward, one a backward motion, the two seen as interdependent:

> (The black stream, catching on a sunken rock,
> Flung backward on itself in one white wave,
> And the white water rode the black forever . . .)

The stark contrast of his complementary figures suggests the imagery of *yin* 陰 and *yang* 陽. After an interlude of Christian metaphor Frost allows the husband to voice at length the most important statement of the poem's cosmology. "'Speaking of contraries,'" he begins, "'see how the brook / In that white wave runs counter to itself.'" The husband's thought then turns to origins. In the image that he has described for us, he asserts, "'we get back to the beginning of beginnings,'" to "'the stream of everything that runs away.'" "'Existence,'" he says, thereby naming the stream, some conceive of as traditional male and female clowns dancing "'forever in one place. But,'" he adds, offering his own (and Frost's) view, "'it runs way, / It seriously, sadly, runs away / To fill the abyss' void with emptiness.'" The last word that Frost has used often translates the Buddhist *kong* 空, a generative principle out of which—as in the vision of the Dao—things are seen as emerging. The husband goes on to elaborate his description of this river of existence, his figures becoming more and more grandly metaphorical. "'It flows,'" he says,

> "beside us in this water brook
> But it flows over us. It flows between us
> To separate us for a panic moment,
> It flows between us, over us, and *with* us.
> And it is time, strength, tone, light, life, and love—
> And even substance lapsing unsubstantial."

These final two lines, with their elaboration of metaphor, suggest the richness of the Buddhist conception of Emptiness. At this point, however, the husband's thought appears to veer from that doctrine, redefining the river as a "'universal cataract of death'" spending to "'nothingness,'" a turn in argument that emphasizes only half of the oriental view of universal process. Once again, however, the argument shifts, returning to the earlier topic of the river's "'strange resistance in itself.'" This "'throwing backward on itself'" the speaker calls "'sacred,'" seeing in it the principle "'sending up our life,'" "'sending up the brook,'" "'sending up the sun.'" With these figures Frost confirms the other half of the oriental doctrine; at which point his protagonist concludes:

> "It is this backward motion toward the source,
> Against the stream, that most we see ourselves in,
> The tribute of the current to the source."

At the last moment then, in a rather Romantic, western way, the poem humanizes the universal force. But in the course of his character's monologue Frost has given us a complex of images that suggest oriental doctrines which we have discussed, among them the Daoist return (*fan* 反) in its motion toward nothingness (*wu chang* 無常). As was the case with Williams' thought, Frost's cosmology is also reconcilable with modern physics, in particular with the contemporary Big Bang Theory of an expanding and contracting universe, but also with the more recent conception of a universe constantly creating itself out of nothing at the subatomic level. What Frost has done is to synthesize western and eastern ideas, combining scientific thought from the former with philosophical and religious notions from the latter, enfolding into this mix other, partly contradictory, western ideas. The whole, which is governed by a fundamentally Heraclitean metaphor, is arrived at intuitively, which is to say poetically.

So much, then, for the presence of oriental ideas in Frost. There remains one poem of interest not so much for its thought as for its geography: "The Bearer of Evil Tidings," collected in *A Further Range* (1936) and listed with two others in *The Complete Poems* under the heading "Outlands." Composed in ballad stanzas, it tells a story of Frost's own invention. Set in the Himalayas, in a country named Pamir, it concerns a Chinese princess, who in ancient times had left her homeland in a royal progress toward the West, where she was to marry a Persian prince. Midway there it is discovered that she is with child (through no fault of her own, or anyone else's: "a god was its father"). When the fact is discovered, her retinue, Frost reports, came "to a troubled halt": "it had seemed," he says, "discreet to remain there / And neither go on nor back." "So they stayed and declared a village," adds the poet bumptiously, "There in the land of the Yak."

The main action of the poem, however, picks up centuries later, as a messenger makes his way to the court of Belshazzar, King of Babylon. With evil tidings to bear (news of the king's overthrow), this Westerner welcomes a fork in the road and takes the way leading off "into the wild unknown." Traveling through the mountains and "the Vale of Cashmere," he eventually arrives at "a precipice valley," where he meets "a girl of his age" and is taken home.

Now the child that had come of the princess had "established a royal line," and "his mandates were given heed to / Because he was born divine." That, says the poet, "was why there were people / On one Himalayan shelf." And so, "The bearer of evil tidings / Decided to stay there himself.

> At least he had this in common
> With the race he chose to adopt.
> They had both of them had their reasons
> For stopping where they had stopped.

"As for his evil tidings," Frost concludes, "Why hurry to tell Belshazzar / What soon enough he would know?" It is a curious little fable, one which remains unexplained by anything else that we know of Frost, except perhaps for his desire to come to terms with the Orient. His other attempts to do so, both earlier and later, seem somewhat inconclusive. By contrast, this one has the finality of myth. Accordingly, its elements bear a moment's inspection.

Like myths the world over it tells of the intervention of gods in the affairs of men, echoing other stories of the founding of a royal line. It tells of a frustrated marriage of East and West, one transformed by circumstance into a cultural transplantation of China into Central Asia, perhaps a reversal of the more famous transplantation of Buddhism into China. Nonetheless, its original motive, an intercultural marriage, is finally realized, this time as the result of the West traveling to meet the East halfway. In the second part of the story, we might note, the time, though historical, is still remote, dating from the fall of Babylon. There is something desperate in the situation of both parties. The original princess had no choice but to stop; likewise, the western refugee, had he not been hospitably received, Frost tells us, "might be running yet." The original girl's descendant tells him the story of how she got there but also teaches him "her tribe's religion," one passed down through the original princess's divine son, a figure who again suggests historical parallels. The Westerner in one sense has been irresponsible, failing to report his news; however, knowing what we do about evil tidings, he also must be judged sensible. At any rate, what he had had to say was soon to become self-evident, as by now the meaning of the parable in the present context should be.

4

Poetry and Philosophy in the *Lao-zi*

When the man of highest capacities hears Dao
He does his best to put in into practice.
When the man of middling capacity hears Dao
He is of two minds about it.
When the man of low capacity hears Dao
He laughs loudly at it.
If he did not laugh, it would not be worth the name of Dao.

(XLI, trans. Arthur Waley)

上士聞道，勤而行之。
中士聞道，若存若亡。
下士聞道，大而笑之，不笑不足以爲道。

Introduction

The Dao De Jing 道德經 (*The Way and Its Nature*), China's greatest wisdom text, traditionally ascribed to the shadowy figure of Lao-zi 老子 and therefore referred to as the *Lao-zi*, is a work of poetry. Written for the most part in metrical language with rhyme, it is divisible into sections whose relationship to one another is like that of the poems one finds in a long poetic sequence. The language of the text is poetic, everywhere concise and elusive. Conventional poetic figures (simile, metaphor, symbol, analogy) are employed from time to time; parts of the text represent traditional sayings. The individual "chapters" are argued as aphoristic poems would be. But the *Lao-zi* is also poetic in a larger sense. As Homer expresses the poetry of *epos*, as the *Bhagavad Gita*, a poetry of religious vision, so the *Lao-zi,* what we might call the poetry of wisdom. This wisdom, or philosophic truth, is embodied in its poetic language, rhetoric and structure.

Western thought, with its penchant for reductive or essentializing categories, loves the abstract. The highest moment in a western text is summary. Its ground and method are both idealist. Chinese thought, with its object of practical advice, tends to be more concrete. We move from one to another aperçu without the western concern for system. Lao-zi, no less than Confucius, is a realist: pragmatic, sensible, anti-idealistic.

The philosophic truth of the *Lao-zi*, then, lies not in the abstract principles deducible from it (as in the summary treatments of western or westernizing historians of Chinese thought—Frederick W. Mote, Fung

Yu-lan 馮友蘭) but in the poetic texture and dynamic of its argument. Likewise, its true poetry lies not so much in its diction, meter, rhyme and suchlike as in its broader conception of things: its practical doctrine, its attitude to experience, its view of thought itself. Since the text—an eclectic assemblage of traditional wisdom, not an argument or essay in the western sense—moves organically from one thing to another, to grasp its meaning we must read it *as it unfolds*.

This raises a problem. For just as the language of the text is uncertain—virtually every line as been debated, emended, cut or moved—so the order of the chapters is open to question. Some texts have Part II (the so-called De Jing 德經) before Part I (the so-called Dao Jing 道經). In fact it has been argued that only the opening chapters of those sections justify this designation of the two parts. Much of the controversy here, as elsewhere, I would suggest, arises from a misapprehension of the nature of the text. For just as the vexed problem of Lao-zi's historicity disappears if we regard the text as traditional, so the problem of its order disappears if we regard it as an anthology of related sayings. There *is* a cumulative effect, but the effect does not depend upon any precise route of accumulation. There *is* a body of thought, but one that we arrive at not so much through progressive argument as through poetic consensus. The analogy of the New Testament Gospels is pertinent: our perception of the Christian message does not depend substantially on the order in which we read them.

What I propose to do, then is two-fold: (1) expound the philosophy of the *Lao-zi*, as it appears sequentially in the text that we have, and (2) demonstrate its poetic element. Part I of the text—the Dao Jing (or Classic of the Way)—is more doctrinal, and I shall use that section to demonstrate Lao-zi's thought. Part II of the text—the De Jing (or Classic of the Nature of Things)—is more practical, pithy, and poetic—in the customary sense. I shall use it primarily to demonstrate the poetic element. But these divisions, both of labor and text, are artificial and should not be misunderstood. For just as the two parts of the text depend upon one another, so philosophy and poetry in the text are interdependent. The first half of my essay, then, will deal with what we might call the poetry of philosophy, the second, with the philosophy (or significant form) of poetry.

1

The text opens with the poetry of epistemological paradox (unless otherwise indicated, all quotations henceforth are from D. C. Lau's translation):

71

> The way that can be spoken of
> Is not the constant way;
> The name that can be named
> Is not the constant name.
> 道可道非常道，名可名非常名。

Much of the poetry of the *Lao-zi* is a kind of anti-poetry: of namelessness; of secrecy and paradox:

> Hence always rid yourself of desires in order to observe its secrets;
> But always allow yourself to have desires in order to observe its manifestation.
> 故常無欲，以觀其妙。
> 常有欲，以觀其徼。

The doctrine is also in a sense anti-philosophical, for, as Wing-tsit Chan says of Chinese philosophy, "Most schools insist on the correspondence of names and actualities and accept names as necessary and good: Daoism, on the contrary, rejects names in favor of the nameless." (Citation of those commentaries listed at the end of the essay refer to the notes to whichever chapter of the text is under discussion.) The poetry of namelessness is by no means exclusively eastern (one thinks of Jehovah's ineffability), nor is the *Dao*'s secrecy (one thinks of the Christian life that is lost before it is found). In fact the poetry of secrecy is a mark of the high religious tradition (one thinks of Buddhist exclusivity as well as western Hermeticism).

Identity and diversity, the mystery of the One and the Many, is the burden of Chapter I's closing lines:

> These two are the same
> But diverge in name as they issue forth.
> Being the same they are called mysteries,
> Mystery upon mystery—
> The gateway of the manifold secrets.
> 此兩者同出而異名。
> 同謂之玄，玄之又玄，眾妙之門。

As Chapter I closes with paradox, so Chapter II opens:

> The whole world recognizes the beautiful as the beautiful, yet this is only the ugly;
> The whole world recognizes the good as the good, yet this is only the bad.
> 天下皆知美之為美，斯惡已。
> 皆知善之為善，斯不善已。

(The form of the paradox might itself be seen as paradigmatic of Lao-zi's whole method: the step-wide reduplicative exfoliation of meaning.) Unlike western categories—such as Plato's *to kalon*—Lao-zi's categories are not consistent, are in fact contradictory; and yet it is precisely with what Chang Chung-yuan calls "the self-identity of contradictions and the wonderful achievement to which it leads" that Chapter II is concerned. It is only one abstractive step to Zhuang-zi's 莊子 "Construction is destruction, destruction is construction. This is also that, that is also this." Though at odds with much western philosophy, in its concern with the interpenetration of reality and appearance, the passage is thematically consonant with much western poetry. This quality, which we might denominate the poetry of reciprocity, extends to other entities:

> Thus Something and Nothing produce each other;
> The difficult and the easy complement each other.
> 故有無相生，難易相成。

Lao-zi next introduces two concepts of great importance to Daoist thought: actionless action and wordless wisdom, both recommended as a consequence of the foregoing observations. "Therefore," he says,

> the sage keeps to the deed that consists in taking no
> action and practices the teaching that uses no words.
> 是以聖人處無爲之事，行不言之教。

Implicit in the chapter, awaiting later development, is yet another theme: the unity of the subjectivity of man and the objectivity of things. By this process of adumbration philosophic points are often prepared and reinforced. (Later we shall speak more specifically to the question of the resolution of the subject-object problem.)

The personal ridding of desire and the taking of no action, enunciated respectively in Chapters I and II, are then applied in Chapter III to the realm of government, where the sage is said to keep the people "free from desire" and to do that himself "which consists in taking no action." As a consequence, says Lao-zi, "order will prevail." Waley sees the chapter as "bait for the Realists [Legalists]"; Chang, reading it metaphysically, sees it as illustrating "the non-differentiated knowledge" or "the knowledge of no knowledge," which he compares with Hegel's "immediate knowledge." (Hegel had first lectured on the Dao De Jing in 1826.) This influence of Lao-zi on western thought extends to the poeticization of philosophical thinking, especially in the work of Martin Heidegger.

Chapter IV introduces the famous metaphor of emptiness, to which we shall return in our discussion of poetic rhetoric. Chapter V opens with a much-glossed passage:

> Heaven and earth are ruthless, and treat the myriad creatures as straw dogs;
> The sage is ruthless, and treats the people as straw dogs.
> 天地不仁，以萬物爲芻狗。
> 聖人不仁，以百姓爲芻狗。

As Chan's translation ("Heaven and Earth are not humane") makes more evident, the passage may be read as a contradiction of the Confucian principle of *ren* 仁 (humanity or benevolence). "Actually," says Chan in his comment, "the Daoist idea here is not negative but positive, for it means that Heaven and Earth are impartial, have no favorites, and are not humane in a deliberate or artificial way." The strategy of this paradoxical passage reflects what we might call the poetry of the unexpected, the deliberate reversal of the reader's expectations. The quietism of the chapter's closing lines ("Much speech leads inevitably to silence. / Better to hold fast to the void" 多言數窮不如守中) has been seen as at odds with Confucianism. Chang reconciles the two by adducing a passage from the Confucianist Doctrine of the Mean 中庸: "When delight, anger, sorrow or joy have not yet emerged, this is called *zhong* 中 ["center"; by extension: speechlessness, emptiness] . . . . *Zhong* is the great foundation of the entire universe." Characteristic here is the reconcilability of Daoist with Confucian and Buddhist thought.

A late Han commentator links this final image of Chapter V with the opening line of VI ("The spirit of the valley never dies" 谷神不死): "When intelligence and thought diminish to nothingness, the spirit of the valley unceasingly remains." Chang elaborates: "When idle thoughts no longer obscure the mind, the reality of the emptiness of the mind exists continuously." We shall return to discuss the symbol of the valley.

The principle of passivity, "the mysterious female" of Chapter VI, is extended in VII to Heaven and Earth, which are here described as "enduring." Combining the concepts, Lao-zi then recommends for man an enduring passivity:

> The sage puts his person last and it comes first,
> Treats it as extraneous to himself and it is preserved.
> Is it not because he is without thought of self that he
> Is able to accomplish his private ends?
> 是以聖人後其身而身先，
> 外其身而身存。
> 非以其無私耶，
> 故能成其私。

For Zhuang-zi, "The perfect man has no self."

The famous first line of VII, "Highest good is like water (上善若水)," may also be rendered (as it has been by Wang Bi 王弼, most ancient of the commentators), "The best man is like water." Chang underlines the relationship between VIII and VII and draws a contrast between their joint image of man and that of the Confucian *ren* 仁: "The man of *Dao* is free from self, free from reputation, and free from claiming credit . . . . Although Confucianism also teaches humility, it is a humility that merely modifies one's ambition or ego. Primarily, ambition and a strong ego persist at the center of one's being." He goes on to compare the Daoist

74

attitude here with the Buddhist concept of "every-day mindedness."

A metaphorical connective with Chapter IX is apparent in its opening lines:

> Rather than fill it to the brim by keeping it upright
> Better to have stopped in time . . .
> 持而盈之，不如其已。

The chapter as a whole recommends retirement, but, as Chan points out, "only after one's work is done: The Daoist way of life is not that of a hermit, although hermits have taken its name." He goes on to draw another parallel with Confucianism: "Mencius said that it was the way of Confucius to withdraw quietly from office when it was proper to do so."

Chapters X and XI are concerned with complementary concepts, Embracing the One ("When carrying on your head your perplexed bodily soul can you embrace in your arms the One / And not let go?" 載營魄，抱一，能無離乎?) and the Unity of Multiplicity. Both are inherently poetic ideas. In XI the utility of non-being is exemplified in a series of images—the wheel hub, the cart, the vessel, doors and windows—all which represent useful emptiness. In XII, Lao-zi contrasts outer and inner worlds—to the advantage of the latter ("the sage is / For the belly / Not for the eye" 聖人爲腹不爲目). Waley calls the section "a reply to the Hedonists." Chapter XIII, though more practical in orientation, is nonetheless linked philosophically:

> The reason I have great trouble is that I have a body.
> When I no longer have a body, what trouble have I?
> Hence he who values his body more than dominion over the
> Empire can be entrusted with the empire.
> 吾所以有大患者，爲吾有身。
> 及吾無身，吾有何患。
> 故貴以身爲天下，則可寄於天下。

To establish the link Waley quotes the *Lu Shi Chun Qiu* 呂氏春秋: "He alone may be entrusted with empire who does not let empire interfere with his own life culture." Inwardness, or accommodation with the void, is a precondition for outwardness, or dealing with the world.

The final lines of XIV, though they appear to deal only with prehistoric origins, are linked by Waley with the foregoing theme of subject and object. Where Lau reads "The ability to know the beginning of antiquity / Is called the thread running through the way" (能知古始，是謂道紀), Waley reads "For to know what there was in the beginning . . . ," which he glosses: "Macrocosmically, in the Universe. Microcosmically, in oneself." Thus a concern with origins, often asserted to be absent from Chinese thought, makes its presence felt.

Almost casually, in a simile (the sage is "thick like the uncarved block" 敦兮其若樸), XV introduces the concept of *pu* 樸 (in Chang's phrase, "original non-differentiation"). The poetic form of the sage's portrait shapes and surrounds the concept. Likewise poetic form figures importantly in XVI, where a passage of poetic concatenation provides both a philosophical summary and, in its linkage of lines, something analogous to the linkage of chapters or ideas that informs the whole text:

> . . . should one act from knowledge of the constant [*rong* 容]
> One's action will lead to impartiality [*kong* 公],
> Impartiality to kingliness [*wang* 王],
> Kingliness to heaven [*tian* 天]
> Heaven to the way,
> The way to perpetuity . . . .
> 知常容。容乃公。
> 公乃王。王乃天。
> 天乃道。道乃久。

Progressively the four key terms describe, in Chang's words, "the stages of contemplation, or quietness, after the achievement of enlightenment. In the realm of the absolute void," he continues, "there is interfusion and interpenetration of self and others." It is the naturalness and inevitability of the resolution of the subject-object problem which western philosophers find so attractive. The notion of naturalness then links XVI and XVII, where attention is turned to the ruler (though what applies to the ruler applies as well to the individual).

Chapters XVIII and XIX are related rhetorically as negative and positive forms of the same idea. XVIII, a caustic deflation of supposed virtues, is cast in the form of a *vituperatio:*

> When the great way falls into disuse
> There are benevolence and rectitude;
> When cleverness emerges
> There is great hypocrisy;
> When the six relations are at variance
> There are filial children;
> When the state is benighted
> There are loyal ministers.
> 大道廢，焉有仁義。
> 智慧出，焉有大偽。
> 六親不和有孝慈。
> 國家昏亂有忠臣。

XIX, the corrective, counters with poetic exhortation:

> Exterminate benevolence, discard the wise,
> And the people will benefit a hundredfold;
> Exterminate benevolence, discard rectitude,
> And the people will again be filial.

絕聖棄智，民利百倍。
絕仁棄義，民復孝慈。

Again the uncarved block is called into being, this time through metaphor, with no concern for further definition:

> Exhibit the unadorned and embrace the uncarved block,
> Have little thought of self and as few desires as possible.
> 見素抱樸，少思寡欲。

Whereas XIX closes with prescriptions for the self, XX takes that self and allows it to flourish in the voice of the sage speaking for the first time *in propria persona*. His poignancy here suggests the voice of a Tang poet:

> I alone am inactive and reveal no signs,
> Like a baby that has not yet learned to smile.
> Listless as though with no home to go back to.
> 我獨泊兮其未兆，
> 如嬰兒之未孩。
> 儽儽兮若無所歸。

The philosophical point is fully embodied, half in the tone or persona, half in what he says: "Vulgar people are clear. / I alone am drowsy" (俗人昭昭，我獨昏昏). "I alone am different from others (我獨異於人)," he concludes, "and value being fed by the mother 而貴求食於母," a phrase that catches up the earlier simile quoted above.

In complement to the *yin* 陰 (the mother) of XX, XXI offers the *yang* 陽: "Fathers of the multitude 眾甫," the abstract external origin that we know because we know its concrete internal counterpart:

> How do I know that the fathers of the multitude are like that? By means of this.
> 吾奚以知眾甫之然哉？以此。

Thus the *Dao* manifests itself in this poetry of bipolar origins. The parallel of the *Brahman-Atman* exchange suggests itself, and, as Chang points out, the Buddhist sense of no origin is also relevant: "Although one tries to see the beginnings of all things, there is actually no beginning. The beginning of no-beginning is the subtlety of all things."

Chapters XXII to XXIV function as a group. XXII introduces the principle of humility through a sequence of metaphors, which culminate in its iteration: "The sage embraces the One and is a model for the empire" (是以聖人抱一為天下式). He does so, as the remainder of the chapter makes clear, for self-preservation. XXIII extends the principle of humility to the principle of conformity to the way. XXIV, which an ancient commentator combines with the preceding chapter, further exemplifies the principles of XXII and XXIII.

Chapter XXV, by way of periodic repetition, offers a major definition of what Chang, citing an ancient sources, refers to as "the totality of *Dao* itself," the "thing" (*wu* 物) referred to in the opening line. Lao-zi's method here is the reprise of earlier passages, a poetic (repetitive) strategy that also serves as a means to reiterate principles:

> There is a thing confusedly formed,
> Born before heaven and earth.
> Silent and void
> It stands alone and does not weary.
> It is capable of being the mother of the world.
> I know not its name
> So I style it "the way."
> 有物混成，先天地生。
> 寂兮寥兮，獨立而不改，
> 周行而不殆，可以爲天下母。
> 吾不知其名，字之曰道。

The lines that follow offer another poetic chain, which is capped by and introduces the important concept of the Return. "Hence the way," the argument continues, "is great; heaven is great; earth is great; and the king is also great" (故道大，天大，地大，王亦大). Then, reversing the order of his key terms, Lao-zi, with an echo of the passage quoted from XVI, concludes, this time making more explicit the principle of naturalness enunciated earlier:

> Man models himself on earth,
> Earth on heaven,
> Heaven on the way,
> And the way on that which is naturally so.
> 人法地，地法天。天法道。道法自然。

Chapters XXVI and XXVII offer, in alternating passages, a mixture of practical advice and metaphysical conclusions. In contrast to the relative formlessness of these chapters the rhetoric of the next four places them among the most tightly argued in the text. Chapter XXVIII, to which we shall return to examine rhetorical structure and the poetic use of symbol, opens as follows:

> Know the male
> But keep to the role of the female
> And be a ravine to the empire.
> 知其雄，守其雌，爲天下谿。

The second line picks up and repeats an idea expressed in X ("Are you capable of keeping to the role of the female? 能爲雌乎?), the third, an image from VI ("The spirit of the valley never dies"), uniting them here more explicitly than before. Philosophical commentators have noted in the chapter the source of the Neo-Confucianist notion of the Non-ultimate, which, added to the Great Ultimate of the Book of Changes 易經, lead to a metaphysical bifurcation of reality. Chan resolves the problem as follows: "the Non-ultimate is the state of reality before the appearance of forms, whereas the Great Ultimate is the state after the appearance of forms"; "the two," he asserts, "form a unity."

Chapters XXIX to XXXI are highly practical in their emphasis and interesting in their modes of argumentation. We shall also return to look at them in more detail; but we can summarize the burden of their argument here by quoting briefly:

> Whoever takes the empire and wishes to do anything to it I see will have no respite.
>
> (XXXIX)
>
> 將欲取天下而爲之，吾見其不得已。

> One who assists the ruler of men by means of the way does not intimidate the empire by a show of arms.
>
> (XXX)
>
> 是以道佐人主者，不以兵強天下。

> Arms are instruments of ill omen, not the instruments of the gentleman. When one is compelled to use them it is best to do so without relish.
>
> (XXXI)
>
> 兵者不祥之器，非君子之器。不得已而用之，以恬澹爲上。

The quietistic philosopher's concern with the practice of warfare has seemed to some contradictory. Two answers to the objection are available: (1) If war is inevitable, one should conduct it according to Daoist principles, remaining detached and quiescent; (2) Lao-zi is not so quietistic as is sometimes imagined.

The last six chapters of the Dao Jing are among its most elegant and demanding. Philosophically acute and poetically serene, they require of the reader both an outward attentiveness (to the text) and an inner attentiveness (to himself). "The way is for ever nameless" (道無常名), XXXII begins, thereby defining the *Dao* as something beyond reasonable apprehension. In the next verse Lao-zi reintroduces the elusive image of the uncarved block, about which he says, "Only when it is cut are there names." By joining the abstract concept of namelessness, which we can render concrete only by an irrational leap, with the concrete image of the uncarved block, to which we can ascribe meaning only by a rational act of abstraction, Lao-zi places in tension two opposed tendencies of the mind. These he then reconciles by an appeal to the principle of moderation:

As soon as there are names
One ought to know that it is time to stop.
Knowing when to stop one can be free from danger.
名亦既有，
夫亦將知止。
知止所以不殆。

The subsequent leap to a final generalization ("The way is to the world as the River and the Sea are to rivulets and streams" 譬道之在天下，猶川谷之於江海) seems to reflect the state of safety Lao-zi has spoken of. Naturalness, earlier posited as a principle, now becomes implicit in the analogy itself.

Though more conventional in form, XXXII pursues this poetry of relentless truth, demanding that the reader attend intellectually to the general form of what is said but, at the same time, and with a self-questioning sincerity, apply the principles to himself:

He who knows others is clever;
He who knows himself has discernment.
知人者智，自知者明。

The chapter is brought to an end with two truths disguised within banalities:

He who does not lose his station will endure;
He who lives out his days has had a long life.
不失其所者久，死而不亡者壽。

In sayings such as these the very discrepancy between banality of observation and depth of insight forces the reader to comment; his effort to elucidate in turn often draws further comment. Hence the tradition of commentary. So Chang quotes Zhuang-zi: "One must learn to see where all is dark, and to hear where all is still . . . . Thus one can penetrate to the furthest depths and grasp spirituality." And then is moved to comment himself on Zhuang-zi: "To grasp the spirituality of one's self is to be aware of one's self. To be aware of one's self is to retain one's source and to be long-lasting."

Chapter XXXIV presents the paradox of greatness in smallness. "It is because it never attempts itself to be great that it succeeds in becoming great (以其終不自爲大，故能成其大)." "The way," Lao-zi argues, "claims no authority," speaking himself with the voice of authority.

After the definitions of XXXIV, XXXV recommends what in psychological parlance would be called an internalization of the *Dao*. The following lines, in which "the great image" stands for the *Dao*, embody the familiar triad of self, way and world:

> Have in your hold the great image
> And the empire will come to you.
> 執大象者天下往。

Discipline is the key (on the practical plane) to the gaining of authority, (on the metaphysical plane) to the resolution of subject and object. The concluding lines of the chapter subtly contradict the earlier advocacy of action, stressing instead the naturalness of the *Dao*, its ineffability (these two themselves in *apparent* contradiction); its inexhaustibility:

> The way in its passage through the mouth is without flavor.
> It cannot be seen,
> It cannot be heard,
> Yet it cannot be exhausted by use.
> 道之出言，淡兮其無味。
> 視之不足見，聽之不足聞，用之不可既。

Chapter XXXVI at first appears more modest in its intentions, retreating from images of ultimate paradox to more commonsensical maxims:

> If you would have a thing shrink,
> You must first stretch it;
> If you would have a thing weakened,
> You must first strengthen it . . .
> 欲將翕之，必固張之。
> 欲將弱之，必故強之。

As we examine and reexamine the couplets, however, they seem less referential, less concerned with the world of the senses, than at first appeared. Moreover, they seem to partake of a rhythm—difficult to specify, but present—of parturition (Lin Yutang 林語堂 titles the chapter "The Rhythm of Life"). Its final line represents yet another of Lao-zi's deliberate "non sequiturs":

> The fish must not be allowed to leave the deep
> The instruments of power in a state must not be revealed to anyone.
> 魚不可脫於淵。
> 邦之利器不可以示人。

Whatever its relationship to the line that precedes it, the final line invites, and has received, two distinct kinds of interpretation. Thus Waley reads it as practical advice to princes, Chang as a statement of metaphysical principle, and translates: "The best arms in the nation are those that remain invisible."

Without enumerating every article of faith therein, the concluding chapter (XXXVII) nonetheless epitomizes the meaning of the Dao Jing. Poetic form greatly aids in this effect. Like the first chapter, the last opens with the phrase, "The way"; as the first closes with the idea of mysteries about to be revealed, so the last closes with the idea of an imminent peace, naturally achieved. Each chapter, then, is informed by an envelope of *yang* and *yin*. The last chapter elaborates this form into the pattern A B B₁ A₁. Where A = lords and princes; B, the myriad creatures; B₁, the narrative "I"; and A₁, the empire. Within this envelope appear other elements: the two important principles, spontaneous transformation and the uncarved block (also designated as nameless), and, between them, desire:

> The way never acts yet nothing is left undone.
> Should lords and princes be able to hold fast to it,
> The myriad creatures will be transformed of their own accord.
> After they are transformed, should desire raise its head,
> I shall press it down with the weight of the nameless uncarved block.
> The nameless uncarved block
> Is but freedom from desire,
> And if I cease to desire and remain still,
> The empire will be at peace of its own accord.
> 道常無爲而無不爲。
> 侯王若能守，萬物將自化。
> 化而欲作，吾將鎮之以無名之樸。
> 無名之樸，夫亦將不欲。
> 不欲以靜，天下將自正。

Thus Lao-zi unites the individual and the collective through their mutual participation in the principle of the way.

2

> How is virtue to be attained? It is to be attained through *Dao*. How is virtue to be completely fulfilled? It is through non-being as its function. As non-being is its function all things will be embraced.
> —Wang Bi

> 何以得德？由乎道也。
> 何以盡德？以無爲用則莫不載也。

In an epigraph to the present essay I quoted Waley's translation of the opening lines of XLI. The chapter continues with a series of paradoxes from the Qian Yan 千言, here in Lau's translation:

> The way that is bright seems dull;
> The way that leads forward seems to lead backward;
> The way that is even seems rough.
> 明道若昧。
> 進道若退。
> 夷道若纇。

In stressing the discrepancy between appearance and reality Lao-zi emphasizes the difficulty of the *Dao;* in choosing paradoxes drawn from traditional wisdom to define it he supports the thesis that the philosophical element in the text most often finds its crucial expression through poetic figuration. After five more lines of comparable gnomic figures Lao-zi leaps to another mode: "The great square has no corners" (大方無隅). Suddenly we find ourselves in a realm of mystic apprehension:

> The great note is rarefied in sound [or has no sound].
> The great image has no shape.
> 大音希聲。
> 大象無形。

The sequence concludes with the reassertion of the *Dao*'s ineffability ("The way conceals itself in being nameless" 道隱無名), this higher poetry of namelessness reiterating the thought with which the Dao Jing had begun. But so far Lao-zi has said nothing new, nothing, that is, that we have not heard before. In the final line of the chapter he strikes a new note: "It is the way alone that excels in bestowing and in accomplishing (夫惟道，善貸且善成). The notion of accomplishment (or bringing to fulfillment) is the key to the De Jing. As Chan notes, *"Dao* is not for contemplation but for diligent practice. The goal of *Dao* is not simply peace of mind or purity of heart but the full realization of all things." The fulfillment, then, of the *Dao* lies in the accomplishment of *De*, which in turn represents the appropriate manifestation of the way.

Is there not here an analogy between this relationship and another, between the philosophical and poetic elements in the text? Should we substitute "philosophy" for *"Dao"* and "poetry" for *"De,"* we might paraphrase Wang Bi's statement, quoted above, as follows: How is poetry to be achieved? It is to be achieved through the exposition of philosophical truth. How is poetry to be completely realized? Through the abnegation of the traditionally poetic. As this abnegation is completed, thereby driving out the extraneously decorative, non-doctrinal element, a poetry of total reality is achieved.

The process of realization in the De Jing begins with the application of metaphysical principles to conduct. Hence its beautifully practical embodiment of philosophy, as in XLIV:

> Your name or your person,
> Which is dearer?
> Your person or your goods,
> Which is worth more?
> Gain or loss,
> Which is a greater bane?
> That is why excessive meanness

Is sure to lead to great expense;
Too much store
Is sure to end in immense loss.
Know contentment
And you will meet with no danger.
You can then endure.

名與身熟親？
身與貨熟多？
得與亡熟病？
是故甚愛必大費。
多藏必厚王。
知足不辱，知止不殆，可以長久。

Though fully rhetorical, this chapter nonetheless represents poetry wholly in the service of truth.

Dichtung und Wahrheit: opposed or correlative? one and the same, or separable? We begin with Chapter XXXVIII, the first of the De Jing.

A man of the highest virtue does not keep to virtue and that is
why he has virtue. A man of the lowest virtue never strays from
virtue and that is why he is without virtue. The former never acts
yet leaves nothing undone. The latter acts but there are things
left undone. A man of the highest benevolence acts, but from no
ulterior motive. A man most conversant in the rites acts but when
no one responds rolls up his sleeves and resorts to persuasion
by force. Hence when the way was lost there was virtue; when
virtue was lost there was benevolence; when benevolence was lost
there was rectitude; when rectitude was lost there were the rites.
The rites are the wearing thin of loyalty and good faith
and the beginning of disorder;
Foreknowledge is the flowery embellishment of the way
And the beginning of folly.
Hence the man of large mind abides in the thick not in the thin,
in the fruit not in the flower.
Therefore he discards the one and takes the other.

上德不德，是以有德。
下德不失德，是以無德。
上德無爲而無不爲。
下德爲之而有以爲。
上仁爲之而無以爲。
上義爲之而有以爲。
上禮爲之而莫之應，
則攘臂而仍之。
故失道而後德，
失德而後仁，
失仁而後義，
失義而後禮。
夫禮者忠信之薄，而亂之首也。
前識者道之華，而愚之始也。
是以大夫處其厚，不處其薄，

處其實，不處其華。
故去彼取此。

Philosophically, the passage represents a poetry of worldly wisdom, which by its nature is paradoxical: true virtue subverts apparent virtue; the highest action lies in non-action; rectitude and rites provide no guarantee of good behavior; the greatest principles of worldly order produce disorder. Life is in the living; its proper conduct dictates the renunciation of mere propriety.

Poetically, the passage represents a philosophical proof based on forms of logical argumentation. It divides into four parts: (1) an introductory chain of paradoxes, all thematically related; (2) a series of consequent truths, linked in a chain argument; (3) a series of moral precepts presented in the guise of definitions ("The rites are the wearing thin of loyalty," etc.); and (4a and b) the two concluding sentences. We might schematize the chapter as follows:

A history of the degeneration of the *Dao* (1 and 2)
B general historical principles induced therefrom (3)
C a general moral principle induced from B (4a)
D a method deduced from B and C (4b)

In another relationship of Truth to Poetry the major philosophical concepts of the Dao Jing appear to have generated corresponding poetic principles. Thus virtueless virtue gives rise to an anti-poetic poetry. Actionless action finds its counterpart in what we might call negative poetry (we have already mentioned and shall later consider examples of negative images and metaphors). The poetry of compressed, seminal statement corresponds to the notion of the uncarved block; the poetry of ineffability, to the concept of namelessness.

Likewise, in a larger sense, the experiential nature of Daoist thought finds its counterpart in the poetry of a chapter such as LXIV, whose method might be designated as the gathering of wisdom (and, behind it, experience) under a single rubric (in this case the principle of non-action). I quote the Waley translation:

"What stays still is easy to hold;
Before there has been an omen it is easy to lay plans.
What is tender is easily torn,
What is minute is easy to scatter.
Deal with things in their state of not-yet-being,
Put them in order before they have got into confusion.
For the tree big as a man's embrace began as a tiny sprout,
The tower nine stories high began with a heap of earth,
The journey of a thousand leagues began with what was under the feet."
He who acts, harms; he who grabs, lets slip.
Whereas the people of the world, at their tasks,
Constantly spoil things when within an ace of completing them.

"Heed the end no less that the beginning,"
And your work will not be spoiled.
Therefore the Sage wants only things that are unwanted,
Sets no store by products difficult to get,
And so teaches things untaught,
Turning all men back to the things they have left behind,
That the ten thousand creatures may be restored to their Self-so.
This he does; but dare not act.

其安易持，其未兆易謀，
其脆易破，其微易散，
爲之於未有，治之於未亂。
合抱之木，生於毫末。
九層之臺，起於累土。
千里之行，始於足下。
爲者敗之，執者失之。
是以聖人無爲故無敗，
無執故無失。
民之從事，常於幾成而敗之。
慎終如始，則無敗事矣。
是以聖人欲不欲，不貴難得之貨。
學不學，以復眾人之所過。
以輔萬物之自然而不敢爲也。

Here, then (to paraphrase Wang Bi), is Lao-zi's virtuous embrace of all things, poetic in the capaciousness of its vision, philosophical in the way in which the sage "also shows the world the degree to which ordinary life can be molded to the pattern of the *Dao*" (Waley). But poetry and thought in Lao-zi are finally inseparable.

Poetry and argument, argumentative poetry, poetic argumentation. Chapter LXXVII affords one of the most complex examples of these interrelationships. Its central philosophical statement, one to which its argument leads, and upon which it turns, reads: "Who is there that can take what he himself has in excess and offer this to the empire? Only he who has the way" (孰能以有餘奉天下？惟有道者). Who is Godlike? He who is like God. The underlying structure, like the structure of the chapter at large, is chiasmic (though not tautological). "Is not the way of heaven like the stretching of a bow" 天之道其猶張弓乎? the chapter opens in simile, then moves with parallel rhetoric to elaborate that figure into conceit (emphasis added):

> The *high* it presses *down*,
> The *low* it lifts *up*;
> The *excessive* it *takes from*,
> The *deficient* it *gives to*.

高者抑之，
下者舉之，
有餘者損之，
不足者補之。

Then, by means of chiasmic elaboration, the *applicatio:*

> It is the way of heaven to take from what has in excess in order
> To make good *what is deficient.* The way of man is otherwise [antithetical turn].
> It takes from *those who are in want* in order to
> Offer this to *those who already have more than enough.*

天之道，損有餘而補不足。
人之道，則不然。損不足以奉有餘。

The sage way of heaven having found its embodiment in the heavenly sage, the chapter concludes with a syllogistic combination of terms:

> Therefore the sage benefits them yet exacts no gratitude,
> Accomplishes his task yet lays claim to no merit.

是以聖人爲而不恃，功成而不處。

Lest the chapter be read as a program for positive action, Lao-zi appends a monitory coda: "Is this not because he does not wish to be considered a better man than others?" (其欲不見賢邪？) In the sage, then, we have neither God nor mortal but the exemplification of what Chan calls "the doctrine of the equality of all things." The suavity of argumentation here puts the Jesuit to shame.

The western mind is prone to mistake Lao-zi's grace for languor, his elegance for desuetude. In fact syllogistic structure, with changes rung thereon, frequently characterizes his argumentation. Chapters XXIX to XXX provide convenient examples. In the first of his arguments Lao-zi offers three examples of the rashness of action; induces a series of general statements illustrating the world's division into categories; and concludes with a deduction of principle ("Therefore the sage avoids excess, extravagance, and arrogance" 是以聖人去甚，去奢，去泰).

Chapter XXX departs from strict syllogism in its doubling of major premises and laxity of conclusion. It begins by stating its principle in negative terms; it replaces the syllogistic minor premise with a reason ("This is something which is liable to rebound"); and adds *exempla.* It then asserts its principle in positive form ("One who is good aims only at bringing his campaign to a conclusion and dare not thereby intimidate"); elaborates in a series of exhortations ("Bring it to a conclusion but do not boast; . . . bring it to a conclusion but do not intimidate"); and then concludes by analogy and recourse to antecedent principle:

A creature in its prime doing harm to the old
Is known as going against the way.
That which goes against the way will come to an early end.
物壯則老，是謂不道。
不道早已。

The analogy poetically multiplies as we ponder it: the creature in its prime doing harm to the old is like the mortal ruler intimidating an immortal empire. His unnatural conclusion of life is the obverse of the ruler's inability to bring his own campaign to conclusion; this in turn brings the ruler to an early end. The glosses of philosophical and religious commentators indicate that extratextual analogies also readily suggest themselves to the Chinese mind. More immediately, the argument has its analogues in the arguments of adjacent chapters; more broadly, in those general recommendations for the conduct of the prince which form so much of the substance of the text at large. Moreover, there is something in the partite organization of argument that encourages this kind of analogical (or poetic) extension of meaning.

Lau's text of XXXI may, as he says, represent not Lao-zi's words but Wang Bi's commentary. Lau recommends certain transpositions but retains a poetic core, poignant in itself and interesting in its use of/departure from syllogistic form. Again I quote the central passage:

> Arms are instruments of ill omen, not the instruments of the gentleman. When one is compelled to use them, it is best to do so without relish.

The form of the argument is of interest. The first sentence (A) defines the nature of the gentleman, the nature of arms, and their incompatibility; the second (A$_1$), their compatibility, with conditions. The text continues:

> There is no glory in victory, and to glorify it despite this is to exult in the killing of men. One who exults in the killing of men will never have his way in the empire.
> 勝而不美。而美之者樂殺人。
> 夫樂殺人者，不可以得志於天下矣。

The first sentence (B) defines the nature of glory and vainglory; the second (B$_1$), the consequences of vainglory. After intervening material, the chapter ends with a passage that serves as a practical pendant to A and B:

> When great numbers of people are killed, one should weep over them with sorrow. When victorious in war, one should observe the rites of mourning.
> 殺人眾多，則以悲哀泣之。
> 戰勝者則以喪亂處之。

Curiously, either sequence, ABC or BAC, may be read as syllogism, and perhaps it is this very ambiguity that lends to the sentiment expressed its poignancy. But enough for the stricter forms of logical argument.

As in most early traditions, especially in their poetry, parallelism is a more common form than syllogism. Chapter XXVIII, one of the most sophisticated in argumentation, combines parallel structure with logic, weaving in and out of its argument some of the most powerful and poetic symbols of the text. I have quoted the opening lines, but we must have them before us again:

> Know the male
> But keep to the role of the female
> And be a ravine to the empire.
> If you are a ravine to the empire
> Then the constant virtue will not desert you
> And you will again return to being a babe.
> 知其雄，守其雌，為天下谿。
> 為天下谿，常德不離，復歸於嬰兒。

Rhetorically as dense—if not as personal, allusive or obscure—as any western poetry, these lines affect the reader at all levels of his consciousness: the male-female-babe sequence draws upon what I have earlier called the rhythm of parturition, the intervening image of the ravine functioning here, subliminally, both as vaginal and uterine metaphor. At this level, Chang's translation—a work of Heideggerian abstraction—provides material for comparison and contrast:

> To be aware of the positive, yet to abide in the negative is to be the
>   abyss of the universe.
> To be the abyss of the universe is to not deviate from real attainment
>   and to remain like an innocent child.

Superficially less poetic (in verbal texture, in imagery, in human associations), it nonetheless speaks to the deep polarities in human nature and experience, serving to crystallize the same archetypes, perhaps more surely for the room which its vagueness allows the reader's own imagination.

That the opening two lines (in Lau's version) quote the traditional wisdom of Lao Dan, that the next two refer us backward to an earlier point in the text, that the final two draw an image of infancy into the central concept of the Return creates another pattern of great depth—but also one of great delicacy and erudition. At a more literary level of rhetoric, the six lines form a mirror construction. *Anadiplosis* links 3 and 4, serving to emphasize their central doctrine; 2 and 5, 1 and 6 complement one another in remarkable ways. The passage partakes of the dynamism of poetry, reinforced by this particular chain of images; but it also partakes of the stasis of the Daoist view, its backward movement to infancy reinforcing this contradictory, paradoxical tendency. At the level of rational argument, we note the simple but compelling structures: the timeless verbs (in lines 1-3), the conditional structure of causality (in line 4-6), and the relationship of those two structures to one another.

The relationship of the first six lines to the subsequent "sixains" also requires some comment:

> Know the white
> But keep to the role of the black
> And be a model to the empire.
> If you are a model to the empire,
> Then the constant virtue will not be wanting
> And you will return to the infinite.
> 知其白，守其黑，爲天下式。
> 爲天下式，常德不忒，復歸於無極。

Each line, in fact each image, glosses its double in the first six lines: white, male; black, female; model, ravine; not wanting, not desert you; the infinite, a babe.

The third sixain reads:

> Know honor
> But keep to the role of the disgraced
> And be a valley to the empire.
> If you are a valley to the empire.
> Then the constant virtue will be sufficient
> And you will return to being the uncarved block.
> 知其榮，守其辱，爲天下谷。
> 爲天下谷，常德乃足，復歸於樸。

So rich are the associations (*the babe, the infinite, the uncarved block),* both individually and in combination that quotation speaks more eloquently than paraphrase.

After using three repetitive sixains—parallel but antithetical, independent of one another but cumulative in their meaning, Lao-zi shifts tactics:

> When the uncarved block shatters it becomes vessels.
> The sage makes use of these and becomes the lord over the officials.
> Hence the greatest cutting
> Does not sever.
> 樸散則爲器。
> 聖人用之則爲官長。
> 故大制不割。

Images of magic parturition, fantastic dominion and dreamlike paradox underlie, contradict and augment the rational meaning of these conclusions. Moreover, the coda as a whole stands in a double relation to all that goes before: it brings a sequence of evocative images to argumentative conclusion and yet, in its non-sequentiality, seals them off as an independent unit still active on another plane of consciousness.

Conclusion

Truthful words are not beautiful; beautiful words are not truthful.
Good words are not persuasive; persuasive words are not good.
信者不美，美者不信。
善者不辯，辯者不善。

The poetic means employed in the *Lao-zi* are manifold, ranging from simple simile ("Governing a large state is like boiling a small fish" 治大國若烹小鮮 [LX]) to commentated parable (the description of utopia in LXXX). Its quintessential poetry, however, is, as I earlier suggested, a kind of anti-poetry; it lies not in conventional figures but in their subversion.

The way is empty, yet use will not drain it.
Deep, it is like the ancestor of the myriad creatures.
Blunt the sharpness;
Untangle the knots;
Soften the glare;
Let your wheels move only along old ruts.
Darkly visible, it only seems as if it were there.
I know not whose son it is
It images the forefather of God.
                                                                    (IV)

道沖而用之或不盈。
淵兮似萬物之宗。
挫其銳，解其紛，
和其光，同其塵，
湛兮似或存。
吾不知誰之子，象帝之先。

This is the poetry of emptiness, of absence, of the void—the void of ultimate reality. Its imagery is negative, its metaphors abstract. But for all that it is no less poetic, no less fecund, no less sensuous:

Is not the space between heaven and earth like a bellows?
It is empty without being exhausted:
The more it works, the more comes out.
                                                                    (V)

天地之間，其猶橐籥乎？
虛而不屈，動而愈出。

Each positive has a negative, each negative a positive. Though it seems reductive this in fact is a poetry of inclusiveness, a way of opening the world so that the world itself becomes poetry.

91

> The way begets one; one begets two; two begets three;
> Three begets the myriad creation
>
> (XLII)
>
> 道生一，一生二，二生三，三生萬物。

It is a poetry of ultimate origins and ultimate manifestations, but also a poetry of continuous creation and natural transformations. Lao-zi's method is organic: chapter follows chapter in an exfoliation of meaning. Word alternates with word, thought with thought, sentiment with sentiment, as day with night. Thought gives way to poetry, poetry to thought. "Thus," says the master, "a thing is sometimes added to by being diminished and diminished by being added to (故物或損之而益，或益之而損 [XLII]."

Lao-zi's poetry is a poetry of thought in the absence of thought:

> The further one goes
> The less one knows.
> Therefore the sage knows without having to stir.
>
> (XLII)
>
> 其出彌遠，其知彌少。
> 是以聖人不行而知。

It is practical and metaphysical, its practicality metaphysical, its metaphysics practical. It teaches how to live and is therefore doctrinal ("doctrine" is one meaning of *Dao*).

Since it derives, in part, from the poet's experience, it is therefore, in part, personal, as in the famous passage from Chapter XLVII:

> I have three treasures
> Which I hold and cherish.
>> The first is known as compassion,
>> The second is known as frugality,
>> The third is known as not daring to take the lead in the empire . . .
>
> 我有三寶，寶而持之。
> 一曰慈，二曰儉，三曰不敢爲天下先。

But what it has to say is really general:

> Being compassionate one could afford to be courageous,
> Being frugal one could afford to extend one's territory,
> Not daring to take the lead in the empire one could afford to be lord
>> over the vessels.
>
> 夫慈故能勇。
> 儉故能廣。
> 不敢爲天下先，故能成器長。

Though sometimes enigmatic, it is more often explicit:

> Now to forsake compassion for courage, to forsake frugality for expansion, to forsake the rear for the lead, is sure to end in death.

今舍慈且勇。舍儉且廣，
舍後且先，死矣。

And though it speaks through metaphor it does so in order to speak the truth:

Through compassion, one will triumph in attack and be impregnable in defense. What heaven succors it protects with the gift of compassion.

夫慈以戰則勝，以守則固。
天將救之，以慈衛之。

Though the *Lao-zi* may seem to be religious, it is really practical. And herein lies its highest value. For this is not transcendent vision but the poetry of worldly wisdom.

Translations and Commentaries Cited

Chang Chung Yuan. *Tao, A New Way of Thinking: A Translation of the Tao Te Ching*. New York: Harper and Row, 1975.

Lin Yutang. *The Wisdom of Laotse*. New York: Modern Library, 1948.

Tao te Ching. Trans. D. C. Lau. Baltimore: Penguin Books, 1963.

Arthur Waley. *The Way and Its Power: A Study of the Tao Te Ching and Its Place in Chinese Thought*. New York: Grove Press, 1958.

Wang Pi. *Commentary on the Lao Tzu*. Trans. Ariane Rump, in collaboration with Wing-tsit Chan. Honolulu: U. Press of Hawaii, 1979.

The Way of Lao Tzu (Tao-te Ching). Trans. Wing-tsit Chan. Indianapolis: Bobbs-Merrill, 1963.

5

Allegory and the Western Epic

Perhaps we have so much trouble [understanding allegory] because we still think of poetry as an end in itself rather than as a medium. The purpose of allegorical rhetoric is to create a particular experience within a person. The words of the poet stimulate this experience. Partial as it is, the *lógos prophorikós* [the spoken word] requires the auditor to complete the poem himself, and in the process he enters into the thought-modes of the poet. He sees through the poet's verbal veil into the poet's mind and there finds truth, but a truth which does not correspond to our notions of truth. He finds not a fact or a concept but a way of looking at things which reveals to him his own divinity. As if he saw lightning flash in a clear night sky, he suddenly perceives that he, simply by being man, transcends his own world, and the more he thinks mythologically, the less he is bound by the chains of contingency.

—Michael Murrin

Persuasive allegory does not duplicate. . . . It releases a counterplay of imagination and thought by which each becomes an irritant to the other, and both may grow through the irksome contact.

—Edgar Wind

Allegoria does not use metaphor; it is one. By definition a continued metaphor, *allegoria* exhibits the normal relation of concretion to abstraction found in metaphor, in the shape of a series of particulars with further meanings. Each such concretion of sensual detail is by virtue of its initial base *already* a metaphor.

—Rosamund Tuve

In addition to *allegory* and *metaphor*, *thought* and *imagination*—the attentive reader will have noticed—our epigraphs have also introduced the terms *myth*, *divinity*, *truth*, and *experience; concretion* and *abstraction*, the *particular* and, by implication, the *universal*. Together with the title they have raised certain questions about the relationship among the *poet*, the *poem*, the *auditor* and, by extension, the *reader* of epic. It has seemed best to lay these cards on the table at the outset. We shall return to our terms for fuller consideration as occasion requires, but none in this essay will be given final definition. To do so would allow our topic, The Allegorical Element, to preempt our subject, The Western Epic. Let us proceed at once to our thesis, to wit, *that the western epic, from beginning to end, is allegorical.* This view is not so much new as neoclassical. In his *Traité du poëme épique* of 1675 Le Bossu had said, of epic action, that "it is *Universal*, it is *Imitated*, it is *Feign'd* [imaginative], and it contains *Allegorically*, a Moral Truth." This truth, he goes on to say, is veiled behind an action which, though "invented by the Author . . . yet will seem to be taken out of some *History* and *Fable*." A fable is of course an imaginative story that has a moral. *Moral* and *allegory* for Le Bossu are practically the same. Do not all epics have a moral? Are they not then all allegorical? What has happened to our sense that allegory requires a special rhetorical machinery, a "continued metaphor" (Quintillian), a "sequence of metaphors" in which "the sense of the words is totally altered" (Cicero), a distinguishing degree of abstraction, as in the general modern conception of the form?

The fact of the matter is that we have made some progress in our understanding of allegory, which we now recognize as a mode, not a form; as an unstable counterplay of terms (Edgar Wind), not an homogeneous expression; as a discourse hard to schematize, not the regularly leveled *quatre-sens* of medieval-Renaissance theory. "The more allegory exploits the divergence between corresponding levels of meaning," Jon Whitman observes, "the less tenable the correspondence becomes. Alternatively, the more it closes ranks and emphasizes the correspondence, the less oblique, and thus the less allegorical, the divergence becomes." Allegory is beginning to sound like literature itself, the hermeneutic exegete like the modern critic. Some will agree, some disagree: if everything is allegory, then nothing is allegory.

Our subject here, we recall, is not, however, literature but the western epic. What in *this* tradition is allegorical, what not? Or to turn the question around, who within the tradition would regard himself as allegorical, who not? Dante regards himself as allegorical. Does Byron? Does Homer? Neither pronounced on the topic. Let us, then, turn the question another way. What in Dante is lacking from other perspectives? From the pre-classical point of view he is not mythic; from the modern point of view he is not historical. Or is he? Auerbach describes him as "the first to configure what antiquity had configured very differently and the Middle Ages not at all: man not as a remote legendary hero . . . but man as we know him in his historical reality, the concrete individual in his unity and wholeness." As for his Christian belief, is it not also mythic? For Gregory Nagy myth represents a "collective expression," "an expression that society itself deems to be true and valued. From the standpoint of the given society that it articulates," he adds, "myth *is* the primary reality." Nagy has in view Homer's society, but he might as well be speaking of Dante's. Dante, then, is mythic, historical *and* allegorical. Moreover, since he represents his personal experience, he may be called experiential as well.

What is it, then, that separates *myth, history, allegory* and *experience?* Many things: they are by no means identical. And yet in epic expression they coalesce. Homer and Vergil, Dante and Ariosto, Spenser and Milton, all are mythic writers, yet all have historical subjects; all represent experience, yet all are allegorical. This inclusiveness is one feature that distinguishes the epic from other literary modes. Furthermore, we may say that all major epic is *sacred, cosmological, geographical* and *philosophical*, in varying degrees of course. It is this variation by degree that gives the sub-genres and that makes the larger mode so resistant to unitary definition. We might explore all these aspects of the epic. Instead we shall concentrate upon only one, the allegorical; but in so doing we must situate that element in relation to the others. The Western Epic is a large subject. We shall limit ourselves to examples drawn from pre-classical Greece and Alexandria; ancient Rome; medieval Italy; Renaissance Italy; seventeenth-century Spain; and sixteenth-, seventeenth- and nineteenth-century England.

1

We begin with Homer. Subject to allegorization at the hands of scholiast, Athenian philosopher, Roman critic, neoplatonist, medieval, Renaissance and later commentators, Homer nonetheless continues to provoke the question, is the text itself allegorical? The modern reader, who takes his fiction in the form of novel, cinema, television series, is all too prone to regard Homer as essentially naturalistic, a novelist with divine machinery, a few allegorical trappings, a certain amount of fabulous improbability (a one-eyed monster, a horse that talks). Accordingly, he is largely unsympathetic toward the great tradition of allegoresis and instinctively recoils at the notion that Homer himself was an allegorist. "Homer no more dreamed that nonsense," said Rabelais, "than Ovid in his *Metamorphoses* dreamed the Gospels." Seneca, in a more balanced statement, remarks, of the philosophical exegetes, "None of their doctrines are in Homer, simply because they are all there, all contradicting one another."

What then is *there*, and how do we prove that it is? The modern allegorical reader of Homer is in much the same position as the teacher of unlettered students. He must convince his audience that what meets the eye is not all there is, and he had best do so without recourse to authority. Not only poetry but critical reading begins with Homer. Let us admit, then, in all candor that the lines between mythic shape, historical significance, allegorical meaning and thematic content are not easy to draw. What to one reader is mythic to another is historical (does the Fall of Troy portend the ascendancy of Occident over Orient?). Likewise, what to one reader may seem allegorical, may to another seem merely thematic. Yet another reader may regard the Odyssey but not the Iliad as allegorical. As to the question of Homer's intentions, it seems to this reader highly unlikely that a poet of such consummate artistry, at the end of such a long poetic tradition, could have been unconscious of his allegorical import. Moreover, he may have been capable of articulating allegorical readings of his work wholly alien to later understanding. What, after all, do we know of the history of this legend between the time of its nominal events and its redaction in Homer?

Let us pick up where Aristotle left off, with his three influential terms: *mythos* (myth), *plasma* (fiction), and *istoria* (history), all counterpoised against actuality or present experience. Is Homer mythic? According to Nagy, "the primary narrative of Greek epic, which is the Trojan War, is self-motivated by the Indo-European social principle of counterbalancing praise and blame," the paradigm for which he finds in the Judgment of Paris, which "entailed the *blaming* of the goddesses Hera and Athena along with the praising of Aphrodite." "Myth," says Nagy elsewhere, "in societies where it exists as a living tradition, must not be confused with fiction." But in Homer's hands it *is* a fiction. Is it not also an allegory? Surely so. Is it also an historical event? It is at least legendary, a part of the *epos* that Homer has inherited. Thus the Judgment to some degree fits all three of Aristotle's categories.

Homer, then, is mythic, but is he also religious? Hera, Athena and Aphrodite figure not only in the underlying paradigm but also as central powers throughout the epic. Zeus, in Xenophanes' description, resembles a monotheistic god: "he remains in the same place . . . , but without toil he shakes all things by the thought of his mind." In Nausikaa, Odysseus sees Artemis, the daughter of Zeus. It was Apollo, not you, who killed me, Patroklos tells Hektor; in Ovid, Neptune exhorts the same god to slay Achilles.

If Homer is religious, is the Iliad *sacred?* By the standard of Tasso or Milton, yes. *Cosmological?* Surely the Shield of Achilles demonstrates that. Is he not then also *allegorical?* What must we do to make the case? Without exhaustively surveying every book, let us touch on some high points. Though not theological in the sense of a Dante or Milton, Homer nonetheless raises questions about the relationship of the gods and men in ways that sometimes suggest Christian argument. What was the reason for all this suffering, past, present and to come? asks Book III. Perhaps the Rape of Helen is but another version of Original Sin, Satanic Paris, uxorious Menelaos, Helen in her pride and sorrow another Eve. The gifts of the gods—Helen's beauty, Paris' charm—are a kind of Fate, not to be cast away. The will of the gods overrides practical and moral consider- ations. The allegorical Menelaos and Paris, responsible husband and profligate prince, having agreed to duel, are nonetheless helpless to resolve a conflict larger than theirs, for Helen (Passion) inhibits its resolution. She, says Homer, is like a goddess. More important than *her* role is that of Zeus; larger still than *his* is the role of Fate. Paris and Menelaos not so much fight as display their allegorical temperaments. As in Spenser, Homeric allegory is complex, psychological as well as moral and theological

Book IV depicts a Council of the Gods in an allegorical parallel with an earlier human council. In Book V Athena, Aphrodite, Apollo and Ares intervene in the battle. Toward the middle of the action Diomedes attacks Aphrodite; dropped by his mother, Aeneas is rescued by Apollo, who fashions him into a brilliant image. How carefully Vergil must have studied this emblem: the Trojan prince as Apostle of Civilization. Book VI, like Books I, IX, XVI and XXIV, all notably naturalistic, brings earlier theological discourse down to an *experiential* level, as Diomedes asks Glaukos why humans go to war. In Book VII, replete with the allegorical episodes of Zeus's golden cord and golden scales, the gods again intervene. What are they but allegories of the invisible world, of its psychological, scientific, cosmic modalities: Energy (Apollo), Culture (Artemis), Strife (Ares), Wisdom (Hermes), Fecundity (Hera), Power (Zeus), Love (Aphrodite), Time (Chronos)? More allegorical episodes follow in Books XIV and XV: the lovemaking of Zeus, instigated by Hera, in turn abetted by Sleep and Aphrodite; the fettering of Hera's feet with anvils. The conclusion of Book XVIII offers the Iliad's most extended allegorical episode, a miniaturized cosmology: Earth, Sky and Sea's Water; Sun, Moon and the Constellations; the Ocean River, all on a work of art so magnificent and incongruous in its context that Ovid's Ulysses is moved to ask Ajax why Thetis would have thought to arm such a rough and foolish soldier as her son with such celestial accoutrements. Thus is the allegorical principle of episodic relevance and incongruity observed.

As the Iliad moves toward closure, its allegorical element increases. Book XXI treats us to an elemental battle of Water vs. Fire along with a series of multilevel parodies, emblematic gods squaring off in human-style conflicts: Athena vs. Ares, Apollo vs. Poseidon, Hermes vs. Leto, Hera vs. Artemis, Hephaistos vs. Xanthos, all foreshadowing on a lower level the climactic battle of the semi-divine Achilles and the mortal Hektor. Only the anagogical figures of Zeus and Aphrodite refrain from contest, as though in comment on their lesser counterparts. In Book XXIII athletic games serve as an extended peaceful metaphor of the poem's more extensive martial action. Book XXIV, with its type scenes (divine visitation, supplication, funeral), involves Hermes in its scenario of reconciliation. As he brought to conclusion his Poem of Wrath (whose other allegorical figures include Fear and Terror; Hate, Confusion and Death; Ate, or Blind Folly), did Homer think of Hermes, the figure of Wisdom, as a bridge to the more hermetic Odyssey? Undoubtedly so. For just as Achilles appears at the end of that poem, so Odysseus' reappearance is predicted at the end of this one.

Iliad and Odyssey: from a whole cycle of epics, why have these two alone survived? Because Heroic Mind complements and completes Heroic Body. Likewise Penelope (Fidelity) balances Helen (Infidelity). Such are Homer's allegorical pairings, unlike the merely modal oppositions that balance the two works and distinguish them from one another (tragedy vs. comedy; Aristotle's simple and pathetic Iliad vs. his complex and ethical Odyssey). Like the Iliad, the Odyssey too is theological, as Athena's domination of Hera and Aphrodite indicates.

Throughout history the Odyssey has been far more subject to allegoresis than the Iliad, and the reason is not far to seek: Odysseus himself in his narrative (Books 9-12) is a blatant allegorist, and Homer, though far more subtle, scarcely lags behind in his activity. Moreover, Homer himself is engaged in allegoresis, reworking presumably rougher, less developed material, refining and allegorizing it. The Odyssey overtly refers to many elements in the Iliad and may even be taken as an allegoresis of the earlier poem's theme of withdrawal and reentry.

Though also concerned with the family, friendship, and the principle of leadership, the Odyssey focuses on the solitary spirit (or in more allegorical readings, the Soul). Laertes, an only child, is the father of an only child, our hero, in turn the father of Telemakhos, another only child. Individual Man, then, is Homer's allegorical hero; his temptation, parallel with that of Paris, occasions heroic resistance: to Circe's wand, to the Sirens' song, to the temptation of Helios' Kine. The last episode is a parable of Original Sin, a temptation foretold at the poem's outset, one to which the leader's companions, but not the leader himself, fall victim. Likewise Penelope resists temptation, though her serving-girls fail to. She is part of a quartet of allegorical female figures that includes Kalypso, Circe and Nausikaa. In a similar configuration Odysseus is placed among another allegorical foursome that includes Agamemnon, Menelaos and Ajax. This kind of symmetry is not naturalistic.

Allegorical elements in the Telemakhiad are easily overlooked. When Menelaos tells Telemakhos of Proteus, Heraclitus recognizes in this figure the Origin of the Universe (and we, a *cosmological* dimension of the Odyssey); for Bacon, Proteus stood for Productive Matter; in a common classical view, for Truth. Who are we to say that Homer was unaware of such allegorical meanings? In Book 5, like one of Ariosto's knights, Odysseus sets out from Kalypso, The Concealer's, island for a series of more openly allegorical encounters with Hermes, Poseidon, Leucothea and Athena. In Book 6 he gazes at Nausikaa, according to some accounts the Mirror of the Soul. The Phaiakia episode as a whole represents an *allegorical topos*, an Ambiguous Paradise, much imitated in later tradition. There Demodokos ("Popular," as opposed to merely "Famous," as Phemius, the poem's other bard's name suggests) sings of the quarrel between Achilles and Odysseus in an *allegorical epitome* of the Homeric corpus. After an interlude of games (multilayered in their significance, here as in the tradition at large) there follows a song of Ares and Aphrodite, another *inset allegory*, cosmologically construed by the neoplatonists, and certainly another metaphor for the themes of Iliad and Odyssey.

Odysseus himself sings of such allegorical subjects as Cyclops ("Circle Eye"), Symplegades ("Clashing Rocks") and Nemo ("Nobody"). The modern reader tends to regard the second half of the epic as essentially naturalistic, but we must not forget that it is introduced by a Voyage in a Magical Boat; the Hero's Encounter with the Goddess of Wisdom; and her Transformation of him into a Beggar in his own Realm. These romance motifs are easily allegorizable, as are Odysseus' reunions with Eumaios and Penelope (above ground), with Achilles and Agamemnon (below ground, in a second Nekyia); likewise, the victory of Good over Bad, which culminates an extended allegory of Intelligence, Fidelity and Loyalty against the forces of Anti-mind (Antinous), Duplicity (Amphimous) and Treachery.

2

When the classical epic is incontestably allegorical, as in the Theogony, we shall not bother to make an argument. The only question is where Hesiod's allegory leaves off, if at all. For in addition to cosmological elements such as Void, Darkness and Light, abstract principles such as Law, Wisdom and Peace, bodily states such as Sleep, Death and Old Age, moral agencies such as Retribution and Strife, Hesiod includes both major and minor divinities, the Muses, the Giants, the Nymphs and the Fates. At the poem's conclusion he points this all in the direction of Jason, Odysseus, Anchises and Aeneas. Are we to suppose that these heroes were for Hesiod less allegorical than the rest of his cast? For some readers another question remains: is the Theogony really an epic? The ancients thought so, as did those in the allegorical tradition. That we today even entertain the question indicates how far we have shifted the epic genre's definition away from allegorical expression toward naturalistic narrative.

3

The whole Alexandrian enterprise of miniaturizing, ironizing and modernizing the epic represents a form of Homeric allegoresis.

Callimachus does in a few hundred lines what the pre-classical epic did in a book; Theocritus turns Polyphemus into a jest; Apollonius, through a kind of psychological allegory, refashions pre-Homeric Jason into a modern urban soul. Since space is limited, we shall take up only the Argonautica, and then only the introduction to Book III. Under the muse of Erato rather than Calliope (love poetry rather than epic), Apollonius has Hera and Athena supplicate Aphrodite in a plot to make Jason and Medea fall in love. This imitation of the Judgment of Paris thus builds one allegory atop another. Power and Wisdom must first be reconciled before they can solicit the help of Beauty and Love (Eros) to do their bidding. It is a fable in which Strife (Eris) is supplanted by the principal of Cooperation.

Apollonius' version is also a tale of Married Love as opposed to Adultery. It merges themes of the Odyssey (where not only Odysseus and faithful Penelope, but Menelaos and unfaithful Helen are reunited) and opposes them to the theme that propels the Iliad (where Paris and Helen, Agamemnon and Briseis and, no doubt, many others are engaged in adultery). Apollonius also gathers up other elements in the tradition, for Medea's violent treachery *within* the family recalls Klaitemnestra's murderous act. His depiction of Aphrodite and Hephaistos in marital harmony supplants Demodokos' model in his song of Ares and Aphrodite. Of Hephaistos the Alexandrian writes, "He had gone early to his forge and anvils in a broad cavern on a floating island, where with the blast of flame he wrought all manner of curious work." In that sentence Apollonius' audience would have seen an allegory of Fire, Water and Earth, a topography of Mainland, Island and Cavern, figurations that we are less familiar with. The first three terms belong to a permanent elemental drama, the latter three to a permanent Greek geography. One of the subgenres of the epic is the *geographical*. In the Iliad we resituate ourselves in Troy; in the Odyssey we return to Greece, taking time out for expansive excursions; in the Argonautica we travel much farther afield but always with one foot in Alexandria.

4

Despite our advances in understanding allegory, there remain many modern misapprehensions: that a work must be overtly allegorical to qualify as such; that its allegorical elements must be consistent; that allegory can exist without allegorical reading. Vergil seems an appropriate point at which to dispose of such misconceptions, for with the Aeneid sophisticated allegorical reading becomes institutional, both on Vergil's part and on the part of his critics. Servius, who had to invent the word "polysemous" to accommodate this poet's work, initiates an

102

enterprise that is alive today and includes the early Christian Fulgentius (who discerned in Aeneid I-VI the course of life from youth to old age), the medieval Bernard Sylvestris (who found in the poem "truth in the veil of fiction"), Dante (who treated his master under the head of Human Wisdom), and Landino (who saw in the work a quest for the highest good). Poets from Boiardo to Milton likewise had their own Aeneids. We must, however, remind ourselves that our principal concern lies not with what readers have found in Vergil but what in the work enabled them to find it.

The Aeneid is an allegory built, we might say, out of a synthesis of earlier allegoresis. There is nothing naïve in Vergil. The Homeric influence competes with the Alexandrian, the Athenian and the Roman, the allegory compounding the *mythic, historical, theological* and *experiential* levels in a way that will prove especially sympathetic to Renaissance and later readers. The first epic of complex historical consciousness, the Aeneid is an allegory of Past, Present and Future. In his representation of Rome, Vergil is also an allegorist: political, religious and amatory. Undoubtedly his contemporaries saw much more in the poem than we do. Only after two centuries of scholarship are we beginning to catch up with Vergil's allusions.

His allegoresis of Homer is a more straightforward subject, for which we now have the basic analysis but not as yet the full interpretation. Only gradually, for example, are we giving up the notion that the Aeneid's first half imitates the Odyssey, its second, the Iliad, a Renaissance idea as imprecise as another coeval critical chestnut, the assignment to the poem's two halves two different themes: the *via contemplativa* and the *via activa*. Likewise the crudity of earlier characterology, as in Scaligero's view that Aeneas represents the fortitude of Achilles (his temerity removed) and the prudence of Odysseus (his cunning transferred to Sinon).

We cannot here discuss the whole Aeneid, though by concentrating on its central story, that of Dido and Aeneas, we may find a key to its structure. As with Homer, Apollonius and others in the tradition, Vergil indicates that his theme is the Fall of Man, when he says of his hero and heroine's outing, "that day was the first cause of death, and first of sorrow." Like Apollonius' Hera and Aphrodite, Vergil's Juno and Venus have colluded in arranging a tragedy, one that Mercury's visit at Jove's behest precipitates. Aeneas himself blames his departure on Apollo and Fate. Here the allegory is theological and moral. Like Milton, Vergil chastises his heroine for her evil deed; unlike Milton, he leaves it for us to surmise its consequences (what will her suicide mean for her subjects?). Though compounded of many characters, historical as well as literary (she echoes Homer's Penelope, Helen, Nausikaa, Kalypso and

103

Circe, and like Ajax commits suicide; she is modeled on Euripides' and Apollonius' Medea; she reflects both the historical founder of Carthage and her modern successor, Cleopatra), Dido is nonetheless an original, as is Aeneas. For though he too combines literary with historical precedent (Homeric Odysseus, Hektor, Achilles, Agamemnon and Paris; earlier representations of Jason; historical figures such as Antony and Augustus), he matches Dido in a brilliance of multivalence that has given life to the pair for two thousand years, in nearly a hundred operatic representations alone. Moreover, this couple (they may well have been married in that cave, for Roman law required no ceremony) stand behind Milton's Adam and Eve and collapse into Spenser's Britomart. No major poet has escaped their charisma.

By reexamining them through the lenses of Spenser and Milton we gain some insight into their character. Like both Dido and Aeneas, Britomart is both chaste and lascivious. Like Britomart, Aeneas and Dido are one: as we read their speeches we feel that we are listening to two sides of Vergil's own personality, in what we might call an allegory of Self and Soul. Both Dido and Aeneas are political leaders who found empires, are exiles who betray their vows and, as a consequence, meet in Hades. We recall Dido vividly from this encounter in Book VI, and of course from her tragedy in Book IV, but we tend to forget that she is also present in Books I-III. Moreover, she is shadowed forth in Books VII-XII. The possibilities of an epic with two central figures, male and female, could not have been lost on Milton. Alive, Dido is anti-type to Creusa; dead, type to Lavinia's anti-type. She dies on Aeneas' sword, of a self-inflicted wound, her pyre recalling Hektor's; Aeneas is Hektor *redivivus*, his Achillean sword the agent also of Turnus' death, the latter another Hektor, or Dido. Nothing in Vergil is simple.

Aeneas' infernal descent is an anti-type of the two infernal descents in the Odyssey. Homer had troped his first with his second; Vergil now tropes both of Homer's. As though obsessively allegorical in his method, the Roman poet forces upon us encounters with Chaos, the Fiery Stream, Grief and Cares, Disease and Old Age, Dread, Hunger and Want. Death and Toil are followed by Homeric Death's own brother, Sleep, Death-bringing War and Discord (that Eris who had provoked the Judgment of Paris). We continue with Aeneas on past the Centaurs, past Scylla, Briareus and the Lernaen Hydra, past Chimaera, Gorgon, the Harpies and Geryon. And this is just the opening scene. No wonder that Vergil's complete geography of Hades sufficed to inspire Dante's Inferno. As Vergil himself makes clear at the end of Book VI, Aeneas' descent is not a real but a false dream. It is, in fact, a dream allegory, personal and psychological but also cosmological, historical and prophetic. Are cosmology, history and prophecy chimerical too? Prophecy will prove especially important in Vergil's Christian successors. Dante will appropriate Vergil's history and cosmology. As Seneca said of Homer, all the doctrines (in this case theological, philosophical, political) are there, all contradicting one another. Again Vergil has taken his master seriously.

In our brief survey of his allegory we must at least touch on Vergil's allegoresis, in Book VIII, of The Shield of Achilles. The Shield of Aeneas, we recall, is made by Vulcan at the request of Venus. (We note in passing how Vergil extends Apollonius' account of a reconciled Hephaistos and Aphrodite.) Like the Greek shield, the Roman places a microcosm within a macrocosm, a common device of ambitious allegory. Landino had allegorized the Aeneid according to a theory of macrocosmic and microcosmic correspondences; one now sees where he found his sanction. Like Homer's Descent into Hades, but not like his Shield of Achilles, Vergil's Shield of Aeneas is prophetic. The Shield of Aeneas combines, then, *myth*, *history* and *prophecy*, a combination that proves essential to the later phases of the tradition.

In Book IX, *contra* Apollonius' Erato, Vergil invokes Calliope, as he moves toward closure. In Book XI Aeneas is spoken of as "first in reverence for the gods." Consequently, some later readers take him for a priest rather than an epic hero, though others regard his piety as confirming the new theological direction that the allegorical epic will take.

5

We need not await Prudentius, much less Dante, those Vergilian devotees, to witness the new theological direction, for within a generation of Vergil comes Ovid, to enact, as he devours his mighty predecessor, the most stupendous succession struggle known to literature, some of its consequences emblematized in the tales of Phaeton, Icarus and Ovid's own exile at the hands of Augustus. As for theology, where could we find a more compendious redaction than the Metamorphoses? In the Bible? An Imperial Roman who begins his epic with accounts of the Creation, Original Man, Universal Sin, The Flood and its aftermath could hardly have been ignorant of Hebrew belief. To ask if he had read the Bible is to miss the point: like Shakespeare and Whitman, this cosmopolitan was a great talker. He learned of Israel as the Londoner learned of Italy, the New Yorker of India, both in and out of books. Along with Confucius, Ovid is for Ezra Pound one of the two reliable guides to religion. A man without much sense of humor, Pound took his Ovid seriously, as for the most part have western poets for two millennia. What has this to do with allegory?

Quite a bit, for one may say serious things in ironic form. Some classical rhetoricians regard allegory as a form of irony, others as a mode of personification, yet others as ornament (*kosmos*, in Aristotle's term). Ovid is the first fully ironic poet, in the sense that he projects at least two contradictory attitudes in everything that he writes. He also creates what D. C. Feeney calls "personification allegory," "an alternative way of reflecting on human behavior, one which was eventually to emerge triumphant in European verse narrative." According to Angus Fletcher, *kosmos*, or the allegorical image, emphasizes "the visual modality," more specifically "visual or symbolic 'isolation,'" and signifies both "a universe" and "a symbol that implies a rank in a hierarchy." According to Gordon Teskey, allegory is paratactic, digressive, and episodic and introduces iconographic details irrelevant to its narrative. Taken together, these observations about the nature of the mode throw a good deal of light on Ovid's practice. As the *Ovide moralisé* and Renaissance readers attest, we are not the first to regard Ovid as bound up with the allegorical. We may, however, be the first to claim that he is quintessentially so.

Let us begin with parataxis. Notoriously Ovid strings together two-hundred and fifty stories in such a way that to this day, though we can recognize thematic and major structural groupings, we cannot discern any general principles of subordination or unity. Even metamorphosis is not an adequate principle. Though most epic narratives digress, Ovid is the first to interrupt a train of thought or story line for the sake of doing so. No other long poem before his is more episodic, that is, composed of such allegorically self-contained units. Only with Petrarch and his sonnet sequence will someone go further toward minimalizing the allegorical segments of a long poem. With Tennyson and other moderns the fashion grows for composing long poems episodically. Generally, then, we may say that Ovid emphasizes "the visual modality," as his legion of painterly followers attests; that his narrative episodes stand in "visual or symbolic 'isolation'" from one another; and that their iconographic details are often irrelevant to any larger narrative, precisely because no larger narrative exists. The frame of the poem, from creation to the present, is not a narrative, merely a *terminus a quo* and *ad quem*. Ovid's novel personification allegories (see Envy in Book II, Hunger in VIII, Sleep in XI and Rumor in XII) set us on a course that will lead through Dante on to Spenser and Milton.

The Metamorphoses, neither continuous in its action nor clear in its moral, is also tonally ambiguous. Accordingly, interpretative responsibility, as with all allegory, falls upon the reader's shoulders. The poem begins with cosmology, devolving thence into theology, myth, history and experience. Thus is promulgated a five-level allegorical scheme: the cosmic, the divine, the semi-divine, the heroic and the ordinary mortal, strands that are often interwoven. The early parts of the poem emphasize

Love, the later, War, the two themes interinvolved, as were Ares and Aphrodite, whose story Ovid retells. This allegorical interplay will find many friends in the Renaissance, among them Ariosto, Tasso, Sidney and Spenser, who follow Ovid in glossing that allegorical union as the two aspects of Hercules.

We have been speaking broadly of Ovid's allegorical features. Let us return to a single episode, the story of Phaeton and the Chariot of the Sun, an allegory of Hubris. Represented as an *ekphrasis* of the doors of Apollo's temple, Ovid's story, like Homer's and Vergil's shields, is an *inset allegory*. Included in its narrative are the *allegorical figures* of Day, Month, Year, Century and Hours, who, along with the four Seasons, attend Phaeton in his progress across the sky. Ovid digresses to introduce the Houses of the Zodiac, an *allegorical cosmology* elaborated with more allegorical figures in attendance on the Sun: Blazes, Dawn, Fire and Flame. The whole episode is part of an overarching *elemental allegory* that contrasts Fire with the Water of the flood and with mother Earth, who, at the narrative's conclusion, complains about the heat of the sun. These three fecundating elements are of course also complementary.

In the space that remains let us turn from Ovid's allegoresis of Hesiod, Aratus and Lucretius to his allegoresis of Homer, Apollonius and Vergil. In reworking the legend of Troy, Ovid both expands the Homeric frame (he includes the foundation of Troy as well as the Odyssean aftermath) and miniaturizes the epic tale (as in Book XII, where he summarizes the Trojan War in half a dozen lines). Later on he does much the same with Vergil, recounting at length legendary Rome and then, in a two-line summary almost comic in its effect, polishing off the last six books of the Aeneid. In four lines drained of all romantic interest he summarizes Dido's story. As though seeking to overgo himself as miniaturist, in Book XIII he reduces both Odyssey and Iliad to an epigram: "Mind counts for more than muscle." Summary, and its cousin, generalization, then, are essential instruments of Ovid's allegorical technique, whereby story is converted into abstraction. Some techniques of allegoresis he has learned from his masters: how to enlarge the Odyssean element in recounting the Iliad's story (from Vergil); how to epitomize Homer by staging a battle between Ajax and Odysseus (from Homer himself); how to introduce Apollonian material into the account of Troy (Vergil as well as Apollonius had taken his hero to Odyssean sites). Similarly, Ovid adds post-Homeric material, in this following Vergil and pointing a direction for Dante and others. His handling of the departure from Troy links the two Homeric poems by way of another Vergilian allegoresis.

The problematic Book XV, taken too seriously by those who seek in Ovid a consistent philosophy, undoes Pythagoras and the general gravity of classical thought. By endorsing the Pax Romana, Ovid contravenes the myth of Eris. Reversing the poem's overall progress, he memorializes the *political* Caesar as an *historical* figure, then renders him *divine*, reserving for himself alone a *cosmic* position among the stars. In a double irony the mortal Emperor is snatched away by Venus, a goddess on whom Caesar himself had bestowed cult status. Nonetheless, Ovid's divine prophecy overgoes the merely political prophecy of Aeneid VI, whose infernal descent Ovid had already overgone by recourse to the deeper myth of Orpheus.

We must note that Ovid is also *anti*-allegorical, in his agnosticism, in his trivialization of myth, history and politics, in his self-defeating parody. In this he predicts Byron.

6

I have two friends, one a devout Christian, the other a non-believer. The latter, having taken up Dante, delighted in scandalizing the former by reporting that he was reading a long poem by an Italian who had gone on a journey. I have another friend, also a believer, and a Dante scholar, who, though he recognizes allegory in the poet's treatment of The Seven Deadly Sins, does not find the Divine Comedy as a whole allegorical. A non-believer myself, I regard the poem as thoroughly allegorical, though I consider Dante a rather muddled critic of his own work, for it seems both improbable and undesirable that a long narrative should consistently maintain four levels of meaning. How can there be such fundamental disagreement among five readers, all brought up in the same tradition, three of them Christian, four of them living in the same age? Quite simple. What is allegorical is a matter of definition and interpretation.

No friend of Dante's, this reader has nonetheless found the Comedy's argument to be the least controvertible in all literature. What is its universal appeal? So few readers have read the whole poem, in the original, recently, that we shall not dwell on the beauties of its language, imagery, or pathetic affect. What, we shall ask instead, in its epic argument, its Idea, that is, its allegory, is so attractive? But first we must summarize that argument and will turn to Dorothy Sayers for guidance. "Allegory," she begins, "is the interpretation of experience by means of images." Dante's poem "is an allegory of the Way to God," "of the Soul's search for God." Dante "set himself down to write the great Comedy of Redemption and the return of all things by the way of Self-Knowledge and Purification to the Beatitude of the Presence of God." In contradistinction to much Christian allegory, his is "an allegory of symbolic personages" in which "far the greater number of . . . figures are symbolic images." On his journey Dante ("the image of every Christian sinner") experiences Hell ("the image of the deepening possibilities of

Evil within the soul"), Purgatory ("the image of repentance by which the soul purges the guilt of Sin") and Paradise ("the image of the soul in a state of Grace," symbolized by Beatrice). Dante's appeal, she says, may have much to do with the story of a lover who is required to "adventure through the Underworld to find his lost Lady."

What is this Inferno through which one voyages, what this Paradiso at which one arrives, and what this Purgatorio that stands betwixt them? Could it be that Hell is Death and Heaven, Life, or is it the other way round? Now, you see, we are talking allegory: it is up to you to decide. Is it that Hell is the Bad and Heaven the Good, or again do we have the terms reversed? Most readers thoroughly enjoy their trip through Hell, whereas few find Heaven attractive. Among Occidental readers, that is; Oriental readers are more prone to find the poem perfectly symmetrical, presumably as Dante intended. What other schemes did he have in mind, for normally we regard poets in Vergil's direct line as something less than direct? Could it be that Dante has taken the *rota Vergiliana* and reversed it, making of the Aeneid his model for the Inferno, of the Georgics his model for the Purgatorio, of the Eclogues his model for the Paradiso? The inversion and rectification of archetypes may be part of his project.

Curiously Dante's epic does not much resemble a journey, though wit may be expended on accommodating his to Aeneas' progress, or to the older pattern of Odyssean *nostos*. In fact he goes *down* into a pit and comes back *up* a mountain to gaze *higher* toward heavenly images. Have we experienced lows and highs, and do we not seek some higher principle? Dante is quite original and patently universal. He is also personal, candidly admitting his pleasure at others' suffering, egotistical in rehearsing the details of his own mid-life crisis. An exile from country, family and the woman he loves, he is secretly happier than communal souls. As a consequence he appeals to two audiences: those who share his freedom and those who wish they did. He stands, in life, for the happily married man (which he seems to have been) who nonetheless craves his ideal woman; or, in imagination, he stands for the goatish loner with all his various fantasies. For Dante's poem is both a fantasy and an incitement to further fantasy. Its lack of mimetic grounding is what this reader finds its principal defect.

Dante, we have seen, gains by denying what he seeks and seeking what he and others have denied. Dante *is* Aeneas, he *is* Paul, though he denies both identities. His coyness is another feature that this reader finds unattractive. Dante pretends to be the student, of Vergil, Beatrice and others, but he is really the teacher. In poetic theory, since Horace and till recently, we all pretended to seek instruction, but did we really delight in it? Dante has us coming and going, for as *he* experiences delight, it is *we* who are being instructed. Brilliantly he embodies this paradox in his relationship with Vergil, whom he learns from but also dismisses. No such teacher-student relationship encumbers the classical epic (Phoenix and Achilles are a minor exception), though it figures prominently in the Indian epic. The relationship surely serves to universalize Dante's poem, especially since the teacher is in part a figure of failure. Vergil, who has done his best to save his own soul, is not to be spared, at least not within the poem's dispensation. Still, Dante is a lucky man to have such good teachers as Vergil, Statius, St. Bernard—and especially Beatrice!

The poem's consummate quest, for the Justice available in The City of God, is compromised, one feels, by the doctrine of retribution, a symbolic sublimation of the principle of revenge. Dante's Hell is, after all, a sado-masochistic Heaven, a feature which may also render the poem's appeal more universal. Even less attractive to this reader is Dante's cultural prejudice and exclusivity. Nonetheless, his comic resolution of the story of man's woe, so much more comprehensive than the final dispensations of Iliad, Argonautica, and Aeneid, or even of Odyssey and Metamorphoses, wipes away blame, as in theory comedy should. If, in fact, all this has happened. Dante might have taken his Ovid more seriously.

What can we learn about the Divine Comedy from its later reception? Here we shall limit ourselves to epic writers, and then exclusively to the English, among whom Dante has had an illustrious readership: Chaucer, Spenser and Milton; Blake, Wordsworth and Carlyle; Pope, Byron and Joyce. Curiously those who may have studied him most carefully have the least to say about him. Chaucer sidesteps Dante; though the divine poet influences his dream allegory, his effect upon Troilus and Criseyde is negligible. In Spenser there is no mention whatsoever of Dante; in all Milton's works, but a few critical remarks. Both would have been expert readers of the Italian and Latin texts and both, according to scholars, had access to them, Spenser to the Comedy, Milton to the Comedy and more (he "knew the *Monarchia*, owned a copy of the *Convivio*," and "was familiar with the *Vita nuova*," says David Wallace). Perhaps the evidence of Dante's influence is so clearly before our eyes that we cannot see it. For the tri-partite structure of The Faerie Queene (Books I-II; III-IV; V-VI) looks very much like the structure of the Comedy; likewise, what this reader regards as the probable order of Milton's major works: Paradise Lost, Samson Agonistes, Paradise Regained. In the first phase of Spenser and Milton the doctrine of Original Sin is set forth; in their middle phases both are concerned with knowledge of self and other; in their final phases both contemplate ideal worlds, in Spenser, those of Justice and Courtesy, in Milton, Paradise again.

7

Like Petrarch and Boccaccio before them, Ariosto and Tasso respond to the baleful tendencies of Dante. Unlike those adulators, who submit to their mighty predecessor's reputation, Ariosto and Tasso take measures to escape him, though important lineaments in their poems may be traced back to the Comedy, Ariosto developing what we have identified as its fantastic vein, Tasso, its allegorical. Both cinquecento writers eschew the personal in Dante, which Petrarch had intensified, and the escapist, which Boccaccio had echoed, albeit in a secular way (his storytellers flee plague-ridden Florence to a suburban *locus amoenus*). Unlike Tasso, who will merge the romance with an original allegorical theory, Ariosto contents himself with his romantic materials, rerendering them in a manner at once more fantastic and more realistic than his medieval predecessors. In so doing he predicts the liberation of mimetic narrative from its allegorical restraints that will only fully emerge in the novel. Like Vergil, Ariosto celebrates an empire, the more restricted House of Este, for which he offers a foundation myth, basing his upon Vergil's. In another sense, however, like Dante before him, he enlarges the Roman empire to include all Europe. Finally, through his frankly erotic thematology he subverts the sublimated pieties of Dante and others who had struggled to reconcile their adoration of Christ's celibacy and Mary's virginity with their own sexuality.

Although the Orlando Furioso embodies many allegorical figures, episodes and larger motifs, Ariosto is in a sense the least allegorical writer in the tradition that we have given that name. Unlike most of our epic poets, he produces a poem for oral recitation. Its statements of moral principle serve largely to salve the conscience of an audience whose more pressing requirements appear to have been delight and self-flattery. Unlike Tasso, Ariosto does not provide an allegoresis of his own work; nor does he Christianize his themes beyond the terms of his received polemic; unabashedly he privileges the amatory over the martial, though both are important themes. In the brilliance and exuberance of his originality he outranks all but Ovid and may well be the most imaginative epic poet. His decision to *continue* Boiardo's already monumental narrative with an equally monumental one of his own reverses the tradition of palimpsest imitation that runs from Alexandria through Dante and resumes with Spenser and Milton. That decision alone bespeaks his liberating genius.

Beneath its romantic surface and despite its mercurial disjunctures, the Orlando Furioso reflects deeper allegorical programs characteristic of medieval and Renaissance thought. Like Dante's work, and in accord with the poetic principal of *movere et docere*, it embodies an allegory of

111

education. In imitation of Vergil, and more appositely sixteenth-century ways of reading him, it embodies an allegory of the perfect prince. The model here, for both Orlando and Ruggiero, is Hercules, a composite hero whose twelve labors allegorize the twelve aspects of his personality. We know Hercules' story from his birth to his death and beyond; this is not true of Odysseus or Aeneas. Accordingly, he provides what we might call a *compressed* (as opposed to extended) *metaphor* for the heroes of Ariosto and others. He also serves as one of two poles in an opposition between Good and Evil, the other represented, in Renaissance typology, by Paris (see, for example, Landino's debate between the evil choice of the latter and the virtuous choice of the former). Similarly, Ariosto's narrative is organized about an opposition between the Heavenly and the Earthly Venuses, another Renaissance *topos*.

8

Since anyone with an eye for capital letters may scan the Orlando Furioso and Gerusalemme Liberata for allegorical figures, we shall not here compile lists of them nor offer commentary on these largely conventional—classical, medieval and Renaissance—abstractions, however adroitly Ariosto and Tasso deploy them. More helpful to our understanding of the allegorical tradition might be a summary of Tasso's contributions to its theory, in his *Discorsi del poema eroico*, in the *Allegoria* to his own epic, in his letters and other critical writings. An extravagantly gifted critic, Tasso, despite occasional irrationalities and frequent contradictions as his thought evolves, stands as the most influential theoretician of the epic since Aristotle. So highly regarded was his work that Spenser may have paused in the composition of The Faerie Queene to absorb the latest edition of the Gerusalemme; his theory, which Milton knew, virtually defines the project of Paradise Lost.

Like most Italian Renaissance critics, Tasso has one eye on Aristotle most of the time. Regarding the romance as equivalent to the classical epic, he explains that Aristotle could have had no opinion in this matter, since he had never read one. Tasso goes on to argue the superiority of episodic plot over single-action plot. It is truer, he says, to the Italian genius and language to have many actions. Out of a passage in the Poetics Tasso develops the notion that the distinguishing feature of the epic is the *marvelous*, which he ingeniously assimilates to the *verisimilar*. In extension of Aristotle he proclaims that the epic may imitate divine actions and works of nature as well as human deeds. In a similar extension, one that merges the Rhetoric and the Ethics with the Poetics, he argues that narrative is substance, not just rhetoric; decorum ethical, not just stylistic. In a more important and even more imaginative transformation of Aristotle he defines allegory as *the verisimilar imitation of the universal*. Following the epideictic Aristotle, he says that epic, as distinct from tragedy, requires *admirable agents of the highest virtue and piety*, in whose discourse we take the highest pleasure. *Contra* Castelvetro, a stricter Aristotelian, who had argued for history, Tasso argues for *invention* as the higher principle in epic. Since history is interinvolved with religion, the highest epic Truth, says Tasso, will be found in Christian history. *Contra* Mazzoni, a Platonist who had argued for the fantastic imagination, Tasso argues for the icastic, which, he says, constructs *idoli* of reality. Love, Tasso pronounces, is the greatest theme for epic, but then, in a characteristic non-sequitur, he argues that Faith, Church and Empire are even greater ones.

Of compelling interest to us is Tasso's definition of allegory. The epic (or heroic) poet, he says, shapes his poem as God shapes His creation. Its allegory is its *Idea* (cp. Sidney's "fore-conceit"), its *Truth*, its *Soul*. It is nothing less than "the glassed figure of Human Life." The higher Truth toward which the epic poet strives is the truth of Universals. In a redefinition of Aristotle, *Imitation* becomes the representation of merely external realities, for allegory alone, says Tasso, can represent the internal, ethical life of man. Allegory takes over at the point where the literal, or historical, leaves off; where *Imagination*, that is, begins. *Poetry*, which Tasso has now identified with allegory, he calls "an imitation of human action, fashioned to teach us how to live." In one final, breath-taking reversal, Imitation, which Tasso earlier had opposed to Allegory, now, through the power of Imagination, becomes the very method whereby the poet achieves Allegory, which itself has been defined as "the Universal Idea."

9

The cinquecento Italian theory of epic and romance had a formative effect upon the structure and allegory of The Faerie Queene. Minturno distinguishes the epic, which, he says, "imitates a memorable action carried to its conclusion by an illustrious person," from the romance, which "has as its object a crowd of knights and ladies and affairs of war and peace." "In this group," he continues, "the knight is especially taken whom the author is to make glorious above all the others." Spenser will call that knight Arthur and his consort Gloriana. "The romances readily devote themselves to several deeds of several men," writes Ariosto's biographer Pigna, but "they concern especially one man who should be celebrated over all the others. And thus they agree with the epic poets in taking a single person, but not so as taking a single action." Toscanella recommends that the poet place "several virtues in several individuals, one virtue in one character, and another in another, in order to fashion out of all the characters a well-rounded and perfect man," the last phrase a reflection of the Renaissance idealization of Aeneas. Petrarch, who in the fourteenth century had already summarized Vergil's "end and subject" as "the perfect man," adds in wonderment, "It is as if Vergil were not describing Aeneas, but the brave and perfect man under the name of Aeneas."

This collective way of thinking leads to Spenser's scheme for his own romance-epic, in which Arthur, the paramount hero, is successively embodied in half a dozen of the dozen, or even two dozen avatars that Spenser had originally planned for. His six *allegorical* virtues he represents in six books (Holiness, Temperance, Chastity, Friendship, Justice and Courtesy), to which he appends a *philosophical* conclusion, an *Allegoria* of sorts. For some have surmised that the Books of Mutability form the first half of a twelve-book plan, according to which Spenser would have offered us six more Books of Constancy. At any rate, the extant books have other important allegorical arrangements: the even-numbered are Christian, the odd-numbered, classical; the even-numbered have as their heroes Knights, the odd-numbered, Elves. Though profoundly influenced by Vergil and Ovid, Spenser's general conception is less classical than medieval (his knights represent what Aquinas called *infused* virtues, his elves, *acquired* virtues); less medieval (it lacks the *quatre-sens* of historical, allegorical, moral and anagogical levels) than Renaissance (the whole constitutes a Christian Humanist synthesis); less Renaissance than curiously modern (as in Dante, all is internalized, if not in the figure of the poet himself, then within the reader's psychology).

His architecture is not as symmetrical as it seems, for the poem is shaped by a temporal, or experiential dynamic. The Book of Holiness lays the doctrinal ground for the rest of the poem and consequently has more importance than other individual books (Milton will counter Spenser's choice of *Revelation* as his scriptural text with his own choice of *Genesis*, in a move like that of Apollonius to assert his priority over Homer by recounting an older story). Likewise, the first two books, which balance and synthesize Christian and classical elements, establish a model that contains the whole poem's method. In this they are like the first two cantos of Dante's Comedy and the first two books of Paradise Lost, all three examples epitomizing the larger works of which they are part. In each of his books Spenser deposits an *allegorical episode* that serves to focus his theme: The House of Pride (I), The Bower of Bliss (II), The Garden of Adonis (III), The Temple of Venus (IV), The Temple of Isis (V) and Mount Acidale (VI). That The Garden of Adonis is "classical" but occurs within a "Christian" book helps us to understand another dynamic: Christian thesis (I), classical antithesis (II) and

Christian Humanist synthesis (III), a pattern repeated in Books IV, V and VI. Books III and IV, one of three pairs of contrasting books, constitute a continuum as well. Under the banner of Vergilian allegoresis, whereby Britomart subsumes both Dido and Aeneas, Spenser further allegorizes her and her quest as Love and War, or Venus vs. Mars in the terms of a *dialectical allegory*. In two of her avatars, Belphoebe and Amoret, Britomart figures another allegory, the Heavenly and Earthly Venuses. Third in a triad, Florimell, reconciling the first two, transports Love onto a cosmic plane. In response to this allegorical grouping, Book IV introduces the figures of Ate, Lust and Discord. Book V is then linked to III and IV by Britomart, whose pursuit of Artegall overflows the boundaries of Book IV. In fact each book of The Faerie Queene, beginning with Book II, serves to complete the preceding book, thereby generating another series of allegorical pairings. In Book V Spenser offers us a *political allegory*, basing his treatment of Justice on an allegoresis of Hercules. Book VI steps out of the allegorical and into the romantic mode, as though to foreshadow what will become of the allegorical in the Romantic tradition. In The Faerie Queene's progression from atavistic allegory through cultural syncretism to a polyvalent mode of romance we might even see a survey of western culture.

But what is the unifying principle of the poem? "Clearly some close relation obtains between Arthur and the liberating faith in the person of Christ," writes C. S. Lewis. "However, any direct leap from the literal Arthur to the theological would . . . have horrified Christian feeling," he goes on to say. "The platonic level provided a meeting-ground between. It was unobjectionable to present an Arthur with philosophical overtones, and the Platonic Arthur was in turn easily syncretized with the Christian." The Faerie Queene, Lewis implies, is a sacred as well as a philosophical poem. As we have seen, it is also *theological* and at points *historical*. Is it mythic too? In other words, is Spenser's poem an epic or just a romance of platonized Christianity? We have begun with C. S. Lewis, a Christian believer, precisely because Spenser of late has fallen into agnostic hands, those of critics who find, for example, that all is relative, his method a "closing up of truth to truth": Holiness leads on to Courtesy, Mount Acidale represents "the poem's allegorical core." For the Christian, however, the poem's allegorical core must be the doctrine of Man's Fall and Redemption.

Spenser is hard to pin down, perhaps because in certain ways he is like Dante, who, though strictly Thomistic in his theology, as an allegorist is personal and modern. We have seen how, despite his explicit denial, Dante *is* Aeneas, *is* Paul. Likewise Spenser, who, through the internal or psychological allegory of Guyon's struggle, represents a process akin to ours or to his own. His poem as a whole may be indebted to another

Renaissance allegoresis of Aeneas, one which allegorizes a process of the spirit. It may also be directly indebted to Dante. "Guyon," says Frank Kermode, "passes from the lower temperance of natural habit to the virtue of a hero, which includes all the cardinal virtues," in "a purgatorial process from human to semi-divine virtue, from a human to a divine *phronesis*." The model for Guyon he finds in the New Testament representation of Christ in the Wilderness. In short, Guyon, as an avatar of Arthur, is a figure of the heroic Christ. He too is Paul and Aeneas. As Jon Whitman argues, allegorical reading is akin to Christian scriptural exegesis, a process that tends toward *conversion*. Spenser's elfish hero, through his conversion, becomes a kind of Christian gentleman, "the general end," we recall, that Spenser had in the Letter to Ralegh specified for his educative epic. Through his own participation in the process of Guyon's redemption, Spenser, like Dante, points the way for reader and poet alike.

10

> On the first pages of some ideal anthology of the period he does so much to initiate, one might find the poet Petrarch, confessing that he has made a holy thing of his beloved Laura—in other words, an Idol. The last pages of this same anthology would bring the reader up against a crazed hidalgo posted on a road in Spain—the mad one is trying to compel a group of traveling merchants to confess with him the supereminent beauty of a partly nonexistent lady whom he may never have seen. Behold, this dreamer cometh. . . . After all, it is not Shakespeare, but Don Quixote, of whom one could truly say that his whole life was a life of allegory.
>
> —James Nohrnberg

In the Proem to Book II of The Faerie Queene, Spenser encourages Elizabeth to behold England "in this faire mirrhour," "thine owne realmes in lond of Faery." *Inversion*, as well as its counterpart *conversion*, is an allegorical stock-in-trade (*inversio* was a Roman term for allegory). "Spenser," says Michael Murrin, "has inverted an age-old convention whereby the real world is mirrored in the ideal by asserting instead that the ideal world is mirrored in the real." Is this not too the method of Don Quixote's madness? And does it not derive from the same source as Spenser's — the world of romance? "Renaissance literature," says Nohrnberg in sentences omitted from the epigraph above, "though it can hardly be said to put the relation of subject and object on that ideal basis of independence that leads from Descartes to Kant, might well be described as a critical engine for insinuating the unavoidable subjectivity of the mind's construction of both the object of knowledge and the object of love."

Cervantes' masterpiece includes two allegories, one an *inversio*, in which the Don imagines the ideal world reflected in the real, the other a *conversio*, in which the world of romance leads to Christian faith. This explains why critics who see only one of the allegories (Nabokov, for example, for whom only the inversion exists; Unamuno, for whom only its opposite) cannot understand Cervantes. Closer to the truth is the critic who sees in the book "the last and greatest epic" and "the first and greatest novel." But is Don Quixote really an epic? And for that matter, is it really a novel? It fact it is neither, if by those terms we mean, on the one hand, something tragic, on the other hand, something realistic. If, however, we add the term "comic," then Don Quixote is both epic and novel. Let us turn to the question of its allegory.

Since we all recognize the Don as an Idealist and Sancho as a Realist (their roles of course also reversible), we shall not belabor the point. If the work is *allegorical*, does it also meet our other requirements of the epic, that it be *mythic, theological, historical* and *experiential?* In "The Captive Captain's Tale"—to look no further—Cervantes transparently rehearses his own experience. Scholars have shown that the book reflects the history of sixteenth-century Spain. Christian theology is everywhere present, in the form of parody as well as serious doctrine. What remains is to identify its governing myth, but that we must do without recourse to previous mythology. For the myth is precisely Don Quixote, the man and the book. Out of his own independent Kantian "experience" Cervantes has created an epic.

11

Despite his classical erudition Milton is most profoundly indebted for the grounding of his enterprise to Italian Renaissance theory. The pastoralism of Paradise Lost, to cite one example, would be unthinkable without Minturno's reranking of epic subjects to read, in ascending order, *heroic, philosophical, bucolic,* along with the general example of long pastoral works by Sannazaro, Tasso, Sidney, Spenser and others. Milton follows Minturno in devaluing martial themes in favor of an "argument / not less but more Heroic," one that is philosophical in its cosmological, theological and ethical speculations, and bucolic in its choice of Eden as his setting. In culmination of this elevation of pastoral from a lowly to an ideal status, René Rapin, in 1659, as Milton is composing his epic, redefines the mode as "a perfect image of the State of Innocence."

Having summarized Tasso's new allegorical theory of the epic, let us now apply its leading ideas to Paradise Lost, for Milton's Christian themes and allegorical technique owe much to this reformulator of the genre. Especially important is the Italian critic's sanction of divine actions as a subject for epic imitation, since God's Will and Christ's Word will figure so prominently, the first in Paradise Lost, the second in Paradise Regained. Moreover, Tasso's favorable view of *the marvelous* serves to propel the development of Milton's fantastic allegorical machinery: Heaven and Hell; God, Satan and the Angels; celestial battles and other improbable motifs. His conception of heroism, as reflected in the prelapsarian Adam and the divine Christ, reflects Tasso's Christian memory of Aristotle's prescription: *admirable agents of the highest virtue and piety.* Like Castelvetro, Milton favors what for the Biblical fundamentalist is an historical subject but, like Tasso, favors *invention* as a means of treating it. By way of the novel concept of *imagination* Milton creates a *verisimilar imitation of the universal.* The highest epic Truth, Tasso had said, will be found in *Christian history*, which Milton takes as his theological frame for the delineation of human events from Adam's Fall to Cromwell's Reign to Christ's Second Coming. His poem combines two of Tasso's recommended themes: Love and Faith. Though Milton does not comment on the Italian's theoretical pronouncements, we can still imagine his applause at two of Tasso's notions: that the epic poet shapes his poem as God shapes His creation; and that the higher Truth toward which he strives is the truth of Universals. For Milton acts upon his Biblical clay to create a version of its story whose universal allegoresis quite transcends its original context. How else, from his comparatist perspective, would the modern Christian Englishman have viewed such events except as universally true?

Paradise Lost principally concerns Adam and Eve, our first parents according to Milton's received Biblical myth. Why is it, then, that we, with our post-Darwinian knowledge of evolution, are still so fascinated by the story? Because this allegorically layered fable works on us in other ways. Adam and Eve represent our *actual* parents, from whose hereditary disposition we are descended and from whose ethical choices we have profited or suffered. Moreover, Adam and Eve represent ourselves (for women, Eve; for men, Adam), as well as our significant others (for women, Adam; for men, Eve). Accordingly, this domestic and personal drama has a more direct appeal than most other epic stories. As did Vergil with Dido and Aeneas, so does Milton make it ambiguous as to whether Adam and Eve are married (there was no Church in Eden). Beyond these levels, and perhaps deeper than they, is the psychological configuration of the story. To use Freudian terms, God appears as a stern Superego, Satan as a rebellious Id; to shift to Jungian terms, Adam and Eve create an androgynous figure known to myth and depth psychology alike: for women, a Self and Animus; for men, an Anima and Self. We note in all this that, except for the celibate or homosexual reader, the relationships that Milton describes are universal. Could he have known that he would find an avid readership throughout the world? Undoubtedly so. He was a student of universality, an allegorical exegete and a practicing allegorist of the archetypes.

As Tasso redefines the genre, Paradise Lost is fundamentally allegorical. Its "Idea" is the doctrine of Original Sin, its theology the elaboration of that germ into the drama of the Fall, the Expulsion from Eden and the subsequent Redemption of Man. Its allegorical figures exist on interpenetrating levels, requiring of the reader an interpretive involvement that leads him theoretically to conversion, if he is not already convinced of Milton's belief. So much is obvious. Of greater interest is the novel method required of Milton's novel subject. For despite his indebtedness to Homer, Vergil and Ovid, and for all his assimilation of Dante, Tasso and Spenser, Milton had to go it alone when it came to actually writing his epics. (In this regard, Paradise Regained, with its unprecedented form, must have posed an even greater challenge than Paradise Lost.) Tasso, we recall, had elevated the status of the romance. In a sense its pattern of *agon, pathos* and *anagnorisis* is more relevant to Paradise Lost than those of classical epic and tragedy which Milton himself adduces. Milton's masterpiece is also a theatrical epic, grounded in the Italian tradition of the *sacra rappresentazione*, whose main performers enact a revel of love and subsequent fall. Masque, pageant and prophetic show, all allegorical forms, provide models for Milton's work as essential as those of epic or romance.

That Milton chose a Biblical subject by no means dictated his particular solution. "Christian writers of heroic story," Leland Ryken observes, "had struggled for centuries to reconcile the theological and literary traditions of the hero," in "holy war" epics, such as Tasso's; in "romance allegories," such as Spenser's; in "divine poetry," such as the Biblical epics of Milton's contemporaries. For Ryken and others the Bible itself, regarded as an epic, provides another important model, not only for its narrative but also for its traditions of allegorization. Moreover, "In the epics of Genesis, Exodus and Revelation," Ryken argues, "Milton found a pattern, respectively, for his substitution of domestic values for heroic ones, his substitution of divine strength and human weakness for the epic motif of human glory, and his substitution of spiritual for physical versions of some common epic motifs." This illuminating scholar goes on to cite Ian Watt's designation of Paradise Lost as "the greatest and indeed the only epic of married life." Like Cervantes, Milton is a figure astride two ages, voraciously gathering up all that had gone before him but with equal strength preparing the way for much that is to follow.

How, then, does Milton's project tally with our definition of epic?

More fundamentally *mythic* and more expansively *theological* than Spenser's, Milton's is also more comprehensively *historical*, moreso than any earlier model. It has many *allegorical* aspects in addition to those already noted: its *allegorical episodes* observe the principle of relevance and incongruity; its grandly abstract discourse maintains an *allegorical distance* from its simple story; likewise, its narrator sustains a tension between its *verisimilar* and its *marvelous* elements; it is *psychological* as well as *ethical*. In short, like Dante and Spenser's epics, Paradise Lost is *experiential*, though in ways that English readers will not fully grasp until Blake, Wordsworth and Byron develop the implications of Milton's innovation.

12

> Allegory belongs to the fallen world, the world of Plato's cave-dwellers; it is an invention of mind on its own, trying to make sense of experience in a benighted world.
>
> —Isabel G. MacCaffrey

As critics we cannot live without definitions, for criticism is a branch of philosophy, and philosophy, at least its western branch, begins with definitions. Nonetheless, it serves no purpose to string the noose of definition about the neck of literature, especially when the terms defined are *allegory* and *epic*. It is in the interest of neither literature, philosophy, nor criticism to do so. Byron is an allegorist in a sense both old and new, according to MacCaffrey's definition of the mode. A most attractive figure, as brilliant a critic as Tasso is a theorist, he is an even more innovative practitioner than Milton. Would that he had lived to write his planned hundred cantos instead of the mere sixteen plus that we have. One suspects that after Juan had visited Paris, to witness the Revolution, had he not lost his head, he would have accompanied Byron on travels yet more universal: to America, to India, to China. In a sense Whitman and Pound fulfil these promises. In another sense they bury themselves in books. For when MacCaffrey speaks of *experience*, it is not of the Kantian kind.

Though every writer in a sense has an open-ended plan—his life, his ongoing work, Byron literalizes this and so puts an end to the closure that characterizes epic from Homer through Milton. His precursors here, as in other matters, are Ovid and Ariosto. Accordingly, he stands among those whom Pound called writers that would be read whether or not they were taught in school. A *young* critic, Byron cannot decide whether he belongs to the line of Homer, Vergil and Dante (he is planning his own "panoramic view of hell") or the line that he knows is truer, Milton,

Dryden and Pope. By Milton he means the Apostle of Liberty, though his reworking of Adam in Juan shows that he has grasped the Poet's importance too. He himself is not so much Homer as Odysseus, for Byron equals Juan equals Odysseus. His poem is autobiographical and philosophical, but also epic and mythic (it is not by accident that he has chosen Don Juan as its hero). Like Milton, Byron is a student of *Genesis*, which, along with Hesiod, Lucretius and Ovid, influences his decision to "begin with the beginning" (that is, with Juan's birth), a move at once liberating and impoverishing, for it restricts the multiplicity of perspectives otherwise available to the poet who begins *in medias res*. Having done the Oedipal triangle once, Byron does it again and again. This reader suspects that he committed incest not only with his half-sister but with his mother too (see Juan's encounter with Catherine the Great). Perhaps Byron's inability to resolve the Oedipal complex resulted from such an horrendous event; at any rate, unresolved it remained. In an open-ended work such as Don Juan, everything can be changed, or nothing can, for the fundamental terms of such an epic have never been determined. Significantly, the *myth* of Don Juan is itself repetitive and open-ended. Though *theology* brings it to closure, Byron does not live to finish his own version of the story. In Don Juan *history* is present, but present history is a contradiction in terms, and so gives way to *experience*, by itself an inadequate basis for epic, as the novel has shown.

6

The Universal in English Literature

> Nothing can please many, and please long, but just representations
> of general nature. Shakespeare is, above all writers, at least above all
> modern writers, the poet of nature . . . . His characters are not modified
> by the customs of particular places, unpracticed by the rest of the
> world . . . . In the writings of other poets a character is too often an
> individual: in those of Shakespeare it is commonly a species.
>
> —Samuel Johnson

> This universality, this necessity, is an extra-logical psychological
> fact, resultant of a purely automatic act of the mind: it is not a logical
> conclusion from adequate premises—
> We express our belief in logically unjustifiable language — a
> universal statement is really a particular statement about the nervous
> apparatus of thought.
>
> —Oscar Wilde

1

In their enthusiastic espousal of current doctrines neither Johnson nor
Wilde gives us a very balanced statement of the age-old problem, What
is particular and what universal? Johnson might better have said that
Shakespeare creates characters who are *both* individuals *and* species.
Wilde might better have said that expressions of common belief are *both*
particular *and* universal. Nor is the individual less individual for
belonging to a species, the universal less universal for being also
particular: uttered in a given language by a given speaker at a given
moment. Emphasis upon the particular is now favored in some circles
over what was once called a more cosmopolitan view of things.

Do universals exist? we have asked—if not from the beginning of time
at least from the beginning of philosophical speculation. In a common, as
opposed to technical, sense, of course they do. We are all born, we all die;
we all speak a language; we share certain needs, emotions, ideals. That
these phenomena come to focus in individuals does not make them less
universal. In fact for Augustine the most *individual* voice, that which
speaks within us, is the most *universal* voice, the voice of Christ, of
Truth — of the Parmatman, however we designate it. In short, the
universal is always particular, the particular always universal.

The universal, like God, like existence, is not readily susceptible of
logical proof. This Wilde takes note of, as he reduces philosophy to

psychology. But the two are not the same. Western philosophy has long sought to define the universal, and a cursory review of such efforts might be of interest. Aristotle, the so-called "empiricist," taught us to generalize by seeking the immanent universal in things. His view has much to do with the generalizing tendency of later classical — not to mention neoclassical—literature. Horace, for example, in the realm of literary criticism, reduced Aristotle's theory of genre to a doctrine of fixed types. The classical view favored ethical norms, proportions of beauty, principles of decorum, all which tended to regularize esthetic theory and practice.

By its appeal to tradition Christianity reinforced this conservative strain in western thought. "What has been taught always, everywhere and by all," said the fifth-century saint, Vincent of Lering, "is to be believed." The medieval debate between particular and universal — termed *nominal* vs. *real*—see-sawed back and forth, as had the classical, though the more permanent realist view tended to prevail. For Aquinas the essential feature of the mind lies in its ability to grasp universals, those categories which transcend the knowledge provide by the senses.

The debate extended into the Renaissance, where Telesius (1509-1588) asserts that knowledge must be grounded in the senses but Campanella (1568-1639) that the senses must unite us with the universe. As Pomponatius (1462-1524) had attributed all religions to the operation of cosmic laws, so later Renaissance thinkers such as Hooker, Tyndale and Grotius developed the concept of the *law of nature*, a kind of concrete universal that prefigures Hegel.

Out of this concept of *nature* the Enlightenment produced the concept of *human nature*, which in turn led to the *general nature* of Johnson's pronouncement. "It is universally acknowledged," Hume had observed, "that there is a great uniformity among the actions of men, in all nations and ages, and that human nature remains still the same, in its principles and operations." The new doctrine of uniformity extends it throughout space and time. In an Aristotelian move, the Enlightenment reduces multiplicity to unity by subsuming the particular in the general. Like Plato it sometimes regards the general as transcendental. Samuel Johnson, in his oriental tale *Rasselas* (1759), says of the writer that he

> must divest himself of the prejudices of his age or country; he must consider right and wrong in their abstracted and variable state; he must disregard present laws and opinions, and rise to general and transcendental truths, which will always be the same.

The English neoclassicist has arrived at a doctrine of universal truth that is culturally relative and metaphysically absolute.

From the love of clarity that characterizes the Enlightenment we turn to the love of mystery that characterizes much Romantic thought. Here the neoclassical preoccupation with general statement gives way to a preoccupation with symbol, as in Goethe's reflections on its relation to idea, image and language:

> The symbol transforms the visible into an idea and the idea into an image in such manner that the idea in the image stays infinitely potent and unattainable, remaining unutterable even if spoken in all languages.

There is something unitary and therefore universal in poetry, something that crosses the boundaries of culture and resists expression in words. For the more philosophical Coleridge, influenced by Goethe's coevals of the German idealist school, the goal of poetry is to manifest "Unity or Revelation of the *One* in and by the *Many*." By taking Goethe and Coleridge together we identify the process — if it still remains a mystery — whereby the intransigent particular becomes the luminous universal. In a movement parallel with Kant's assimilation of subject to object in Experience (*Erfahrung*), Goethe speaks of symbolic objects as evoking in his mind "pertinent and similar as well as foreign ideas" — native as well as exotic ideas, we might say. "Consequently," he continues, "from within as well as from without they claim a certain oneness and universality." *Symbol*, then, vies with Kant's *Experience* as the modality for the integration of subject and object. It remained only for Hegel to reknit this contrariety, to claim for the marriage of subject and object not only, as Kant did, truth, but also both particularity and universality: "Everything that is genuinely true, in mind as in nature, is inherently concrete, having both subjectivity and particularity in itself, as well as universality." At last the *concrete universal*, having replaced *Experience* and *symbol* as the term of ultimate synthesis, attains its full philosophical dignity and force. Despite later developments we are still under the sway of Hegel's generalization, which is neither fully concrete nor merely abstract. The protest against his high valorization of the universal also stems philosophically from Hegel himself.

What, then, of the universal principles of literature or the universal elements in a particular branch thereof? Aristotle, in a view later reinforced by the neoplatonists, says that poetry — what we would call literature — is itself universal, meaning that it generalizes from experience. For our purposes we require a more specific sense of the ways in which it can be universal. The subject at hand, the universal element in English literature, is two-fold: English literature, and its bearing in the world. Accordingly, we might divide the question: What about English literature is *inherently* universal? And what about it is *practically* so?

Practically speaking, since English has become a universal language, English literature has become a subject of study for those who wish to master it. We might therefore say that English literature has become universal, that is, a world-wide subject of study. But even in translation it has achieved a notable international popularity. In other words, it is universal not only under duress but also in its general appeal. Some of this is no doubt due to several centuries of British hegemony. But much is not. Keats and Eliot, Dickens and Lawrence are read in countries that never fell under the cultural sway of the British Empire. We need not rely upon the overwhelming evidence of Shakespeare's appeal to claim a universal appeal for the English classics, nor need we presume that they are read merely because of politics or economics.

English literature also has qualities that make it *inherently universal*. Here we may distinguish between two senses of our new term. English literature is inherently universal because it is preternaturally syncretistic and inclusive, modeling itself on and incorporating Greek, Roman, modern continental European, and latterly Asiatic, African and other literatures. Like western literature generally it is also inherently universal because it is concerned with the origin and structure of the universe: the myth of creation, the myth of divinity, the myth of original parents.

The Bible, with its many Western Asiatic origins, along with the classics of Greece and Rome, serve as the principal sources of traditional cosmology and theogony. These sources also provide western literature with the material for its recurrent revival of exotic motifs (Adam and Eve, the life of Christ, the matter of Troy, Roman history). We tend to forget that ancient Hebrew and Christian, Greek and Roman cultures were for the early English writers very exotic. The inclusion of these sources also produced a ground of historical retrospection, one which vastly extended in space and time the island world of early provincial England. The recursion to biblical and classical traditions became a less constant technique as the British Empire gradually attained its scope and influence.

The Bible, an anthology of widely diverse traditions and genres, itself served at the well-head as a standard of eclecticism. Moreover, its rhetoric of type and anti-type, prophecy and fulfillment, wisdom and commentary provided a model for the dialectic of ancient and modern. That much of the biblical story points to a future, as well as to a past and a present, further universalized time and encouraged English writers as diverse as Chaucer (in *Troilus and Creseyde*), Ralegh (in his plan for *The History of the World*) and Blake (in *Jerusalem*) to adopt this comprehensive pattern. As a multiple but also singular book, the Bible again served to centralize literary influence and thereby standardize, or universalize, the tradition.

The Greek and Roman classics were likewise influential in this regard. The early process of canon formation served to concentrate *them* as a

125

source and moreover to provide a model for later canon formation. Again a bipolar system emerged, providing for all European cultures a common tradition of old and new. Though the Bible had its imitators and theorists, the classical principle of imitation, already encoded within the tradition itself, was more explicitly elaborated than the biblical. The imitative theories of Plato and Aristotle operated alongside late classical, medieval, Renaissance and neoclassical practice to provide both a common doctrine for that practice and a model for later theory.

As its adherents are fond of telling us, the word of God is universal, Christ the universal truth and savior. Much the same of course may be said of Allah. Do such claims contribute to Christian and Muslim literatures a principle of universality? And if so, does their universality depend upon belief, or simply upon the unified structure that monotheism lends to a culture? Whatever the answer, the question itself suggests yet another universal aspect of English literature. For Chaucer, Spenser and Milton, Wordsworth, Tennyson and Auden cannot be read apart from the belief system that dominates their work. Though early English writers were universally Christian, later writers either fitfully endorse the faith or implicitly model themselves on those who had once professed it.

The classics, I have argued, exerted a universal influence on later western literature. In the early Renaissance, however, the *idea* of the classical assumed the status of a universal. As the monotheistic faith of Christianity began to wane, this new universal faith came for many to supplant, or at least supplement, their earlier faith. And so by the time of the neoclassical period western cultures defined themselves in terms of yet another centralizing doctrine.

I have spoken of the Bible as the original anthology and of the classics as the original canon of heterogeneous particulars. The Middle Ages were profoundly determined by both biblical and classical examples. But there also arose a new practice and accompanying principle, the *collocation* of contemporary sources, for example in the compilations of the Arthurian materials. In the later Renaissance, collocation gave way to deliberate *syncretism*, whereby classical and biblical traditions were merged with the modern. In the period that followed, syncretism in turn gave way to an enlightened *eclecticism*, whereby meaningful tradition was broadened to include materials that lay outside Europe or beyond the pale of previous cultural definitions.

In enumerating our catalogue of universalizing tendencies we have so far largely overlooked the role of interpretation. Biblical hermeneutics and classical allegoresis played a central role in unifying western literature. Moreover, as the ground of a critical tradition that moralizes and generalizes the canon, the two practices have been especially instrumental in determining the character of such later branches of western culture as English literature. It is not only that later literature became more critically conscious, inherently comparative, deliberately cosmopolitan; its very nature was determined by its absorption and perpetuation of the traditions of hermeneutics and allegoresis.

These broader traditions have early origins. The Bible is itself hermeneutical. Homer himself, I have argued, is an allegorist, or at any rate is soon the subject of allegoresis. These two methods of interpreting texts, once established as standard critical procedure, then began to affect the way in which primary texts themselves were composed. The formation of the Roman Catholic Church, that centralizing institution which determined the nature of so much early literature, depended in large part upon a hermeneutical activity that developed into theology. Vergil centralized himself as much through his allegoresis of Homer as by his allegorization of Rome. Early on the two modes of interpretation were combined. Vergil became the object of both Christian hermeneutical scrutiny and neoplatonic allegoresis. Meanwhile medieval traditions of allegoresis—themselves not wholly independent of Vergil, but more dependent yet on biblical commentary—had spawned a fully allegorical literature that fed into the work of such Renaissance writers as Tasso, Spenser and Du Bartas. The critical theories of Tasso came to have a crucial role in the formulation of later literary projects, notably Milton's. The point here is that all this exegetical, allegorizing and theoretical activity, creative as well as critical, served to abstract, hypostasize and universalize the tradition. Due to its belatedness, English literature modeled itself on other literatures until, by developing its own criticism, it achieved a self-awareness. Once its own critical tradition had matured, English literature was in a position to perpetuate its own classics, with their inherently universalizing tendencies, even in the teeth of the broadly naturalistic movement that followed.

So far I have spoken of general tendencies, the most influential traditions, and critical techniques. Before we turn to individual authors and their works it remains to mention several specific themes which, because they persist as motifs from beginning to end, serve to universalize English literature. We return to the Bible for its primary influence. Not only is the idea of God a universal but also the notion of his singular incarnation. In this doctrine we note both a universalization of the particular and a particularization of the universal. The figure of Christ, compounded of Adam, provides a model for the emergence of the individual, whether in the form of a medieval *genus humanum* (Everyman), a suffering Renaissance stage hero (where classical models reinforce the tendency), or the singular protagonists of eighteenth- and nineteenth-century novels. The medieval and renaissance recovery of classical epic reinforces this centralized image of man, in his struggle with nature and the gods, on his journey through life, in his effort at constructing a world. Other motifs that may be traced to the classics or to the Middle Ages but which blossomed in the Renaissance include the interaction of microcosm and macrocosm; the chain of being; the theory of correspondence; and the themes of time, mutability and immortality. The Enlightenment introduced a whole new vocabulary of philosophical universals, governed by a new goddess named Reason. The Romantic and post-Romantic periods, returning us in a sense to earlier biblical and classical motifs, refurbished those myths of disorder and order bodied forth in the earliest configurations of chaos and creation.

Cutting across the ages are certain political and emotional *topoi* that the rest of the world has come to see as typically western. Political universals include the ideas of empire and democracy. Among the sentimental motifs, love, whether sexualized or sublimated, is probably the most universal. As a theme it dominates the medieval romance, the early lyric, much of stage history, and the novel. Chaucer, Spenser, Shakespeare and Milton are all preoccupied with the theme, as earlier Homer, Vergil, Ovid and Dante had been. Love may take many forms, spiritual or erotic, comic or tragic, mythic or realistic. Ethically it may be wholesomely domestic or marginally adulterous, incestuous, homosexual. As a theme it has an obviously universal appeal, though in such encompassing profusion it also serves to differentiate western from other less romantic, erotic or spiritual cultures.

2

Despite its Christian element and profundity of theme Old English literature is not cosmopolitan. Revived as a subject of study in the nineteenth century and sporadically emulated in the next, it remains in a special class of things admirable but provincial: Scythian gold, Jain belief, Etruscan culture. Overall it is too morose and fatalistic. True, life is a boat adrift on the cold ocean stream, a bundle of bitter breast-cares; it is, however, also a Fair Field of Folk. Langland, through the abstractive powers of Christian allegory, offers a more balanced philosophy, no less serious for the delicacy and delight of his personal vision. But *Piers Plowman* too is somehow restricted and provincial, restricted by the very conventions that enlarge it, provincial in its lack of the contemporary spirit of Italy that Samuel Daniel, in his *Defense of Rhyme* (1603), was later to call "the miracle and phoenix of the world, which wakened up other nations likewise with this desire of glory." The motive of glory may have compelled Daniel's age more than the age of Chaucer, but it is in the latter's work, as in the work of no other medieval English writer, that we feel the invigoration of Italy, which the poet visited and otherwise absorbed through the work of Dante, Petrarch and Boccaccio. Chaucer mastered the medieval forms—from love vision to revival epic, from fabliau to romance—but enlivened this largely French tradition with a native realism and a seasoned irony hitherto lacking in English. In addition to classical and more recent continental models, his own comprehensive genius also contributed to his universality. In this he is like Shakespeare and Fielding.

A different kind of universalization occurs in the drama that we designate mystery and morality. The medieval mystery plays take as their frame the Christian calendar, as their subject, the mysteries of the birth, death and resurrection of Christ. The calendrical feature unites them with the cultural agenda of the universal church, the themes of course with the Bible. Accordingly, we might say, the mystery play is both externally and internally universalized, the latter by virtue of the spectator's identification with Christ and the reinforcement of his personal faith.

The medieval morality play, a somewhat crude form that dramatizes a single idea, elaborating it with the trappings of allegory, nonetheless demonstrates the power of the stage to give us at once a particular image and a universal meaning. The eponymous hero of *Everyman*, a figure both collective and singular, though timeless, is placed before us at a given point along the continuum of universal time (the history of the world from the Creation to the Apocalypse). All the morality plays have universal protagonists and universal plots that set the microcosm of the individual over and against the macrocosm of God's conception. All are concerned with the Fall and Redemption, the Bible's central doctrine. *Everyman* introduces allegorical figures drawn from tradition, such as the Seven Deadly Sins, along with other medieval types, such as Death, the universal scourge, a figure somewhat unbiblical in his fatalistic persistence. Compelling even to the non-western audience, the play nonetheless reflects a problem known to Dante: Christian Sin, like Hell, is easier to represent than Redemption or Paradise.

Auden once remarked that a Christian art is a contradiction in terms. As the representation of Christ in the Old English poem of that name demonstrates, as his depiction elsewhere in medieval literature confirms, the direct artistic embodiment of such spiritual themes is problematic. Perhaps the best solution is a collocation aimed at conflating Christ in his perfection with a secular figure in all his imperfection. It is some such sublimation of Christian within heroic values that Malory accomplishes, some such collocation of motifs that Caxton in his preface to the *Morte Darthur* may have been pointing to when he listed the Nine Worthies, three pagan, three Jewish, three Christian, as the context for understanding Malory's hero, whom he designates as the greatest of all. For Arthur absorbs something from each of the others, the mythic, military and political virtues, respectively, of Hector, Alexander the Great and Julius Caesar; the prophetic, regal and administrative powers of Joshua, David and Judas Maccabeus; the practical strength and romantic appeal of Charlemagne and Godfrey of Boulogne. Though Malory may be drawing on even deeper archetypes, he explicitly conflates the figures of Arthur and Christ, so as to sacralize the heroic and secularize the religious motifs. Arthur has died, "Yet some me say in many parts of England," Malory reports, "that King Arthur is not dead, but had by the will of our Lord Jesu into another place. And men say that he shall come again and he shall win the Holy Cross. Yet I will not say that it shall be so," Malory comments, "but rather I will say, Here in this world he changed his life." Though apparently rejecting a religious for a secular construction of his hero, he in fact has it both ways. If only in the figure of this semi-divine hero (his plot is too loosely episodic), Malory achieves the unity and depth of continental epic tradition, at least successfully enough to scare Milton off his subject.

Only a generation separates the headstrong Ralegh (1552?-1618) from the volatile Donne (1572-1631), but the difference in their treatment of a single *topos* bespeaks the difference between two ages. In Book I of *The History of the World* Ralegh enunciates the standard, with its biblical roots and medieval trunk:

> Man, thus compounded and formed by God, was an abstract or model, or brief story of the universal, . . . endued with the powers and faculties of reason and other abilities, that thereby he might govern and rule the world and all other God's creatures therein. . . . And because in the little frame of man's body there is a representation of the universal, . . . therefore was man called microcosmos, or the little world.

Ralegh goes on to elaborate the principle of correspondences—"the four complexions resemble the four elements . . . the seven ages of man the seven plants"—in which "also is the little world of man compared, and made more like the universal." Discontent with this balanced view of universal and particular, Donne elevates the latter: "It is too little to call man a little world," he says in his fourth meditation. "Except God, man is a diminutive to nothing." In other words, man is *larger* than the world, is himself a universe. Likewise man is *different* from the world: "For as the whole world hath nothing to which something in man doth not answer, so hath man many pieces of which the whole world hath no representation." Like a universal, capable of transcending the world, he does so through the exercise of mind:

130

> I their creator am in a close prison, in a sick bed, anywhere and any one
> of my creatures, my thoughts, is with the sun, and beyond the sun,
> overtakes the sun, and overgoes the sun in one pace, one step,
> everywhere.

Man through his imagination is therefore a rival creator, the particulars of his own experience rivaling in importance the universals of theology. With a new cosmology, a new science, and a new ethics of inward virtue taking shape around him, Donne postulates a new universe. He and his lover stand at its center ("The Sun Rising"), their eyes both perceiving and containing this new world ("The Canonization"). His poetry, then, is both a reflection of the universe and a universe itself. We are well on the way to Mallarmé. Situated half a generation between Ralegh and Donne is Shakespeare (1564-1616). Less consistent than either of theirs, his view is sometimes harmonious, sometimes discordant, sometimes comic, sometimes tragic. His heroes are often tragic precisely because they mistake their own universe for the universe at large.

The Renaissance signals not the rebirth of an old universe but the birth of a new one. In this the Bible and the classics serve as midwives. Translation is a most important instrument not only for making texts available but also for showing how to bring forth new from old. The Bible, done into English half a dozen times in the period, is fresh and exciting, though by itself not enough for inspiration. As Petrarch had reinvented Rome and through Dante discovered a voice, so Wyatt, Surrey and Sidney reinvent Petrarch, in works that are neither translations nor original poems but something new and syncretistic. Versions of the classics are called for, and they in turn afford more models of how to combine the old with the new.

Sidney, no less than Golding, Chapman and Campion, is one of the great creative translators of the period. Though he sometimes redoes a foreign text into English, it is rather his wholesale transportation of exotic genres into the mainstream of English literature that constitutes his principle contribution. The pastoral romance he naturalizes in *Arcadia*, the sonnet sequence in *Astrophil and Stella*. As if this were not enough, he then syncretizes Plato, Aristotle and Horace, along with his own views, to offer us the first universal theory of poetry in English. Like the world of More's *Utopia*, all the worlds that Sidney creates are superior to this one, hierarchical, holistic, serene. In accord with classical universal theory all science and art are directed toward *architechtonike*, "the mistress knowledge," a goal both breathtakingly ambitious and practical, one that embraces the self, ethics and politics. Poetry itself for Sidney is universal, that is, all-inclusive, capable of imparting "all knowledge, logic, rhetoric, philosophy natural and moral." In an eclectic gesture he gathers together the views not only of the classical theorists but of Bembo, Scaligero, Clauserus, Landino and "the poets themselves." Poetry, he says, "is so universal that no learned nation doth despise it." It belongs, in other words, to the world at large.

Poetically Sidney closes his "Defense" by evoking time, death and love, three prominent universal themes that Shakespeare in his *Sonnets* also associates with poetry. A century earlier Leonardo too had linked them:

> O time, thou that consumest all things! O envious age, thou destroyest all things and devourest all things with the hard teeth of the years, little by little in slow death! Helen, when she looked in her mirror and saw the withered wrinkles which old age had made in her face, wept, and wondered to herself why ever she had twice been carried away.

Though time and death are poignant, and just as universal, they are not so interesting as love. In the classical age Helen had stood as its adequate symbol. Some in the Renaissance tried to revive her. Significantly, Leonardo himself turns to other models, male as well as female, some more sinister, some more mysterious than Helen. A proliferation of types, one that will outstrip classical mythology, is under way. In short, we are witnessing a new theogony, one to which Spenser, Shakespeare and Milton, along with the sonneteers and divines, all contribute.

As Shakespeare had indicated early on, love was to be a major theme. For the most part he is *romantic*, though sometimes disillusioned, sometimes tragically so. Among his works of greatest universal appeal are *Romeo and Juliet, Antony and Cleopatra* and *The Tempest* or, in a lighter vein, *A Midsummer Night's Dream, As You Like It* and *Much Ado About Nothing*. Milton in this regard is closer to Molière and the novel, for his theme is *domestic* love. Milton was not romantically inclined. As a fellow universal writer, however, he shared Shakespeare's generalizing power, his eclecticism and, surprisingly, his common touch. More of Milton later.

What now of Spenser? After Valmiki, Ovid and Dante, after the passionate poets of romance and *amour courtois*, Spenser may be the greatest poet of love. In fact he may surpass them all. More credible than Dante, more ethical than Ovid, more philosophical than the writers of romance, he also subsumes many of their virtues: Dante's spirituality, Ovid's variety, Ariosto's humor. He succeeds despite a decision to invent his own system. On the other hand, his manifold sources and multiple plots give his allegory more particularity to work with than any single tradition or story would have afforded him.

Spenser of course is far more than a poet of love. In his faerie land he has posited a whole world of imagination. It is not, he insists, another world but this world. In other words, it is not fantastic, it is real. This causes a problem for the modern reader who regards as real what can be shown in a photograph. As in Plato, our world is merely a shadow of that ideal world which Spenser delineates, filling it with all the truth and value that he knows of. Who is the faerie queene? Certainly not Elizabeth, who recognized the fact by rewarding Spenser with only fifty pounds a year. A more glorious figure, in her Authurian avatar she is called Gloriana, the king's consort—which again helps us understand why Milton chose another subject. Unlike Eve, who is merely a part of it, the faerie queene comprehends the world, absorbing many of the classical and Christian goddesses and the allegorical figures (Wisdom, Nature, Mutability) with whom Spenser had familiarized himself.

Spenser did not know all there is to know about women, and his poem is less than complete. He planned to continue it to twice its length but died at forty-nine. (Like Shakespeare's, his work is the work of a young man.) Nonetheless, the poem's universality—its inclusiveness, its power of abstraction, its general ethical validity—will probably never be equaled. In this Dante is Spenser's only rival. At certain moments we feel him to be a greater poet even than Vergil. He is a paragon of enlightened self-knowledge and civility. By comparison Milton seems curmudgeonly.

Any discussion of the universal element in sixteenth-century English literature would be incomplete without Marlowe. *Dr. Faustus* stands head and shoulders above his other work, as it does above other attempts to grasp the cultural and philosophical problem of the age. Because that problem has now become universal, Marlowe's play has acquired a universal appeal comparable to that of Eliot's *Waste Land*. Both describe man as caught between traditional and modern worlds. For Marlowe's contemporaries Faustus may be said to stand for all who had left the Roman church. More generally he may stand for anyone who has lapsed from faith. For Marlowe's contemporaries he may be said to stand for those who had dabbled in science, or for those who had come to realize that the universe was no longer hierarchical. Like Donne, Faustus has seen that man is godlike but still subject to God's damnation. More generally again, he stands for those who have seen that man must create the world anew, that the individual must depend upon himself, and that the undertaking is perilous.

Marlowe's (and later Goethe's) Faust, like Shakespeare's Falstaff and Hamlet, Cervantes' Sancho and Don Quixote, Byron's and Mozart's Don Juan, are modern universal myths which, like the figure of Everyman, depend upon the prototypes of Adam and Christ. In their suffering, Faust, Hamlet and Juan all take on a Christ-like burden for the modern reader who has turned for illumination from the Bible to secular literature. Like the figure of Arthur, their universal appeal may in part be attributed to the persistence of an archetype. At the end of the Renaissance Milton makes this archetype explicit by naming one of his heroes Adam, the other Christ.

None of our Renaissance authors calls his hero Everyman, and yet Faustus, Hamlet, Adam and Christ are clearly so representative. Though transparently Christian in his ethics, Shakespeare remains secular in expression, thereby perhaps increasing his universal appeal. Here his variety is also a factor. For just as each age has had its different Shakespeare, so various cultures choose their favorite plays. *Hamlet* is the exception that proves the rule, for it has enjoyed a universal popularity, both historically and geographically, and the reason is not far to seek. Hamlet the character, like *Hamlet* the play, is full of contradictions. For Hamlet everything is problematic: one's relations with the spirit world; with one's family and colleagues; with one's significant other — to say nothing of one's self. Nor are Hamlet's resourceful solutions to these problems satisfactory. If the situation that Shakespeare describes here were not universally perceived to be that of man in general, one doubts that the play would be so popular.

Ben Jonson is sometimes said to have what Shakespeare lacks: erudition, decorum, an ethical realism. For those who like morality there is much edification in the epigrams, the satirical verse, the popular plays and the masques. *Volpone* in certain ways is also universal — in its beast-fable framework, its egoistic theme, its comic motifs that absorb classical precedent. What Jonson, however, demonstrates is that one can be universal but not especially appealing. For poetry is not merely a record of sound procedures and judgment. It must also have the passion, spirit and inspiration that we associate with Shakespeare.

Shakespeare's plays together may be regarded as constituting a world, but it is Milton who wrote the universal Renaissance epic. So unlike his Roman predecessors in the form—Lucretius, Vergil, Ovid—Milton does not much resemble contemporary universalists either. Bacon had promulgated the principles, or at least certain procedures, on which our now universal scientific knowledge is based. Hobbes had begun a similar process in the realm of political theory. Descartes was engaged in a universal philosophical project. By contrast Milton is antediluvian: mythical, biblical, theological. In his double perspective he resembles Thomas Browne, who extends the progression that we witnessed from Ralegh to Donne: "Whilst I study to find out how I am a microcosm or little world, I find myself something more than great." Browne predicts both Milton's inwardness and his capaciousness. "The world that I regard is myself," he says; and again: "There is all Africa and her prodigies in us." Like Browne, Milton is both internally and externally universal. And in matters of authority he shares Browne's independent spirit: "I borrow not the rules of my religion," the physician asserts, "from Rome or Geneva but the dictates of my own reason."

For his epic Milton seeks an adversative biblical myth as fatalistic as Homer's Fall of Troy and finds it in the Fall of Man. The redemptive counterpart to the return of Odysseus he finds in Christ's resistance to the force that had made Adam fall. As Homeric hermeneutics and biblical allegoresis it is impeccable, as is everything else in Milton's art. We must only swallow the pills of original sin and the crucifixion to abort our misery and enter into the heaven of Milton's vision. The mystery lies in how those who cannot do so still admire him. Here he stands with Dante as universal in spite of himself.

Enormously cosmopolitan in one sense, Milton, like Ezra Pound, is provincial in the schoolmaster's zeal with which he turns his mind into a biblical and classical encyclopedia, a dictionary of a dozen languages, a pamphleteering machine. Except to marry a seventeen-year-old girl, whom he then ignores, he never stops reading—until, that is, he reaches the Homeric goal of blindness. For Milton himself is a vast void, a rewind of history to the point of Hesiodic Chaos, a fast-forward to Pater's dissolve into inner sensation. It is in this sense that Milton is most universal: he includes all possibilities. But he himself is not one of them. For he has systematically reimagined himself: as Adam and Eve, as Satan, as God. This is his central work, his central panel. Christ and Samson are pendentives. He does bear relation to the world, for he was very much of it, and in his time. But his relation to it, as Blake saw, was that of a visionary Homer, whose voice Milton imitates more directly in his prose than in his verse:

> Methinks I see in my mind a noble and puissant nation rousing herself like a strong man after sleep, and shaking her invincible locks: methinks I see her as an eagle mewing her mighty youth, and kindling her undazzled eyes at the full midday beam; purging and unscaling her long-abused sight at the fountain itself of heavenly radiance; while the whole noise of timorous and flocking birds, with those also that love the twilight, flutter about, amazed at what she means, and in their envious gabble would prognosticate a year of sects and schisms.

Douglas Bush regarded Milton as the second of English poets, standing next to Shakespeare's throne. In fact, Milton is either the first or the fourth of English poets, depending upon one's attitude to life. If one believes what Milton believed, then Milton is supreme. But if one thinks that Chaucer, Spenser and Shakespeare have taught us how to live, then Milton follows. Wherever evangelical Christianity takes root, there Milton thrives.

Milton's principal followers in the long poem are Blake, Wordsworth and Byron. Each has an original program for further universalizing Milton.

Blake creates a "Universal Man" who absorbs the figures of Adam and Christ but supplants God and supercedes the classical divinities, whom Blake scorns. This "Human Form divine" encompasses the cosmos and comprehends its various stages of development, thereby incorporating history. Among Blake's goals are "universal Brotherhood" and "universal Poetic Genius," by which he means the investment of every man with imagination. ("All," he says, "are alike in the poetic genius.")

Wordsworth discovers his universal principles in nature and his own mind. *The Prelude*, which he subtitles "Growth of a Poet's Mind," imitates Milton's inner voice, narrowing the subject of *Paradise Lost* to the development of the poet's own conception of the cosmos. In this democratization of the universe Wordsworth follows Blake and predicts Whitman. Like Blake, he believes that his own mind is capable of transforming nature. The microcosm—to use our earlier term—absorbs the macrocosm, if not half creating it. In this process of natural research, says the poet, "I looked for universal things" (*Prelude*, III, 109). In lines that follow directly thereon Wordsworth reinvents such universals as "that first paradise," "highest truth" and "Divinity itself."

Byron in *Don Juan* offers a comic reduction of The Fall of Man, repeating its pattern with each subsequent episode. Unlike Adam, who falls into sinfulness, Juan merely falls into experience. Like Byron's poem, and like life itself, experience is open-ended. The unprecedented form of *Don Juan* adumbrates the modern conception of the universe as expanding, organic and incomplete. Byron's hero, like Goethe's Faust a modern mythic figure, is independent of biblical and classical models, though he gathers up and combines Adamic and Odyssean qualities. Juan, again like Goethe's Faust, expresses both the universal and the autobiographical, the latter mode becoming itself increasingly universal as the nineteenth century progresses. Like *The Prelude*, *Don Juan* is related to the *Bildungsroman*. Like Blake's work, Bryon's moves toward a geographical universality, deliberately circling Europe in its extant seventeen cantos, presumably to set off farther afield in its remaining, projected eighty-three. Despite his adamant modernity, Byron, like both Blake and Wordsworth, revives and continues the high tradition of the long poem, absorbing such romantic models as Ariosto, disregarded by his peers. Even in its present form *Don Juan* is a consummate work.

In considering the universal element in nineteenth-century Romantic England, we might glance briefly at continental Europe. Unlike Byron, hell-bent in his escape from English insularity, Goethe embraced, indeed defined German culture, in a work that Schiller described as "the poem peculiar to Germans," a phrase that we could modify to read "the poem universal to Germans." For Goethe is one of the few western writers successfully to design and execute a work of national culture—one thinks of Vergil, Camoens and the Shakespeare of the Henriad as other examples. Like the first, and unlike the later two, Goethe's work also achieved what Schlegel, speaking of the Frühromantiker, whose work followed that of Goethe, described as *"eine progressive Universal-poesie."* Goethe, in other words, not only epitomizes German culture, he projects as well a vision of world culture. It is he, we recall, who originates our conception of *Weltliteratur*, or universal literature. At the middle of the nineteenth century Baudelaire introduces another sense of the universal potential of literature when he defines the poet as *"un traducteur, un déchriffreur"* (a translator, a decoder) who draws upon *"l'inépuisable fonds de l'universelle analogie"* (the inexhaustible stock of universal analogy).

Much of what is universal in English—or more broadly, western—literature, however, develops without a definition of universality and without agreement that universality is itself desirable. Paradoxically, just at the point when western letters take their turn toward particularity—personal experience and realistic representation, universality becomes a topic of discussion. A few highlights in the modern history of the notion may be helpful.

In the sixteenth and seventeenth centuries writers revive the classics of Greece and Rome as models for imitation. Gradually an attendant interest develops in the historical circumstances under which those works had been produced. This in turn leads to definition of the universals that underlie works of all historical periods and cultures. Here science and rational philosophy encourage the formulation of a literary theory of universality that embraces values such as nature, reason and truth, which replace such earlier universals as Adam, Christ and God. In the later seventeenth and eighteenth centuries a canon is established: Homer, Vergil and Ovid from the world of Greece and Rome; Chaucer, Shakespeare and Milton from English literary history. These figures are said to express "nature," or "general nature," as in Johnson's famous pronouncement.

In the later eighteenth century critics begin to defend works that *depart* from the classics. The battle between ancients and moderns continues, with the latter consistently gaining ground. At this point a concomitant shift occurs: from concern with rules to concern with the universal, newly regarded as the defining characteristic of art and as a prescriptive principle. The imitation of models is rejected in favor of the representation of actuality. Greater attention is directed to the creative

137

process, to the poet's imagination, to his "genius." The last of these, regarded as a power that appeals to all men, gradually gains the status of a universal. Emphasis begins to shift toward the *audience* of the work of art. The concept of "general humanity," of the "natural" human being (as in Rousseau), his response to the work of art are all emphasized. Poet and reader, it is felt, share a universal humanity. In these shifts from ancient to modern, from nature to art, from poetry to the mind of the poet to his responsive auditor a new acceptation of "universal" has evolved. For it is no longer the genres, themes or moral lessons of poetry that are so considered, it is that which is most essential, individual, ineluctable.

Let us return now in our review of English literature to those neoclassical English critics who had first defined the universal. In "An Essay of Dramatic Poesy" (1668) Dryden has one of his interlocutors pronounce: "A thing well said will be wit in all languages; and though it may lose something in the translation, yet to him who reads it in the original, 'tis still the same . . . ." The essence of a text, in other words is universal, its verbal expression accidental. Dryden, we might note, is also preparing the way for the use of translation as the foundation for a world literature. Like Pope, and unlike other major poets, he devotes much of his career to translating the classics. But Dryden is also a defender of the modern, a newly emergent universal value. Unlike Johnson, who unfavorably compares Shakespeare with classical models, Dryden advocates the Bard's modernity. Like Johnson, he also stresses Shakespeare's inclusiveness: "He was the man who of all modern, and perhaps ancient poets had the largest and most comprehensive soul." Paradoxically, Dryden's original productions in verse and poetic drama, though they reinforce his respect for the modern, represent a retreat from his critical advocacy of universality. For unlike the cosmological, comprehensive design that we find in Milton, the work of his first major follower is much smaller in scale, more particular in detail.

In this Dryden's work parallels the development of bourgeois expression, such as that of his contemporary John Bunyan, who in *The Pilgrim's Progress* reduces the macrocosm of biblical allegory to the microcosm of the individual Christian's experience. An emphasis upon the individual and his experience is of course a leading feature of the novel, the most original form to arise in the period, and the one practiced by many of the leading prose writers of the next century: Defoe, Richardson, Fielding, Sterne and Austen. It represents, among other things, such universal aspects of experience as *Erziehung* (education) and *Entwicklung* (development), to use the German terms which name two of its sub-types.

In the eighteenth century the term "universal" begins to be used explicitly as a measure of worth. Addison, for example, says of *Paradise*

Lost that "The great moral which reigns in Milton is the most universal and the most useful that can be imagined," a comment that Johnson endorses: "It is justly remarked by Addison that this poem has, by the nature of its subject, the advantage above all others, that it is universally and perpetually interesting." By "interesting" Johnson means "in our interest to know," as his next sentence makes clear: "All mankind will, through all ages, bear the same relation to Adam and to Eve, and must partake of that good and evil which extend to themselves." For both Johnson and Addison universality denotes that which all Christians accept as universally true. Johnson, that is to say, has retreated from the enlargement of the term which he and Dryden in their criticism of Shakespeare had undertaken.

Nor do all eighteenth-century writers whole-heartedly endorse the new principle. More skeptical than Johnson, Swift is ambivalent about the value of universality, especially when it promotes a scientific utopianism. In Part III of *Gulliver's Travels,* for example, he treats with irony his protagonist's enthusiastic hopes for the discovery of universal formulas and remedies, including "the universal medicine," a formula for eternal life. Elsewhere Swift ridicules the idea of a universal language, of a universal monarch, the longing for immortality merely because it *is* universal. Though he includes mathematics in his ideal curriculum, he excludes those hard sciences that are based upon universal laws. In *The Tale of a Tub* he rejects the substitution of microcosm for macrocosm: "For what man, in the natural state or course of thinking, did ever conceive it in his power to reduce the notions of all mankind exactly to the same length, and breadth, and height of his own?"

At the same time, if only implicitly, *Gulliver's Travels* endorses the principle of universality, perhaps more strongly than any other work since More's *Utopia.* Its geographical range, its typology of human vice and virtue, its conception of *l'homme moyen sensuel* all imply the principle. Likewise, the world-wide reception of the book by readers young and old attests to its universal appeal. In fact Swift is one of the first modern western writers—Shakespeare is another—to achieve a universality without relying explicitly on classical or Christian values. Dr. Johnson's remark that once you have grasped the principle of big people and little people you have the essence of the book identifies the central device of Parts I and II but fails to recognize the sources of its universal fascination. Ironically, it is precisely here that Swift appeals to "general nature," whether it be our fantasies of supremacy or our common infantile experience. Like those critics who regard as too simple Cervantes' scheme of skinny idealist and fat realist, Johnson is either blind to Swift's genius or jealous of it. For whereas *Rasselas* is universal in its philosophical generalizations, *Gulliver's Travels* is universal in its

139

appeal: everyone is interested in animals who can talk.

Alexander Pope may be taken as a turning point in the development of English literature. In one sense he is all general principle, in another sense all personal experience. Two of his major works, the *Essay on Criticism* and the *Essay on Man* are fundamentally concerned with universals. "First follow Nature," says the poet,

> Unerring Nature, still divinely bright,
> One clear, unchanged, and universal light . . .

Pope's definition of the central neoclassical principle suggests its *geographical* universality. His definition of wit, on the other hand, suggests Nature's *historical* universality:

> True wit is Nature to advantage dressed,
> What oft was thought, but ne'er so well expressed.

An Essay on Man, the most ambitious cosmological poem since Milton, begins with the topic, "*Of the Nature and State of Man, With Respect to the Universe*," thereby reviving the motif of the microcosm and macrocosm that has often figured in works of universal imagination. In this regard Pope follows the progressive emphasis upon the little world observed in Ralegh, Donne and Browne:

> Know then thyself, presume not God to scan;
> The proper study of mankind is Man.

If the *Essay on Criticism* enunciates universal critical principles, the *Essay on Man* enunciates universal principles of human nature, principles culled in part no doubt from Pope's massive labor of translating Homer and editing Shakespeare, those poets of general nature. That Pope is not only a poet of universal light is revealed in *The Dunciad*, whose final line, "And Universal Darkness buries All," expresses another, equally important principle. "All," another word for the cosmos, taken together with "Universal Darkness" in the sense of extinction, may be read as prefiguring the poet's own death (*Après moi, le déluge*). If so, the experiential and the universal here combine in a single conclusion. Pope's *Paradise Regain'd* (his *Essay on Man*) might be said, then, to precede his *Paradise Lost* (*The Dunciad*), the last line quoted perhaps even echoing the fate of the blind Samson, buried, we recall, under the weight of the Philistine temple.

Nineteenth-century English literature is preeminently a literature of personal experience: lyric poetry, spiritual autobiography, the personal essay, the novel. It particularizes human affairs but is not without its ideals. One such ideal is the universal. Shelley, dragging wholesale into his *Defence of Poetry* the perennial neoclassical values, defines poetry in terms of "its eternal truth," calling it "the creation of actions according to

140

the unchangeable forms of human nature." The poem, he says, by contrast to the story—which is "partial, and applies only to a definite period of time, and a certain combination of events which can never again recur"—"is universal, and contains within itself the germ of a relation to whatever motives or actions have place in the possible varieties of human nature." The universal, that is to say, is holistic, eternal and recurrent. For a more original, philosophical definition we must turn to Coleridge, who reconfigures the classical or neoclassical terms into an ascending order (*individual, special, general, universal*), which he then synthesizes in the manner of the German idealists. Like the Goethe whom we quoted earlier, Coleridge finds in *symbol* the proper instrument for assimilating one to another: "A Symbol," as he defines it then, "is characterized by a translucence of the Specil in the Individual or of the General in the Especial or of the Universal in the General." Coleridge's series of linked terms produces a generality dependent upon particularity. It is also clear that universality has become a permanent Romantic desideratum.

To the Victorians, with their extensive empire and ever-expanding popular audience, the term "universal" comes to acquire a more practical meaning. In this period England achieves universal literacy, universal communication (by rail, telegraph, newspaper, circulating book). For the first time, not only in England but throughout the empire and the former colonies, one can begin to speak of a universal audience for English literature. Furthermore, in this period English develops into a universal language (by the end of the next century the non-native-speaking audience will surpass in size the native-speaking).

"May we not call Shakspeare the still more melodious Priest of a *true* Catholicism, the 'Universal Church' of the Future and of all times?" asks Carlyle, in whose prescient imagination English literature begins to assume its modern status as a quasi-religious institution. Asking us rhetorically to choose between the Indian empire and Shakespeare, Carlyle answers, "We cannot do without Shakspeare! Indian Empire will go, at any rate, some day; but this Shakspeare does not go, he lasts forever with us." Elsewhere, like Johnson, he calls the Bard both "universal and perennial." Other major Victorians evoke the same usage, as they register and encourage the age's expansive catholicity. Ruskin admires the Gothic for its universality and posits a "universal law" in defense of its imperfections. Like Carlyle, he is merely extending the neoclassical acceptation of the term. Likewise Arnold, when he finds in both Greek and Hebrew cultures a "feeling after the universal order." But when the latter also finds in the French Revolution an appeal to "an order of ideas which are universal, certain, permanent," he has ventured onto new ground. For these ideas, like the laws of mathematics ("to count by tens is the easiest way of counting," he says) have a force of truth that goes beyond the mere tradition of a literary canon. The principle of reason, "its prescriptions" enforced by a new political order, are, says Arnold, "absolute, unchanging, of universal validity." Significantly, the universal has now been associated with a modern rather than ancient set of ideas (however much reason—to say nothing of democracy—may owe to the classical world). The future universal order, Arnold implies, will be ideological.

As the last quarter of the nineteenth century began, Pater, in *The Renaissance*, his epoch-making fusion of the historical past and the personal present, defined the problem—his own and the century's—in terms of Winckelmann's:

> For him the problem came to be:—Can the blitheness and universality of the antique ideal be communicated to artistic productions, which shall contain the fulness of experience of the modern world?

It is a problem that exercises Tennyson, Browning, Arnold and the lesser luminaries of the esthetic movement. Browning solves it by amalgamating features of Shakespearean soliloquy, modern historiography and the contemporary novel into a new form, the dramatic monologue.

The greatest Victorian novelists seek other means to universalize their stories, often treating an individual life with such intensity as to enlarge it into an emblem *sub specie aeternitatis*. Dickens, through the voice of Pip, gives us a clue to this procedure:

> That was a memorable day to be, for it made great changes in me. But it was the same with any life. Imagine one selected day struck out of it, and think how different its course would have been. Pause you who read this, and think for a moment of the long chain of iron or gold, of thorns or flowers, that would never have bound you, but for the formation of the first link on one memorable day.

With equal economy the novelist explores those matters most plangent to reader, character and author alike, as when Miss Havisham, Pip tells us, "asked me such questions as what I had learnt and what I was going to be." The changes rung on the formula are legion: "I put my light out, and crept into bed," says Pip in London; "and it was an uneasy bed now, and I never slept the old sound sleep in it any more." Modeling his upon Milton's mythical account of Adam's encounter with Satan, Dickens intimates a reader closing Pip's tale, putting out the light and creeping serpent-like into bed, where, instead of falling into innocent sleep he falls into his own uneasy experience.

Tennyson, employing a strategy of generalization, in a *post facto* critical gloss similarly universalizes *In Memoriam*: "The 'I,' he says of the poem's voice, "is not the author speaking of himself, but the voice of the human race speaking thro' him." In the poem itself Tennyson generalizes perhaps a little too grandly for our present taste, but some such principle of universalization must be inherent in the work, otherwise how account for its world-wide popularity? Beyond Tennyson, the esthetic movement's emphasis upon art extends the Romantic universalization of man so as to define him in terms of a formal activity equal in discipline to those of science, religion and philosophy. Simultaneously, the Romantic particularization of experience, which I shall take up in my final essay, begins to create a problem for the would-be English universalist.

Also partly responsible for his difficulties may be the coming of age of Irish and American literature. For the best — or at least the most universalizing—twentieth-century writers of English are not English. Yeats, Joyce and Beckett, though Irish, are also international, not only by virtue of their geographical dislocations but also by a conscious linguistic design, Yeats mastering an alien tradition of English poetry, Beckett alternating English with French, Joyce at last creating for himself a dubious international language. The Americans, James, Pound and Eliot, are equally dislocated, though two of them, along with Yeats, more or less successfully assume the mantle of English tradition. When we seek for native English writers to measure against the Irish and the American we are left with the likes of Hardy, Lawrence and Auden. Though all substantial figures, none is so imposing, at least in the role of universalist. Hardy and Lawrence express their universality the new way, through a defiant localism which says that we all have a place of origin—if Lawrence too is vagrant. Complementing the English immigration of James and Eliot, Auden emigrates to America. All three are cosmopolitan, but the work of the Americans has greater universal appeal than Auden's, as does the work of Hardy and Lawrence for that matter. In a category apart, Joseph Conrad, Polish by birth but writing in a language acquired as an adult, masters the medium and contributes his cosmopolitan, if not precisely universal, perspective. Perhaps he holds the key for the non-native speaker who would enter and transform the tradition of English literature.

7

Experience in Late Modern British Literature

I have often expressed my regret that Aristotle did not discuss the relation between poetic or universal meaning and particular meaning.

—Northrop Frye

Sage ich ein *einzelnes Ding*, so sage ich es vielmehr ebenso als ganz *allgemeines,* denn alle sind ein einzelnes Ding; und gleichfalls *dieses* Ding is alles, was man will.

—Hegel

[S]trictly considered, what is all knowledge . . . but recorded Experience and a product of History; of which, therefore, Reasoning and Belief, no less than Action and Passion, are essential materials?

—Carlyle

Though gnomic elements abound, the western wisdom tradition, unlike the Vedic or Confucian, is fundamentally experiential. The Bible, no less than the Odyssey, tells a story. Both texts concern ordinary men, godlike men and a God or gods. Of the latter, says Jenny Strauss Clay, speaking of them as they appear in the Homeric Hymns, "Their actions, prerogatives and epiphanies can be called timeless—not, however, in the sense that they are beyond or outside time, but insofar as their unique manifestations are indistinguishable from their eternal ones." We might recast the debate between particular and universal to include a middle term, the hero or demi-god, one that is both unique and eternal, both concrete and abstract, both special and general, both particular and universal. "Tell me, Muse," Homer begins, in Lattimore's version,

> of the man of many ways, who was driven
> far journeys, after he had sacked Troy's sacred citadel.
> Many were they whose cities he saw, whose minds he learned of,
> many the pains he suffered in his spirit on the wide sea . . . .

Though "*andra,*" the first word of his original text, may indicate a human subject, Homer's ritual narrative in fact mediates between man and god, a process in which the "godlike" Odysseus is central. His sacking of Troy's sacred citadel predicts the historical overthrow of a sacred, hierarchical, singular order by a secular, democratic, multiple order. Odysseus is a man not of one path but many. Elsewhere called "*polymetis,*" of many minds, he is here called "*polytropon,*" of many turns. Western literature begins on the road, away from home (in Troy), or on a winding way back (to Greece). Odysseus is a man of many experiences, or of much Experience, to appropriate the term that Locke inscribes on his *tabula rasa* and defines as consisting of sensations ("Many were they whose cities he saw"), that Kant will reformulate as a mental construct ("many . . . whose minds he learned of"). His journey not chosen but fated, Odysseus is "driven" (*"fato profugus,"* as Vergil will say of Aeneas). Driven off course, *"planchthe"* (from a verb that means to seduce or lead astray), he is forced into "far journeys." Homer is being metaphorical as well as literal: the man of many minds travels in many ways. Like Adam, he is our first Man of Experience, falling first from unity into duplicity, thence into multiplicity.

He suffers real physical pains, *"algea,"* but through his *"thymos,"* his spirit, they become his experience of the wide sea. Thus *actual experience* is transmuted into *philosophical Experience*, or, we might say more simply, *sense experience* eventuates in *accumulated experience*. "Of many people he saw the cities," says Homer literally, thereby defining this hero of his geographical epic as the original universalist. The mention of "cities," though, is curious, for we do not recall from the narrative of his wanderings that Odysseus visited many. Perhaps again Homer is being metaphorical: "cities" stand for the different civilizations that Odysseus experiences.

So, his hero is a wanderer—though less by inclination than by happenstance. In Books 9-12 Odysseus offers us and the Phaeacians an account of his wanderings. The Odyssey is the first western narrative that includes within it another narrative, a tale which strikes us on reflection as both unreliable (a man with one eye in the midst of his forehead?) and deliberately allegorical (Circe changes Odysseus' lustful companions into swine). Odysseus, as we know from other contradictory tales that he tells about himself, is a notorious fabricator. Is Homer not also a fabricator, and is not Odysseus' experience somehow related to Homer's? In an earlier essay I have suggested that Homer, like Odysseus, is composing a deliberate allegory. Dorothy Sayers, whom I quote there, defines the mode as "the interpretation of experience by means of images." Is the Odyssey's allegory, then, like Odysseus' own, a proof that the Odyssey is experiential? Or is all literature experiential? How *are* we to limit, that is, define, experience?

At any rate, as we have seen, Homer is hardly naïve. Odysseus' mendacious accounts of himself in Ithaca (see Books 13-16) ask us to consider whether stories are shaped by experience or experience by stories. As he brings his own story to its moral conclusion (in Books 17-24), Homer makes the implicit claim that, far from being the enemy of truth or knowledge, his fiction is their vehicle. With these points none could have been in more substantial agreement than Vergil, who in one sense merely recapitulates and thereby reinforces what Homer has said and done.

For in his Aeneas, Vergil embodies the experience not only of Odysseus but of Hector, Achilles, Paris and others; the experience not only of Troy but of Rome. He compounds in that figure not only personal and fictional but also historical and universal experience. As the source of all their experience he returns his audience to the Fall of Troy, much as Moses had returned his audience to the source of theirs in the Fall of Man. Both allegories culminate in tears, as visualized in Masaccio's "Expulsion of Adam and Eve" or in Vergil's *"lacrimae rerum."* Both images are emblems of *accumulated experience.*

In the thirteen hundred years between Vergil's Aeneid and Dante's Comedy the literature of experience undergoes little development. The first person presence in late classical narrative vanishes, only to be revived by the Florentine, whose very different sort of sacred epic nonetheless, like the classical, offers us a collective experience of history within a deliberate allegorical program. No less than Odysseus, Dante's hero—himself—is an Everyman figure. In his adventures, Auerbach remarks, "Human destiny and the history of the world became once more an object of direct and compelling experience, for in the great drama of salvation every man is present, acting and suffering; he is directly involved in everything that has happened and that happens each day."

"Everything that has happened"—for the historian, at least, a demanding subject. As Carlyle, a student of Experience and a formidable historian, remarks: "The most gifted man can observe, still more can record, only the series of his own impressions: his observation, therefore, to say nothing of its other imperfections, must be successive, while the things done were *simultaneous;* the things done were not a series but a group." At the beginning of the sixteenth century Dante's great successor Ariosto will address this problem in fiction by interlacing his episodes so as to make them occur simultaneously. Meanwhile, his overarching conception liberates us from time and space, those coordinates of Kantian Experience, much as Dante's cosmology had, based as it was on the conception of God. It will remain, however, for the later nineteenth century to define afresh the relation between experience and its ultimate concept, history, in a theory that I shall delay taking up in detail and here merely epitomize instead by quoting Emerson: "This human mind wrote history, and this must read it. The sphinx must solve her own riddle. If the whole of history is in one man, it is all to be explained from individual experience." When we have finished with Romanticism and drawn some conclusions as to how its theory of history may have been affected by the philosophical Idealism set in motion by Kant, we shall be in a better position to say what must be said about experience and its relationship to history, that is, *individual experience* and its relationship to *collective experience*.

To return to Dante then: in one sense, and in keeping with Auerbach's observation, he makes of something personal, something historical; of his own particularity, something universal—just as he transforms the actual Beatrice into the eternal Maria. In so doing he predicts the later grounding of western culture in individual experience. But in another sense he retains the older view, out of Aristotle by way of Aquinas, that the particular (Man) is but a part of the universal (God), that "unity," as he tells us in the De Monarchia, is "the ground of goodness and multiplicity the ground of evil." "We can see," he later adds, "that to sin is to despair and abandon unity for multiplicity." Homer, we recall, having summarized the multiplicity of Odysseus' experience and praised his struggle to save not only his own life but the lives of his companions, turns immediately to summarize *their* tale of Original Sin: "Even so he could not save his companions, hard though / he strove to; they were destroyed by their own wild recklessness, / fools, who devoured the oxen of Helios, the Sun God, and he took away the day of their homecoming." Dante knew Homer only through Vergil and other intermediaries, but he doubtless saw the parallel with Christian doctrine. A man of many paths himself, wandering in a dark wood, he sought the straight and narrow, if he too, driven by his own sin, was forced to divagate.

Within three centuries the Italian Renaissance had blossomed into a fullness of self-expression and individual consciousness that even Dante could not have foreseen. "I hold myself bound, as best I can," says Castiglione, "to bend all my efforts to preserve this bright memory from human forgetfulness and, through my writing, to make it live for posterity." Dante, though as intensely aware of the future as he was of the past, could hardly have imagined that either depended solely upon himself. In Castiglione's sentence something new has entered western consciousness: the suggestion that we write to preserve, yea, to create, our experience. In one stroke of the pen our experience, paradoxically, has come to seem both dependent upon and yet more important than our writing. This will lead to a momentous development toward the end of the century, not in Italy but in Spain.

Like Vergil, the anonymous author of *Lazarillo de Tormes* invents a hero who sets out from home never to return. On the road he receives a moral education in the school of hard knocks. Unlike Aeneas, it is Lazarillo himself who records his tale, in extension of that Odyssean self-narration which Aeneas briefly imitates. The picaró's self-authorship will redefine the foundations of western fiction, not to say theology. For we only have experience, implies the picaresque author, by writing about it. Lazarillo, setting out in adolescence from an already fatherless home, by eventually becoming an author creates the authority that he had lacked, one which he had sought in master, priest, God and other father substitutes. The very Figure of Experience, by recording his adventures he becomes the Master of Experience, an amalgam of life and art, of that Kantian Object and Subject which he anticipates. But in achieving this *knowledge of experience* he has also in a sense achieved the knowledge of God, the ultimate author. In this he predicts the Crisis of Faith.

As a literary staple the *picaró* recurs in succeeding centuries with increasing regularity, gradually replacing his classical heroic counterparts, until those philosopher-critics of Nature, Self and their interaction, Locke, Hume and Kant begin to make sense of his philosophical import. Not by accident are Defoe, Smollett and the inventors of the *Bildungs-* and *Erziehungsroman* simultaneously plying their trade. Eventually novelist and critic conspire to make the picaró respectable, as he and his narrative evolve into *Entwicklungs-* and *Künstlerroman*. Joyce's *Portrait of the Artist as a Young Man* completes this process of introspection. Nor will its author return home, except in imagination.

In the same period another aspect of experience—*expérience* as the French call it—has risen to prominence: "experiment," to translate the term a second way. For all the while that LeSage has been formalizing the principle of the *picaró*, Bacon has been defining the empirical principle of experimental science. *Accumulated experience* and *experimental evidence* go hand in hand. Why then does Kant choose to call his Experience *Erfahrung*? Because he is German, of course, but also because he has come to a new understanding: "*Nur in der Erfahrung*," he says, "*ist die Wahrheit*." ("Only in Experience may we find truth.") Truth, then, is not in science but on the road. (*Erfahrung* comes from *fahren*, to travel.) Yet scientific truth is also known only when recorded, in a form that can be replicated experimentally. Accordingly, our new form of literature, which we sometimes call "experimental," like science has as its ultimate objective the discovery of new realities, new principles, new worlds. Ours is a new age of discovery, in literature no less than in outer space and historical time. But before we arrive at the present, let us first turn to our principal subject, the literature of experience in late modern Britain.

"As the true method of knowledge is experiment," says Blake, "the true faculty of knowing must be the faculty which experiences. This faculty," he concludes, "I treat of." In so saying, England's most notorious visionary connects science with ordinary sense experience. If we look more carefully at his language, we notice that "method" has within it the metaphor of the road (*meta* = after; *hodos* = a road or way). If Blake seems to be on the road to empirical science, however, not so; "Man's perceptions," he asserts, "are not bounded by organs of perception; he perceives more than sense . . . can discover." In connecting religious vision with experience, then, Blake in a sense has connected science with religion and so prophesied another modern development. As poet he composes Songs of Innocence and Songs of Experience, as well as songs of innocence and experience combined. "The Tyger," his most famous lyric, exemplifies this fusion, which connects the religious innocence of his vision with his experience of the empirical world. His major prophetic books merely develop this tendency, setting the Mental Traveller on a road that, like Dante's, connects Heaven and Hell to arrive finally at a new marriage, a new Jerusalem rebuilt "In England's green and pleasant Land."

Wordsworth and Blake, though in many ways divergent, share one great commonality: the principle of experience. Like Blake, Wordsworth "travelled among unknown men" (his, unlike Blake's, actual), returned by way of "an English fire" to "the last green field," a pastoral *topos* of personal reminiscence, a kind of Platonic *anamnesis*, since Wordsworth, like Blake, Milton, Spenser and many others before them, is heavily indebted to Plato. His experience is thus three-fold: *actual experience*, *Kantian Experience*, and a *Platonized experience*, different from Kant's because it so heavily depends upon recollection. Plato had said that the actual world is derived from the ideal world. Wordsworth simply reverses Plato: the ideal world, he says, is derived from the actual. In practice, both doctrines are forms of Idealism. That Wordsworth thought of experience in this way is attested in a comment that he made about his own Immortality Ode: "There may be no harm," he wrote to a friend, "in adverting here to particular feelings, or experiences of my own mind on which the structure of the poem partly rests." Experience for Wordsworth is mental, he no less than Blake a "Mental Traveller."

Save Keats, all the major English Romantics are Platonic. When he asks, "Whither is fled the visionary gleam? / Where is it now, the glory and the dream?" Wordsworth might be speaking on behalf of them all. For if not, as Blake, so minutely in a grain of sand, or, as Shelley, so airily as in the West Wind, Wordsworth in a field of daffodils, or more precisely in his own *anamnesis* of them, can see another world and its animating principle. Even the ambitions of *The Prelude*, that supposed epic of common experience, are defined by a vision of the absolute (I, ll. 261-266):

> This is my lot; for either still I find
> Some imperfection in the chosen theme;
> Or see of absolute accomplishment
> Much wanting, so much wanting, in myself
> That I recoil or droop, and seek repose
> In listlessness from vain perplexity . . . .

Like Blake's, the lessons that Wordsworth learned from Nature are often universal, as those which he and his companion conned as they crossed the Simplon Pass (VI, ll. 544-548):

> With such a book
> Before our eyes we could not chuse but read
> Lessons of genuine brotherhood, the plain
> And universal reason of mankind,
> The truths of Young and Old.

Nature's particulars are not so much the details of individual experience as the eternal symbols of a screed that speaks to the poet (VI, ll. 633 . . . 642):

> As if a voice were in them . . . [they]
> . . . .
> Were all like workings of one mind, the feature
> Of the same face, blossoms upon one tree,
> Characters of the great Apocalypse,
> The types and symbols of Eternity,
> Of first and last, and midst, and without end.

It is not of course Plato pure and simple but a Christianized Plato who informs Wordsworth, as he had Dante, Ariosto, Tasso, Spenser, Milton and others before the Romantics arrived on the scene. But just as Plato has been reshaped by Christianity, so had Christian doctrine been reshaped by Plato. The relationship is reciprocal.

That Wordsworth's vision of experience is Platonic is nowhere more explicitly stated than in his Prospectus to *The Recluse*, the grand plan for his magnum opus (ll. 1-9):

> On Man, on Nature, and on Human Life,
> Musing in solitude, I oft perceive
> Fair trains of imagery before me rise,
> Accompanied by feelings of delight
> Pure, or with no unpleasing sadness mixed;
> And I am conscious of affecting thoughts
> And dear remembrances, whose presence soothes
> Or elevates the Mind, intent to weigh
> The good and evil of our mortal state.

The Christian doctrine of good and evil is invoked only after a pure state of Platonic Mind has been attained. "And if with this," he continues (ll. 93-99),

> I mix more lowly matter with the thing
> Contemplated, describe the Mind and Man
> Contemplating; and who, and what he was—
> The transitory Being that beheld
> This Vision; when and where, and how he lived;—
> Be this labour useless.

The realm to which he aspires, simply put, is that of Plato's Ideas, not Kant's *Erfahrung*. Though his terminology and procedures may often be mistaken for those of German Idealism, he is less the poet of philosophical Experience that he has been represented as than the imperfect precursor of a Shelleyan Ideal.

I have quoted extensively from Wordsworth to support my contention. Coleridge we may consider more summarily. The idealism of his prose has been more frequently remarked upon than that of his verse. But "Frost at Midnight" exemplifies a mystic strain that intrudes upon his representation of experience. To his babe, cradled by his side asleep as the poet ruminates, he expresses the hope that "*thou*," in distinction to himself and his own early experience, "shalt wander like a breeze / By lakes and sandy shores, beneath the crags / Of ancient mountain, and beneath the clouds." In lines that follow thereon (ll. 58-62), the poet's idealism becomes explicit:

> so shalt thou see and hear
> The lovely shapes and sounds intelligible
> Of that eternal language, which thy God
> Utters, who from eternity doth teach
> Himself in all, and all things in himself.

"Great universal Teacher!" Coleridge adds, thereby implicitly connecting those antithetical but embracing principles—*universal* and particular, *eternal* and unique, *immortal* and mortal—without which the western poet seems incapable of grasping his experience. Again, Coleridge's debt to a Platonized Christianity may be greater than his debt to Kant.

One might protest that, whereas "Frost at Midnight" is primarily a poem of actual experience, there are also in Coleridge's oeuvre poems of *philosophical Experience*, such as "Dejection: An Ode." But here too, overwriting the Kantian formulae, are mystic strains, both Platonic ("Ah! from the soul itself must issue forth / A light, a glory, a fair luminous cloud / Enveloping the Earth" [ll.53-55]) and Christian ("Joy, Lady! is the spirit and the power, / Which wedding Nature to us gives in dower / A new Earth and a new Heaven" [ll.67-69]). Though one may argue that Coleridge has merely posed the Romantic problem (Self and Nature) and offered a Romantic solution (Romantic Joy), doctrinally the poem is shifted toward a different dispensation. In the mode of *visionary experience*, as in "Christabel," "The Ancient Mariner" or "Kubla Khan," Coleridge gives even freer reign to this Ideal. "A damsel with a dulcimer / In a vision once I saw," he begins the last poem's final stanza, whose final lines again compound Christian with Platonic vision.

Should we think this all merely a matter of poetic vision, Coleridge in his prose gives unequivocal proof of his belief in the Christian-Platonic ideal: "The fact therefore, that the mind of man in its own primary and constitutional forms represents the laws of nature, is a mystery which of itself should suffice to make us religious: for it is a problem of which God is the only solution, God, the one before all, and of all, and through all!" Against Coleridge's theism we shall shortly return to pose Shelley's atheism, but first we turn to Byron, whom Coleridge may well be characterizing when he says, "in its utmost abstraction and consequent state of reprobation, the Will becomes satanic pride and rebellious self-idolatry in the relations of the spirit to itself, and remorseless despotism relatively to others."

Byron is half Satanic idealist, half satirical realist and thus avoids the philosophical terms of Experience which so preoccupy Wordsworth and Coleridge. What his poetry has that theirs (and Blake's) lacks, is *actual experience* — imminent, dangerous, as yet not fully understood. Only Byron's life is more thrilling than the open-ended adventures of *Don Juan*, or the mysterious crime of *Manfred*, both so palpably grounded in the poet's own life.

"I am no Platonist," Byron announces at the age of twenty-three. "I am nothing at all," he adds, meaning thereby that he has no faith. But if he is no worshipper of Plato, he is nonetheless an emulator of the classic poets, retrogressively of Pope, Milton, Ariosto, Ovid and, as his vision deepens, Homer himself. At twenty-seven he calls Paradise Lost "the finest poetry that had ever been produced in this world." His yet more telling ambivalence toward the Greek and Roman classics, as expressed in *Don Juan*, typifies the love-hate relationship of all classicists with their mighty predecessors. Unlike a Vergil, a Tasso or a Spenser, however, Byron claims to have broken free into pure *experiential improvisation*. "I have no plan," he says famously. No plan, that is, except that by liberating himself from the classics he may overgo them. And yet he characteristically falls back upon them for the terms of his project: "My poem's epic, and is meant to be / Divided in twelve books," he proclaims proudly. As with Whitman, Ezra Pound and later open-ended experientialists, it is the classics — latterly Hindu and Confucian as well as Greek and Roman — that provide the impulse and the standard against which to measure their experiment. The experimentalist, like the

152

experientialist, must start somewhere, for he is grounded, if only by the language that he inherits, in terms that precede his own experiment or experience.

"Tom has spit a leetle blood this afternoon," says Keats of his dying younger brother, in a letter taken up mostly with a lazily even-handed weighing of the relative merits of Milton and Wordsworth. Is Keats really concerned with actual experience, or is he after all a poet of sleep and poetry, a poet's poet, absorbed in his own Psyche, in the song of the Nightingale, in the static bliss of a Grecian Urn? All his major odes, we might say, are saturated with Melancholy and Indolence. A degraded allegorical figure called Autumn offers his most haunting image. Yeats thought of Keats as a schoolboy, his nose pressed against the window of a candy store. The longer narratives this reader finds unreadable; to him the poet's reimmersion in decadent myth seems a dissolute indulgence in "a Life of Sensations rather than of Thoughts," a triumph of the poet's own questionable principle of "negative capability."

Keats represents the underbelly of Shelley, whose personal moral decadence, in his dealings with Harriet, Mary and Claire, prepared a field ripe for Byron's ploughing. We must not forget that Harriet, pregnant and desperate, drowned herself; that Clara and William, Shelley's children by Mary, died of neglect in early childhood. Shelley's death in an accident and Keats' of tuberculosis are merely amoral details. The point is that neither poet of experience controlled his own experience nor in any sense died heroically in the face of it. Each was at least spared the shamblings in old age of a Wordsworth or Coleridge. But none of the four was about to embark on any grand Blakean vision, and Byron was probably right in dismissing the lot of them, including his friend Shelley, as "all in the wrong . . . upon a wrong revolutionary poetic system, or systems, not worth a damn in itself."

That system fundamentally overestimates the value of feeling, beauty and imagination. "I am certain of nothing but of the holiness of the Heart's affections and the truth of Imagination," says Keats. "What the imagination seizes as Beauty must be truth." Though more mature, Shelley's thought is similarly flawed, both morally and esthetically: "The great secret of morals," he says, "is Love; or a going out of our own nature, and an identification of ourselves with the beautiful which exists in thought, action, or person, not our own." It is "negative capability" all over again, and its flaw lies in its naïve idealism. "A man, to be greatly good," he puffs, "must imagine intensely and comprehensively. The great instrument of moral good," he concludes vaguely, "is the imagination."

Thomas Carlyle, born the same year as Keats, is the last, and arguably the best, of the Romantic poets. Though his medium is prose, his *French Revolution*, as Macaulay was the first to observe, is the great English epic of the nineteenth century. Though poetically impassioned, his principal contribution is to reinstitute Thought in Poetry. By turns theologian, moralist, metaphysician and critic, he redefines God and the Imagination in terms of the Kantian duplex of Time and Space in a paragraph that might be regarded as an Ode to and against Experience:

> That the Thought-forms, Space and Time, wherein once for all we are sent into this Earth to live, should condition and determine our whole Practical reasonings, conceptions, and imagings or imaginings, seems altogether fit, just and unavoidable. But that they should, furthermore, usurp such sway over pure spiritual meditation, and blind us to the wonder everywhere lying close on us, seems nowise so. Admit Space and Time to their due rank as Forms of Thought; nay even, if thou wilt, to their quite undue rank of Realities: and consider, then, with thyself how their thin disguises hide from us the brightest God-effulgences! Thus, were it not miraculous, could I stretch forth my hand and clutch the Sun? Yet thou seest me daily stretch forth my hand and therewith clutch many a thing, and swing it hither and thither. Art thou a grown baby, then, to fancy that the miracle lies in miles of distance, or in pounds avoirdupois of weight; and not to see that the true inexplicable God-revealing Miracle lies in this, that I can stretch forth my hand at all; that I have free Force to clutch aught therewith? Innumerable other of this sort are the deceptions, and wonder-hiding stupefactions, which Space practices on us.

"Still worse is it with regard to Time," he adds. "Your grand antimagician and universal wonder-hider, is this same lying Time. . . ." Carlyle's achievement here is nothing less than the reinvention of cosmological poetry, this Englishman the Hesiod as well as Homer of our post-Kantian world, whose basis has shifted within the century and a half since Milton from myth to history, from history to experience, from experience to science, thereby recapitulating the development of civilization. Progressively the western intellectual, moving retrogressively through its phases, attempts to come to terms with each: Descartes with science, Kant with experience, Carlyle with history, Frazer with myth. A giant among giants, Carlyle arrives at a synthesis of all four modes of thought. We shall focus here on his treatment of two alone: Experience and History.

"Examine History," he says, "for it is 'Philosophy teaching by Experience.'" No wonder, then, that Carlyle as historian must first come to terms with Experience, must himself become a philosopher. Unlike the principal Romantic poets, he has understood the untenabililty of Idealism ("pure spiritual meditation"), Platonic or Christian, in the brave new world. God must instead be reinvented out of the new Realities of Space and Time. Next, with the reach and grasp of his own hand as exemplum, he brings his meditation down to the individual, to *individual experience*. Individual experience accumulated, as in Wordsworth, becomes personal history. For Carlyle, the Experiential historian, the problem is how to get from personal to collective history. Perhaps, he suggests, the best way is by fiat:

"History," he says, "as it lies at the root of all science, is also the first distinct product of man's spiritual nature; his earliest expression of what is called Thought." If the cosmos is defined by Space and Time, man is defined by History, a human scientific given. Henceforth, all thought will become historical, all disciplines framed within their own histories, as the great project of the later nineteenth-century now takes root. Science will become the history of science; philosophy, the history of philosophy; theology, the history of theology. For Newman, the history of theology comes to replace theology itself. As Carlyle has it: "Church History . . . did it speak wisely, would have momentous secrets to teach us; nay, in its highest degree, it were a sort of continued Holy Writ; our Sacred Books being, indeed, only a History of the primeval church, as it first arose in man's soul, and symbolically embodied itself in his eternal life." But the personal cannot be eliminated, even by fiat. Newman unconsciously reflects the problem when he says: "I mean to be simply personal and historical; I am not expounding Catholic doctrine." Personal, or historical? Or both? Why not simply one or the other?

Because history is but experience writ large. Moreover, once we have taken the historian's own role into account, we cannot return to objectivity. As with realism in art or certainty in science, we discover that objectivity is illusory. What then are we left with? Experience. In our self-absorption we have no choice but to redefine science, philosophy and theology as the science of experience, the philosophy of experience, the theology of experience, until God can only be captured from our own point of view. That He may have created this point of view is overlooked. If history, experientially reconceived, is our new God, experience, historically reconceived, is our new hero. It is that which mediates, like the demi-god, between particular and universal.

Experience summarizes the Romantic theme of Self and Nature, integrating its principal terms and providing a problematic basis, as we have seen, for history. Ever since we left Shelley behind, we have been slighting another important Romantic principle: the Imagination. As we turn to the novel we find that it makes its reappearance. For this quintessentially Romantic form is less a product of experience or history than of Coleridge's esemplastic power, or of Tasso's predictive *meraviglia*, our integrating sense of wonderment now turned narcissistically upon ourselves, on our self-regulating democratic society with its self-determining political and economic institutions.

Far from the objective mode implied by the labels employed to categorize its phases: historical, realistic, naturalistic, the novel is fundamentally subjective, locating nature within human process, in fact identifying it with human nature. In this essentially popular and secular form we lose the mystery of cosmology and the proportional view of the universe that it implies. In fact, once Experience, with change as its single constant principle, has captured our thought, even science cannot serve to anchor our universe. On this Carlyle puts the bravest of faces: "[C]ould you ever establish a Theory of the Universe that was entire, unimprovable, and which only need be got by heart," he opines, "man then were spiritually defunct, the Species we now name Man had ceased to exist." The novel, then, presents, by definition, only a partial picture—particular, not universal; is constantly in need of improvement—always unique, never eternal; and takes a notoriously unmemorizable form, at least as long as the species Man and his Imagination are to dominate art and art theory, criticism and the literature that it thrives upon. We shall return to reconsider these questions, as they recur in the thought of Ruskin, Arnold and Pater.

If Dickens, as the dominant Victorian figure in the form, represents the apotheosis of Romantic Imagination, if Scott in the Romance represents the inventor of our self-regarding view of History, if Jane Austen but holds up a mirror to improve our Manners, and if varieties of Realism, Naturalism and Expressionism can be assigned to Trollope, Hardy and the Brontës, what to make of George Eliot, the most serious of all Victorian novelists?

Called the most learned woman of the nineteenth century, she is not only novelist but thinker, social historian, theologian. Since the first two roles, but not the last, are often played by the modern novelist, let us pause to ask why Eliot is so concerned with God, with Biblical studies, with theological argument and everything else that goes to make up the Higher Criticism. The answer is simple, if its terms complex: she is engaged in the task of rewriting Paradise Lost and, behind it, the Biblical Genesis. For in *Adam Bede, The Mill on the Floss, Middlemarch* and *Romola*, to look no further, she is redescribing Eden, the Fall of Man, the Expulsion and its aftermath. Science, History and Experience, however well-versed she is in all three, are insufficient terms for her complete understanding. Her undertaking requires a pre-existing myth, which she finds in Adam and Eve. She is the first English novelist to embody one that is so central to western civilization.

Why at this juncture, at this particular distance from Milton and Dante, in this agnostic climate? Surprisingly her practice has not been subjected to detailed critical scrutiny. Or perhaps not surprisingly: many of the most important relationships between nineteenth-century figures and their precursors or successors have been neglected. One thinks of Whitman's relationship to Blake and to Pound, or of Dickens' relationship to Cervantes and to later fiction. The same neglect is typical in our study of other ages of English letters: Shakespeare's relationship to Spenser and to Milton, for example. And who, in the twentieth century, has continued the work of *Middlemarch*, the greatest English novel of the nineteenth century? Have we lost our taste for Adam and Eve, for Paradise Lost and Paradise Regained? If so, we have lost touch with perhaps our profoundest and most enduring myth.

Henry James wrote dismissively of *Middlemarch*, overemphasizing its portrait of a lady, underemphasizing its complexity, and ignoring its mythic element. Henry James himself never managed to write so substantial a novel. What did James believe in, what Eliot, what Milton? Milton believed in God, Eliot apparently in Milton and James in himself. George Eliot was only *curious* about Henry James (invited to her house, he reported that no one had ever been more eagerly received nor more eagerly dismissed). Eliot, on the other hand, was utterly absorbed in Milton and his material. Along with God and herself, she embodies him in the figure of Casaubon. Though also the archetypal old man who foolishly takes a young wife, this scholar of antiquity represents more than meets the eye, for Eliot, adept at the broad, popular effect, was a subtle allegorist as well. The Miltonic project that Casaubon fails to complete, even with Eliot's surrogate, Dorothea, at his elbow, is titled *The Key to All Mythologies*, the key in question being the Bible. In addition to God and Milton, Casaubon represents Eliot's father and that father-figure and lover, George Henry Lewes. But if we read Dorothea as Eve, Casaubon must be Adam, though only in the pre-lapsarian part of the story, the one in which Ladislaw plays Satan. After Casaubon's death—the death of God, of Eliot's father, of Milton, of the first Adam— Dorothea marries Ladislaw (Eve and Satan? Eve and the second Adam?) and lives happily ever after. Are they Saint and Sinner? Not only does Eliot name her heroine after one saint, she pointedly compares her to another, while Mrs. Cadwallader calls Ladislaw "Byronic." Henry James, having never closed his Byron, understood this part; having failed to open his Goethe, he missed some other parallels. For Casaubon is a Faust figure doubling as God; Dorothea, his Gretchen; Ladislaw, his Mephistopheles (in her post-lapsarian good works Dorothea too is a Faust). And we have not even touched on the parallels with Dante, Cervantes, Shakespeare and Bunyan to whom Eliot directs us in her epigraphs. Why, finally, this career-long obsession with Adam and Eve? Because George Eliot is Milton's principal continuator in "the home epic."

As it would be unthinkable to exclude Dostoevskii from a study of nineteenth-century Russian literature or Victor Hugo from a similar study of French, so Dickens must have a place, and a very important one, in any view of nineteenth-century English letters. He is, in my view, the most powerful English imagination since Shakespeare. The question is how he relates to the theme of experience. For it is not enough to say that his work is hugely autobiographical and therefore reflects his own experience; nor, that it is realistic and so reflects the experience of modern London. The work of a diarist would satisfy the first criterion; that of a journalist, the second. That he is popular does not count against him, any more than it counts against Shakespeare or Tennyson; that he makes his living as a professional writer puts him in the same category as Carlyle. Why, one might ask, should we take so seriously the work of the anonymous author of *Lazarillo de Tormes* but not that of Dickens? One had best admit that an airtight case for excluding him cannot be made. Nor is this a matter of personal taste. *Great Expectations* is one of my favorite novels, a marvelous entertainment, by turns hilarious and plangent, full of profound insight into human nature. But all in all it represents neither collective nor personal experience. The novel bears only incidentally upon history; what it derives from Dickens himself has been transmuted by imagination into another world. Though Dickens' mind is not to be underestimated, he is neither philosophically cultivated nor inclined. In short, *Great Expectations* is a work of Romantic Imagination, whose aim is to probe "the Heart's affections." That he had little interest in Aristotle, Vergil, Dante or Kant does not count against him either but rather increases our admiration. For Dickens, by dint of his own capaciousness, has invented a human world that rivals theirs in scope, if not in finesse and meditated purpose. He has, however, precisely, *invented* it, and Invention is not Experience.

For the categorizer Thomas Hardy poses an even more difficult problem than Dickens. His *Jude the Obscure*, for example, has many features in common with the novels of George Eliot. And I have in mind features in addition to their provincial English settings, their backward glance at an earlier age, their use of dialect and other realistic devices. Like Eliot's novels of Experience, *Jude* interweaves amidst its plot of passion and education systems of evocative symbols drawn from Christianity and the classical tradition. Hardy, who composed a long and systematic, if somewhat crude, philosophical poem, could not, like

Dickens, have been unaware of the tradition of thinkers that we have frequently evoked. Naturalism itself, as we are told by those who favor the term, develops from concerns of Darwin, Marx and Spencer, and Hardy certainly knew them. How is it, then, that he too comes to be excluded from the literature of Experience? This time personal judgment enters the picture. For Hardy's thought seems to me not reflective but instinctive, his theology limited to a cosmic irony, his world view the product of a passionate Romantic pessimism and limited by a lack of philosophical reflectiveness. Not surprisingly, he is a more popular figure than F. H. Bradley, but it is Bradley who is concerned with Experience, not Hardy.

We might here pause briefly to reconsider the terms "Romantic" and "Realistic." Though their currency is entrenched and unavoidable, neither is very accurate nor readily definable. One might say the same of "Experiential," but at least this term is philosophically justifiable. There *is* no philosophy of Romanticism or Realism. Since both bodies of literature—and this includes the whole high nineteenth-century European tradition—are encompassed by the phrase "literature of Experience," I would suggest that it be allowed to replace "Romanticism," "Realism," and the equally problematic "Symbolism."

Unlike Byron and Eliot, who through most of their lives were unmarried, Tennyson, like Milton, was thoroughly domesticated. Unlike the Romantic poets, he was genuinely popular, a poet of *collective experience*. To achieve an historical position among the Victorians he resituated himself in antecedent times, variously in the mythic Greece of Tithonus, the legendary Britain of Arthur, his own *personal past*, or a generalized past nostalgically circumscribed by conservative values and traditional culture. Whitman envied Tennyson his democratic appeal but failed fully to grasp the Poet Laureate's shrewd insight: in matters of taste the People are anti-democratic. Tennyson appeals to them through his emotional *reexperience* of the past, sharing with them, as Vergil does with his audience, his own emotional response to a *collective past* that they by themselves are not capable of recovering. Again like Vergil, he addresses three audiences: his heroic predecessors, his contemporary world, and his future readers. Whitman speaks effectively only to the second and third of these—though the Vedic sages may still be listening.

Like George Eliot, Tennyson is a serious thinker, a vocation largely overlooked by his posthumous readers though not by his contemporary, James Stuart Mill. "Every great poet," says Victoria's leading philosopher (he is reviewing *In Memoriam*), "every poet who has extensively or permanently influenced mankind, has been a great thinker;

159

has had a philosophy, though perhaps he did not call it by that name."
What is it that Tennyson is thinking about? About *collective history* in
relation to his *personal history*, in short, about Experience in the sense
that it comes to have for post-Romantic man, be he Hegel or Carlyle. I
would argue that Tennyson is no less a thinker than they. For economy
and convenience let us narrow our focus to a single work, "Ulysses," and
its treatment of our opening theme: the Homeric tradition of experience,
which Tennyson, as we shall see, is both perpetuating and undoing.

In the concluding lines of "The Lotus Eaters," a poem that precedes
the principal object of our scrutiny, the poet writes:

> slumber is more sweet than toil, the shore
> Than labor in the deep mid-ocean, wind and wave and oar;
> O, rest ye, brother mariners, we will not wander more.

Had we not the rest of the text we might wonder who was speaking.
Odysseus, or Aeneas? A nineteenth-century English sailor, or Tennyson
himself? The lines repay four separate recitations in which one imagines
each of those figures speaking in turn. Yet all four are speaking at once,
as is the reader.

From a little Homeric episode, which in 1832 he *expands* (with help
from Spenser and Lucretius), in 1833 he turns to the whole of Homer,
which he *condenses* (with help from Vergil and Shakespeare). Here he
invents a prologue to Dante's famous episode in Inferno 26. Having
returned to his wife, a Hamlet-like Ulysses says, "I cannot rest from
travel; I will drink life to the lees." It was a poisoned cup, we recall, that
killed Shakespeare's Everyman and restlessness that did in Dante's. But
experience, like literature, is on-going; the past, all that he has "enjoyed
greatly," "suffered greatly," Ulysses must leave behind, though its
sensorium ("Much have I seen and known") may be retained as Lockean
experience. After further universalizing Homer's epitome of Odysseus'
travels, Tennyson in a one line Kantian prelude to his own definition of
experience, has Ulysses proclaim philosophically: "I am a part of all that
I have met." His hero then continues:

> Yet all experience is an arch wherethrough
> Gleams that untraveled world whose margin fades
> Forever and forever when I move.

Not only is experience on-going, it is never complete. One might think of
Ginés de Pasamonte's comic response, upon being asked if he has
finished his *Life of Ginés de Pasamonte*: "How could it be finished? I am
still alive." We laugh but then reflect: perhaps life is not, after all,
susceptible of realization. Besides, if we know our experience only by
writing about it, what of that experience that we have not yet written
about? As Cervantes in his critique of the picaresque, so Tennyson in his

meditation on Homer is breaking new ground. Moreover, we notice that Tennyson is speaking of "*all* experience." So much for the whole enterprise! It is all unknowable, he implies.

Like the Esperantist, Tennyson has invented a basic English that makes him attractive to the non-native speaker, though, curiously, to the native speaker as well. His simplifications are especially noticeable in his monosyllabic lines: "How dull it is to pause, to make an end." The experience of reading this line is akin to the experience of translating it into another language. We recall that "Ulysses" is a poem out of a Greek text by way of Latin and Italian texts projected on into English. Monosyllabic phrases are also important: "Life piled on life," "When I am gone," "He works his work, I mine," "You and I are old." Each phrase teeters on the edge of semantic ambiguity. Some of Tennyson's best-remembered passages are also monosyllabic: "The long day wanes; the slow moon climbs," or the poem's final, cumulative injunction "To strive, to seek, to find, and not to yield."

What has this to do with *universal experience*? A great deal, for if we are not all writers, we are all readers, or at least verbalizers of our experience. If we take seriously these monosyllables: "life," "death," "fate," "time," "world," "will," "all," they may tell us how Tennyson has thematized his poem, how it is, in short, that he "thinks." They may also tell us how he wishes us to consider Experience, in relation, that is, to "life," to "death," to "fate," and so on. Is Experience something that one may "hoard"? What is its relation to "work"? "That which we are, we are," says the poet, in a sentence that might seem ridiculous if spoken by someone other than Tennyson. But now that we see how he thinks, we understand that he is pondering the relation between experience and existence. What does Ulysses mean, when he calls his mariners "Souls that have *toiled*, and *wrought*, and *thought* with me"? In the spirit of my thesis—that Tennyson's work is interactive—instead of answering, I shall leave the reader to his own devices.

As in "Ulysses," where he maintains a perspective both personal and historical, so in his own efforts at epic Tennyson balances the modern with the traditional. Both *In Memoriam* and *Idylls of the King* rest on earlier models: his Arthurian cycle, on Malory's handling of the myth; his elegy, on Dante's poem of experience. Both transpose the experience of Christ, as in Arthur "dead" but "come again: he cannot die," as in the linkage of Arthur Hallam with the "strong Son of God." Tennyson himself is less the poet of doubt than a doubting age had imagined, more the poet of a sublimated Christianity. Like Dante's, his delineates the experience of despair, purgation and redemption. As in "Ulysses," where Telemachus prepares to continue his father's experience after the latter's death, Tennyson expresses more literally his interest in *experience beyond the grave*. After we die, do we rejoin the past or do we move into an "untraveled world" of the future? Tennyson's Ulysses contemplates further travel but also imagines a reunion with Achilles. As with Eliot and Carlyle before him, Tennyson returns experience to its mythic roots.

With Browning—for us, perhaps even more than for his contemporaries, the representative Victorian—we have a meeting of minds, an interweaving of the modes whereby the nineteenth-century grasped and reordered reality: *Experience, Imagination, History*. For though he is distant from the Romantics—in time, in culture, in place of residence—Browning is still of their party, a poet of Experience *a fortiori*, half a realist, half a sentimental idealist, and for which combination much beloved. Like the novelists at mid-century, he is essentially a poet of Imagination, recreating his Florentine painters, his Ferrarese Duke, his Bishop, his Sordello by means of an historiography that he shares with Flaubert, Tolstoi and George Eliot. No matter how meticulously they may have researched their subjects, however, neither they nor Browning are really historians.

Browning's dramatic monologues, once set on their course, ride upon their own melting toward nothingness (like Frost's homely ice-cube set atop the stove), expiring as their substance finally evaporates. One-time events — energetic, metamorphic — they still command our attention, precisely because, as performances, they could not be repeated. As we ourselves return to Florence, to his Renaissance masters, Browning's poems continue to recede, as he intended, into a Shakespearean mist. They represent, in short, not history but a new amalgam, as different from Shakespeare as they are from our modern discipline, the history of art, some of whose features they nonetheless anticipate. For Pound, for Eliot, for Yeats, they held a permanent fascination and constituted a profounder influence than has generally been recognized, despite Pound's effort at explaining his own indebtedness.

For Hegel art, like everything else, is inseparable from history. Less an influence upon Ruskin and Arnold than a figure whose thinking prefigures theirs, he nonetheless has things to say about our larger problem, the particular and the universal, which should be mentioned before we take up these later Victorians. To epitomize the second epigraph to this essay, we might say that for Hegel the only thing that is universal is everything. Though in epistemology he begins the shift away from Kant toward Subjective Idealism, his view of Experience is again all-embracing. In a general way he anticipates what Ruskin, Arnold and

Pater, regarded collectively, in their view of Experience are heading toward.

This is not the place to review the general contours of the work of these late Victorian thinkers. Suffice it to say that the history of culture is for each crucial as a way of carrying forward the development of English thought about Experience. Each advances in his own way the general integration of Experience with history, Ruskin by making both more socially responsible, Arnold by broadening our comparative perspectives, Pater by finally dissolving altogether the borderline between the two processes. Each figure goes beyond Hegel in his integration of esthetics with the rest of human knowledge.

"What we have to do," says Pater in his Conclusion to *The Renaissance*, "is to be forever curiously testing new opinions and courting new impressions, never acquiescing in a facile orthodoxy of Comte, or of Hegel, or of our own." Pater not so much opposes philosophical theory as insists that we make use of it to grasp the meaning of life, to heighten our passion, to experience for experience's sake. What, then, does he contribute—aside from a yet more expanded sense of its world-wide scope—to our understanding of experience? A sense, we might say, of its evanescence, of its intermittency, of its indeterminacy. In this he predicts the quantum physicist. "The whole scope of observation," says Pater in his peroration, "is dwarfed into the narrow chamber of the human mind." "Analysis," he continues, as though having established a mental laboratory,

> goes a step farther still and assures us that those impressions of the individual mind to which, for each one of us, experience dwindles down, are in perpetual flight; that each of them is limited by time, and that as time is infinitely divisible, each of them is infinitely divisible also; all that is actual in it being a single moment, gone while we try to apprehend it, of which it may ever be more truly said that it has ceased to be than that it is.

Having defined the Self as a "strange, perpetual weaving and unweaving," Pater intuitively grasps the applicability of that figure to Nature itself, alertly warning us that experience itself is an endangered species. "Not the fruit of experience," he says, departing from Hegel, "but experience itself is the end." His position will influence many figures in the century that follows, none more directly than the Dandy.

After an age of political revolution there follows an age of social revolution; by the twentieth century a third revolution, the cultural, has worked its way into our consciousness. For prescient thinkers such as Alexis de Tocqueville, however, the third revolution was implicit in the second; for the avant-garde thinker, such as Beau Brummel, it was implicit in the first. Brummel is the first Dandy in the dignified modern sense, that is, of a man who creates his own culture, who creates himself out of his own manners. He is an apotheosis of Democratic Man. If we are all equal, not only politically and socially but culturally too, how is the artist to distinguish himself from the average person?

By the middle of the nineteenth century two eccentrics, Charles Baudelaire and Walter Whitman dandify themselves with the aim of establishing their own centrality. Both owe much to Byron. At times both adopt his dress, Baudelaire affecting the airs of the noble decadent, Whitman, in the same costume, the posture of the democratic, self-made man. Baudelaire takes urban evil as his theme (*Les Fleurs du mal*, 1857), Whitman, wholesome nature as his (*Leaves of Grass*, 1855). Between them they divide good and bad, two universal kinds of experience. In the English tradition, the most notable continuator of Brummel and Byron, of Baudelaire and Whitman is Walter Pater's student, Oscar Wilde. In our dramatic argument he enters to answer the question, "How can one have experience without writing about it?" By making of oneself a work of art, Oscar replies. Dressing the part of an *objet d'art*, and on the strength alone of his reputation for wit, Wilde at the age of twenty-seven tours America, delivering at each stop his one lecture on the importance of home furnishing. "We spend our days looking for the secret of life," reads its next to last sentence. "Well," it concludes, "the secret of life is art!" Wilde has mastered Pater's lesson.

He continued to write, though his dandified persona and verbal wit have proved more memorable than his verse or prose. His brilliant *Importance of Being Earnest* also teaches us exactly the opposite lesson: the importance of being something other than one's Self, of being sincere in dismissing Sincerity. Significantly his best work is a *play:* for Wilde life was dramatic performance. In this he predicted Charlie Chaplin, Marcel Duchamp and Harry Crosby. The first of these created of himself the only image that rivals in universal appeal the image of Mickey Mouse; the second made of silence and inactivity modes of activity and expression that echo Rimbaud's decision to quit writing at the age of nineteen. The third, living in the Paris of Picasso, achieved an artist's reputation without becoming an artist. Each has had a myriad of followers. We must remember that not all Dandies are memorable. "Doing one's own thing" has by now become standard procedure for Everyman.

On the threshold of the twentieth century, what had been a radical departure, the Literature of Experience, suddenly becomes an orthodoxy. All valid literature henceforth is assumed to be experiential. We catch a sense of this fossilization of the living creature in Conrad's 1899 characterization of his own work of that year. "*Heart of Darkness*," he says, "is experience too, but it is experience pushed a little . . . beyond the actual facts of the case." That a more demotic "experience" has, in the theory of this hyperconscious practitioner of the point of view, replaced the more philosophical "Experience" is telling. For what is experience "pushed beyond the actual facts" but the novel again, that narrative of Romantic Imagination soon to become, if not already, standard literary fare.

Meanwhile, on the philosophical front, Yeats, though no philosopher himself, nonetheless rises to the challenge, as had Pater, of contributing to the discourse. Within a decade of Conrad, in a diary entry, he will ask, "Is not life the struggle of experience naked, unarmed, timid, but immortal against generalized thought?" His sentiment is again a popularization, here of the struggle of the first Romantic Idealists to overcome the orthodoxy of Enlightenment thought. In one sense Yeats is behind the times, but by flattering the general reader he leads him into the world of advanced ideas. Recapitulating the nineteenth-century enlargement of experience into history, he adds that "personal history in this is the inverse of the world's history. We see all arts and societies passing from experience, that is to say, not what we call its 'results,' which are generalizations, but with its presence, its energy." History, then, for Yeats, and *contra* Aristotle, is generalization; for him and his early Modernist colleagues, its revitalization, its rerendering as experience, will be the designated task. "All good art," Yeats concludes, "is experience, all popular bad art generalization." The volatile notion, taken hold, has solidified into doctrine.

In London during the early years of the century two Americans assume leadership of the Modernist program. Ezra Pound, taking his cue from Walter Pater, shows us how in practice to render history experiential and experience historical. His younger, more philosophical accomplice, T. S. Eliot, in his dissertation on F. H. Bradley, extends the high doctrine of Experience one step further. The problem he identifies as Kant's first step, for once we have divided the world into Subject and Object, he observes, we can never return to a unified knowledge or experience. Kant, as a consequence of Hume's skepticism, had already lost confidence that what we experience is the Thing-in-Itself and so had begun to concentrate on the categories that he felt determine our thinking and are somehow more real than reality. Bradley examines the Subjective Idealism of Hegel and Nietzsche only to wonder aloud whether anything like the Subject actually appears in our thought. He then goes back to question Kant's categories, to ridicule the father of modern thought for saving us from superstition by creating yet more superstition. By the standard of Bradley, Pater is philosophically retrograde, his dream of a world really but Coleridge's primary Imagination again, in the new guise of Subjective Idealism. Bradley sets out to deconstruct the very concept of the self.

In this Eliot follows him. Questioning the Romantic poets as well as their philosophical counterparts, he moves beyond Idealist epistemology to maintain that we may get at reality only through *immediate experience*, whose priority to Object and Subject he asserts. Dismissing Time as discontinuous and therefore illusory, he complements Bradley's dissolution of the Subject with his own dissolution of the Object. In the process he does away with Self and Soul. The only philosophical move that remains is the Existentialist. Sartre proposes that we begin not with essence but with existence itself. We are still working out the problems of that proposition. Until we see more clearly where we have arrived, we cannot confidently apply this body of thought to the body of literature contemporaneous with its development. As yet we scarcely understand the import of Modernism, much less that of later movements.